$f\mathbf{P}$

ORIGINAL SINNERS

*A New Interpretation
of Genesis*

JOHN R. COATS

FREE PRESS
A Division of Simon & Schuster, Inc.
1230 Avenue of the Americas
New York, NY 10020

First Free Press hardcover edition November 2009

FREE PRESS and colophon are trademarks of Simon & Schuster, Inc.

For information about special discounts for bulk purchases,
please contact Simon & Schuster Special Sales at 1-866-506-1949
or business@simonandschuster.com.

The Simon & Schuster Speakers Bureau can bring authors to your live event.
For more information or to book an event contact the Simon & Schuster Speakers Bureau
at 1-866-248-3049 or visit our website at www.simonspeakers.com.

DESIGNED BY ERICH HOBBING

Manufactured in the United States of America

1   3   5   7   9   10   8   6   4

Library of Congress Cataloging-in-Publication Data
Coats, John R.
Original sinners: a new interpretation of Genesis / John R. Coats.
p. cm.
Includes bibliographical references and index.
1. Bible. O.T. Genesis—Criticism, interpretation, etc. I. Title.
BS1235.52.C63 2009
222'.1107—dc22   2009021132
ISBN 978-1-4391-0209-1
ISBN 978-1-4391-1759-0 (ebook)

For Pamela, my wife,
and Virginia, my daughter

What is laid down, ordered, factual, is never enough to embrace the whole truth: life always spills over the rim of every cup.

— BORIS PASTERNAK

CONTENTS

NOAH: IN THREE ACTS,
A STORY FAR MORE INVOLVED
THAN YOU MIGHT THINK

PART II

THE WANDERERS

CALLING

ABRAHAM

PART III

THE BLESSING THIEF:
A STORY IN THREE ACTS

PART IV

THE DREAM READER

ORIGINAL SINNERS

INTRODUCTION

Read the Bible in your own way, and take the message because it says
something special to each reader, based on his or her own experience.
— JOSEPH CAMPBELL

When I was a boy, a measure of goodness was the number of gold stars beside one's name on the chart in the Sunday school room in our church in Pasadena, Texas, these stars earned by a successful recitation of the books of the Bible and regular recitations of select verses. Sunday school, Training Union (think Sunday night school), and Royal Ambassadors (a service-evangelism club for school boys), as many as three church services a week, two weeks of vacation Bible school at the beginning of every summer, plus a week of summer church camp with its Bible study and three services per day, and one or more weeklong revivals a year (a few under large, clay-red tents) — to grow up in the Southern Baptist church of the fifties was to stand beneath a waterfall of words *from* and *about* scripture. Central to Baptist doctrine was the insistence that the Bible was true as it was written, and I accepted this, even as I began to notice what appeared to be discrepancies.

So it was more from curiosity than rebelliousness that I began to ask questions. It seems I asked too many of them — and of the wrong sort — as I was expelled and sent home with a note that read, "Johnny can come back to Sunday school when he stops asking so many questions." With orders from my mother to keep my mouth shut, I was allowed back the following Sunday. But I never quite returned. As the years passed, I continued to separate from the idea of the Bible's literal truth until, finally, I put it away.

Now what? If the stories are not to be taken as literal, as *the* record of the divine presence in human affairs, and of the reasonableness of faith, of what use are they? Certainly, they're valuable as literature, and I did consider them as that, but I couldn't get past the quirk of having regarded Abraham, Isaac, Jacob, et al. as historical figures, people who'd lived as surely as I live. While I could accept that they were *not* that, I could not consider them as entirely fictional. Then, in time, I was presented with an entirely new way of regarding the Bible, its characters, and their stories.

No, I don't believe there was a Garden of Eden, an Adam and Eve, a Cain and Abel, but I do believe in the metaphor — I live inside it, and so do you. The story of Adam and Eve rings with perfect pitch because my own

1

life has been a constant cycle of falling from grace (Eden), regaining it, falling, regaining. I've been my brother's and my sister's keeper, yes, but from my own smallness of spirit, my refusal to forgive, all of it justified by old hurts, like Cain I've also been their killer, and, ironically, my own. In Jacob's penchant for sneaky manipulation, I see myself with greater clarity, and in the cluelessness of Joseph's youthful naïveté and arrogance, I've come to understand the hatred that came my way in the summer of 1967 when, having been disliked from the first day by fellow workers in a shingle manufacturing plant, and for reasons I can only guess at — "College Boy" was more an epithet than a nickname — I showed up for work one day in my own "coat of many colors," a canary-yellow '65 Mustang convertible, my father's gift on my twenty-first birthday.*

For more than forty years, I've witnessed the same dynamics at play in all sorts of people from all walks of life and from all over the world. Jealousy, greed, stupidity, brilliance, cowardice, bravery, hate, love: so much of the ordinary business of just being alive remains the same, even from one millennium to the next, which is why the Bible works as metaphor. And *as* metaphor, it loses all purchase as a measure of one's goodness or badness — loses its tyranny. Instead it shows itself to be a mirror in which to see one's own humanity, one's flaws of character, one's strengths through the lives of the people found in its stories. There is pathos here — Adam and Eve being tossed from the Garden of Eden, the death of a son, the banishment of another, the flood, the sacrifice of Isaac, Esau's grief and anger. And humor, too, far more than you might imagine. As I hope to show you, the narrative is run through by a river of irony that might bring an amused grin and head shake in one moment, a chuckle in another, and even a time or two of laughing out loud.

And therein lies the unbreakable bond we have with the Bible and its stories: whether or not we can ever establish the historical existence of the characters — the *people* — in the stories of Genesis, we have to admit that we can find the same pathos in their lives, the same humor and irony that we find in our own. While researching his book *Abraham*, author Bruce Feiler spoke with a ninety-three-year-old scholar-archaeologist in the old city of Jerusalem, who told him, "All we know of Abraham is in the Bible. In the ground there is nothing . . . If you're looking for history, you'll be disappointed. If you're looking for Abraham, you won't be."[1] Nor will you be disappointed if you are looking for Sarah, or Isaac, or Rebekah, Jacob, Rachel, or Joseph. An unexpected surprise may come, however, when, looking closely at them, you begin to see your own reflection.

---

*The full story is in chapter 97.

*   *   *

A great irony in my life is that, despite my Southern Baptist upbringing, my own journey of the spirit had its genesis in my hometown's Roman Catholic church, where, in the fall of 1958, during a nuptial mass, I had what might be called an "ecstatic" experience,* a split second in which my imagination went off the rails, or something actually happened. Whatever it was, it left me confused, frightened, fascinated, and curious to know what it meant. I still don't have a clue—and therein lies the greatest irony of my life because what I've done with my life, the paths I've gone down, the man I've become, can be traced back to that single moment more than fifty years ago.

It happened again, or seemed to, in the spring of 1968, my senior year in university, this time in an Episcopal church, during the nuptial mass for my college roommate. Then, two weeks later, a car crash left me with two fractured vertebrae, a broken jaw, pulverized gums, and broken teeth. Ten days in the hospital were followed by more than two months in a rented hospital bed in the den of my parents' home. I had little else to do but watch the limited fare of daytime television, read, and think. With graduation impending and the military draft a certainty, my life plan in the near term had been boot camp, advanced infantry training, and Vietnam. If anything followed that, it would be graduate school, or joining my dad in the family business, or something else. But that was then, before the accident. Now, given that it would be at least six months before I could even rise to a sitting position without first strapping on a metal back brace, and that I faced more reconstructive oral surgery, my fitness for military service was in serious doubt. With room to consider the future, and still reeling from that second "experience," I convinced myself that my future was in the church. Within a year and a half, I'd joined the Episcopal Church, married my college sweetheart, moved to Virginia, and had begun my first term at the Episcopal seminary in Alexandria, just across the Potomac River from Washington, D.C.

The idyllic existence of a graduate student had little in common with the lives of the clergymen with whom we worked on weekends, the life for which we were preparing ourselves. Toward the end of my second academic year, with just one more to go before graduation, ordination, and a life I was not at all sure I wanted, I requested and received permission to leave academics for a full-time internship in a local parish, St. Mark's, on Capitol Hill in the Episcopal Diocese of Washington. While I assumed the year would be important, I didn't suspect that my assumptions about

*The full story is in chapter 38.

almost everything were about to be blown sky-high during what would prove to be, to that point, the ride of my life.

By the mid-1950s, the phenomenon known as "white flight" had eroded St. Mark's membership to the point that the diocesan authorities considered closing its doors. Then, with new leadership calling on "Interested Pagans, Bored Christians, and Others," and offering lectures and discussions on topics such as "Christianity and the Intellectual" and "Christianity and the Bored Citizen," the parish began a remarkable evolution, in time gaining a national reputation for its innovative uses of the arts in liturgy, for its revolutionary approach to Christian education, for its policy of *"Whatever you believe, whatever you do not believe, you are welcome at this table,"* and for the commitment, caliber, and enviable talent of its laity. All were welcome to attend services and classes, but membership in the parish was another matter. The first requirement was participation in the the "St. Mark's Confirmation Class" (including Episcopalians previously confirmed), a sixteen-week course that included two mandatory weekend retreats. The next step was to assume one's share of responsibility for the overall well-being of the parish. This included a financial commitment but also a pledge of at least twenty hours of service each month, these spent in groundskeeping, choir, altar guild, teaching (children or adults), or one of the various committees or special projects.

While the rectors of St. Mark's were strong leaders, the organizing principle of the community didn't allow the sort of overwhelming personality found at the center of most successful churches. Instead that center was to be found in the community itself, and in the biblical principle of *accountability*—learning to live by the power of one's word, that is, learning to be *faithful*, without which servanthood is impossible. I learned that one of the undergirdings of faithfulness is *vulnerability*, stretching oneself, with support, toward living the sort of unhidden humanness that Jesus had lived. This called for a reading of scripture that I'd never before imagined—to read it not as admonishments about right and wrong, good and bad, but as a vast, reflective surface in which to see our own lives, individually and collectively. Making that switch, shifting my perspective on stories and characters I'd known since before I could read—regarding it all as metaphor—proved to be its own task.

Among my duties that year would be to deliver the Sunday morning sermon, not once but several times, and to what I considered the most intimidating gathering of human beings I'd ever faced. The congregation at St. Mark's neither expected nor wanted pat answers and theological dazzlements from the preacher, but rather his insight into the human issue at the heart of the scriptural passages for that day, and plain talk, human being to human beings, about how that issue had presented itself in *his* life, and how it had been resolved, or how it continued to have ramifications. In fact, talking about some issue that remained unresolved could be far more useful because it *was* human, after all, to have ongoing struggles, such as character issues, self-doubts, damaged relationships with family and friends. My mentor that year, the rector of St. Mark's, said that if I was honest in telling them about my own struggles, the congregation would love me for it. If I tried to impress them with my education, or manipulate them with sentimentality, it was a near certainty that someone from the congregation would stand and ask me to stop and sit down. If they didn't, he said, *he* would.

Over the coming weeks, I observed that he used a biblical story almost as a morality play, the characters as archetypally human, dramatic elements in the narrative. Without it seeming forced, contrived, sappy, or inappropriately revealing, he would use one or more of the characters as a device for reflecting on some personal experience or some element in his own character. Afterward, whether it was immediate, hours later, or the next day, I might find that something in me had stirred, as if he'd been speaking about me, or on my behalf. Once, for instance, after he'd talked about his own struggles with authority (the scriptural passage may have been from David's conflict with Absalom, his son), I had a better sense of my part in the ongoing conflicts with my bishop and my father. Following the service, people talked about the sermon, how they'd seen themselves reflected in the character(s) in the story. These responses were possible—and here was the key to the method—because the stories are our stories, and the people in them are all of us. That reflective use of scripture in teaching is the only model that makes sense to me. Because it does not require a religious point of view, it makes the Bible available to everyone.

Graduating in 1973, I served parishes in Texas and California. In 1981, I joined a startup training organization, The Life Training (now More To Life), which, by 1990, had opened training centers in the United States; London and Cambridge, England; and Johannesburg and Durban, South Africa. We taught people to change the negative stories they told about themselves that led to repeated failures; it was a psychological but also a spiritual process, the beginning of an exodus from bondage of spirit to freedom, a personal journey to be taken in the company of others on the same path.

By the time I left the organization, in 1995, I had led or co-led more than three hundred two-day trainings, plus evening workshops and lectures, logging more than ten thousand contact hours with groups as diverse as Wyoming cowboys, British nobility, federal prison inmates, white and black South Africans involved in the anti-apartheid struggles, plumbers, housewives, M.D.s, househusbands, electricians, psychologists, psychiatrists, mechanics, CEOs, and high-court judges. I also went into management training and consulting in corporate culture, as well coaching and crisis intervention.

After eight years in the church, having served a wealthy parish, a *fabulously* wealthy parish, and a blue-collar parish, I can say that the human issues in each bore a striking similarity. Yet there and in the groups I've worked with as a trainer, the powerful, the powerless, and those in between virtually always expressed surprise at discovering that they stood on the same human ground. Few of the stories I heard in the course of those twenty-plus years—and none of the stories I lived—would fail to find their parallel among myriad human tales in the Bible.

Above I slipped it in that you, too, live inside the metaphor. I invite you to consider that possibility, to ponder whether these ancient stories resonate with your own. As you will see from my own musings, you need not be religious for this. In fact, if you're alive and breathing and reading this, these stories and their characters have already shaped you, and in greater measure than you might think, as they have shaped us all, religious and nonreligious alike. Their moral, ethical, and spiritual DNA are embedded in the foundations of our civilization, in our awareness of who we are as a people *and* as individuals, our best and worst selves.

Because I'll be referring to it from time to time, a brief overview of what biblical scholars call the "Source Theory"* of the Bible is in order. The first five books of the Bible, known to Jews as Torah, to Christians as the Pentateuch, are composed of an interweaving of four primary strands of source material, known to biblical scholars as "J" (Jahwist, or Yahwist), "E" (Elohist), "D" (Deuteronomist), and "P" (Priestly), each of separate authorship, at times telling different versions of the same story (for example, one creation story is told by P in Genesis 1:1–2:3, another by J in Genesis 2:4–4:24), and, except for J and E, written in different historical periods. Their work was put into its final form by R (Redactors), editors of such genius that some modern scholars regard their work to be a fifth source.

Finally, since this book follows the book of Genesis, I suggest that you also read the biblical text itself, and that you use a modern translation. While I have relied on the translations of Robert Alter, Richard Elliott Friedman, Everett Fox, and others, unless otherwise noted all biblical quotations are from the Jewish Publication Society Tanakh, 1999.

---

*For an excellent summary of the Source Theory, see Richard Elliott Friedman, *The Bible with Sources Revealed* (New York: HarperCollins, 2003).

PART I

THE BEGINNING

Adam and Eve, but Mostly Eve

1

Imagine yourself as the first human being. You've popped into the world inside the body of a full-grown adult. You've gone from nonbeing to being and become fully conscious, although you have no memories, no parents, no siblings, friends, or enemies. No clothes and no language, though it seems reasonable that *from thy bowels*, as our Elizabethan ancestors were wont to say, would arise some expression of, *What th'* . . . ? as you stood, lay, or sat, blank-brained, absorbing those first bursts of fivefold sensory input. This wordless sense of being and identity is just the sort of abstraction that your big *Homo sapiens* brain is designed to ponder and dissect. Advanced queries such as *Who am I?* and *What am I?* will follow, in time.

But all those thoughts require *context*, and at present you don't have any. So your brain, with its capacity for objectification, starts building some. Perhaps you begin by noticing that you and a tree, say, are not the same thing. You have feet, for instance, and trees don't. You can move from here to there; they can't. *Hmm.* Then, suddenly, all about you, as if appearing from nowhere—which they did—are hopping things, jumping things, soaring, crawling, running, buzzing, growling, chirping things. Your second *What th'* . . . ? Your first adrenaline buzz and an inner voice screams, *Run!* Then a louder inner voice shouts, *No! Wait! Look!* So you do and you see that those tiny creatures hovering around the flowers, and that big, stripey one with the huge teeth, and the ones in the trees all have feet; they can move from here to there. As for the *How* and the *Why* of them, well, the same All-Powerful Being who made you lets you know that he also made them, just so you wouldn't be alone—and how nice was that? Now, as you go about naming everything—bird, bee, tiger, horse, platypus—you notice that there are at least two of each of them, but only one of you. *Hmm!*

The facility takes care of your basic physical needs—food, water, shelter, climate control—so there's little for you to do but eat, sleep, hang out with the birds, bugs, plants, and animals, ponder it all, and build those contexts. No hassles. No worries. Except for that one *tiny* wrinkle that came up during the tour when the All-Powerful Being pointed to that one tree and said, *Don't eat the fruit of that one!* He was pretty emphatic, going on about *Good, Bad,* and *Die.* Your software being quite adept at sniffing out danger, even in the subtleties of mood and tone, from the sudden shift in voice inflection, *and* the look, *and* the finger-pointing, *and* the finger-wagging, you'd picked up on the bit about *Don't eat.* (But, *Die?* What's that?) If, however, he'd meant that you were not even to *think* about it, well, too bad, because that tree you might never have noticed is now the most interesting thing in the Garden.

2

ANOTHER CREATURE—ONE LIKE
YOU, SORT OF—SHOWS UP

That is, until that one day when, on waking from a nap, you find a new creature in the garden. It makes you feel all funny. You forget about the tree. Then, sometime later, when the two of you come up for air, you remember to mention it. So now your partner is curious, too, and when you two aren't, um, *involved,* you both can be found at the tree, your curiosity now infatuation, now compulsion, moving you closer each day until, finally, there you are, the two of you, beneath it, contemplating the heavy, hanging fruit of it, dangerously, flirtatiously, close to the forbidden touch. Day after day it hovers there, silent, juicy, *whispering.* Yum.

3

IT'S ENTIRELY POSSIBLE THAT NONE OF
THIS IS WHAT YOU'VE ASSUMED IT TO BE

The above two sections have bits and pieces of both creation stories. Yes, *both.* The Bible's opening line, the familiar "In the beginning . . . ," is the creation of P,* as is the story of the man and the woman who just popped into being. The tree is from the second creation story, J's version, which recounts that the woman was created after the man. (Yes, Genesis can get a little confusing.) There's more. For instance, you probably grew up with the idea that, in Genesis, the first man was *named* Adam. Nope. While P writes that "God created man in His image . . . male and female He created them," he never mentions anyone actually *named* Adam—or Eve, for

---

*See Source Theory overview in the Introduction.

that matter, or a Garden of Eden. In fact, we're well into J's story (which begins at Genesis 2:4b) before the man is referred to as "the man," which makes sense from a linguistic point of view, given that *adam* is the Hebrew word for "human." Yes, *human:* male *and* female. So, *adam* is a common gender noun rather than a proper name, a "Hey, you!," and Eve is as much an adam as Adam. While Eve is given her name by the man, *Eve* means "mother of all that lives"—which is interesting, since she has not yet given birth—and though J does refer to him as "Adam," at least in translation, the first man is never *officially* named. I suppose that, were one to send a formal announcement or invitation, say, the proper inscription would read, *Eve and friend.*

The text that is actually there in Genesis, and what readers *assume* is there, are often quite different. Indeed, among its other functions, Genesis challenges assumptions, a role made necessary by thousands of years of attempts at interpreting its contents, itself a role to which any interpreter, being human, will bring a point of view. Moreover, people tend to defend their assumptions regarding Genesis—or, for that matter, any part of the Bible—with the tenacity of a lioness guarding her cubs. While proponents of this or that assumption, however outrageous, might truly believe theirs to be the product of divine inspiration, some, for their own reasons, likely made it up. Or someone else did, and they believed it. Take Eve, for example.

4

ABOUT THE WOMAN

In the JPS translation, P's account of the creation of the humans reads: "God said, 'Let us make man in our image, after our likeness . . .' And God created man in His image, in the image of God He created him; male and female he created them." The URJ translation of the same Hebrew text reads: "God now said, 'Let us create human beings in our image, after our likeness . . .' So God created the human beings in [the divine] image, creating [them] in the image of God, creating them male and female." Note that the latter translates the Hebrew *adam* as "human beings," not "man," as in the JPS and most English translations. Note also the use of the plural, "human *beings.*" About that, Bible scholar Tamara Cohn Eskenazi writes,

> This translation resorts to the plural to avoid using misleading masculine pronouns later in the verse. Literally, the Hebrew has: "And God created the *adam.* In the image of God he created *him/it*; male and female he

created *them*" (shifting the object pronoun from singular to plural). By referring to *adam*, the text is not describing an individual but a new class of beings that comprises female and male from the start, both of them in God's image . . . The shift from singular to plural does not convey that man was created before woman . . . Rather, it seems to say that our humanity, as *adam*, precedes our division into sexual categories. Our humanity comes first; our sexual identity next.[1]

J's account of the creation of the humans is earthy, intimate, and hands-on. In chapter 2, verse 7, Yahweh fashions the man from the soil (earth, *adama*) then breathes into him "the breath of life," which, *breath* and *spirit* being the same word in Hebrew (*nephesh*), is an act of infusing the human with life *and* the divine spirit—a significant act. Then, to provide the man with companions, Yahweh fashions, again from the soil, the birds and animals. Still, since the man has no proper mate, at verse 21, Yahweh puts him to sleep, takes one of the man's ribs, and creates one.

But, one *what*, exactly?

In Hebrew, the phrase is *'ezer kenegdo*, which, for centuries, has been translated into English as "helper" or "helpmate," and taken to mean something akin to "the little woman." "The Hebrew," writes Robert Alter, in his commentary on Genesis, "is notoriously difficult to translate. The second term means 'alongside,' 'opposite him,' a counter-part to him. 'Help' is too weak because it suggests a merely auxiliary function, whereas *'ezer* elsewhere connotes active intervention on behalf of someone, especially in military contexts, as often in the Psalms."[2] Alter translates the phrase as "sustainer beside him [the man],"[3] Richard Elliott Friedman as "a strength corresponding to him."[4] In other words, the woman was created in order to provide the man with a partner—an equal partner. This leaves us with nothing in either creation narrative that places the woman in an inferior position to the man—not her sex, not her place in the order of creation, and not the reason she was created. Yet thousands of years of inventive speculation and creative writing about the book of Genesis, efforts that would yield "proof" of Eve's (and her sex's) inferiority to Adam (and his sex), have given us most of what we assume to be true about Eve—even though no validation of those assumptions exists in the original text.

How *that* came about is its own story.

5

WHO ARE WE?
THE RISE OF THE INTERPRETERS

If you build your house on the southeastern shore of one of the Florida Keys, you must expect that, one day, a hurricane will take it away. Likewise, if you establish your homeland on a piece of geography that, for centuries, has been a principal invasion corridor (think *interstate highway*), then you will, in time, be invaded. If you do either on the premise that you are under divine protection from such consequences, only to have your house blown away, or an invader roll over your land, you'll likely arrive at one of two conclusions: your premise for choosing that location was faulty, or your premise was correct, but something you did, or failed to do, *really* annoyed the divine protector.

In his masterwork, *Traditions of the Bible: A Guide to the Bible as It Was at the Start of the Common Era*, James Kugel reveals that, over the centuries, passages from the Bible were interpreted this way, then that way, then another; each interpretation, in the context of place and time of its origin, seemed to be correct. Therefore, what we might assume to be *the* interpretation of the Bible might well be but the product of the latest interpreters. "Who nowadays, for example," writes Kugel, "does not automatically think of the story of Adam and Eve as telling about some fundamental change that took place in the human condition, or what is commonly called the Fall of Man."[5] Yet the early Israelites made no such assumption, until after the Babylonian invasion. Known in Jewish history as "the great divide," the year 586 B.C.E. witnessed the fall of Jerusalem, the destruction of the first Temple, and the beginning of nearly fifty years of exile from the promised land, a national trauma expressed with affecting poignancy in Psalm 137:

> *By the rivers of Babylon*
> *there we sat,*
> *and we wept*
> *as we thought of Zion.*
> *There on the poplars*
> *we hung up our lyres,*
> *for our captors asked us there for songs,*
> *our tormentors, for amusement:*
> *"Sing us one of the songs of Zion."*
> *How can we sing a song of the Lord*
> *on alien soil?*

Then, in 532 B.C.E., soon after the Babylonians fell to the Persians, Cyrus the Great, king of Persia, granted the Israelites the option to return. Some remained—what had been a foreign land to their grandparents was the only home they'd known. Those who chose to go back to Zion were haunted by the idea that, somehow, their ancestors had tweaked the divine nose and lost the protective shield. As for *what* their ancestors had done, nobody had a clue. The Israelite elders who might have remembered were dead, along with their knowledge of the sacred texts and their meanings. Besides, even if they'd found a key to that old knowledge, they no longer spoke the old language. Fifty years of immersion in Babylonian culture had created new words and given old words new meaning. Too much of the past was out of reach. Still, with no place else to look but their holy books, when answers weren't forthcoming with sufficient clarity, the role of the *interpreter* was born.

None was a woman.

6

THE FRUIT OF THE TREE OF THE
KNOWLEDGE OF . . . EXACTLY WHAT?

The first clue about free will and human nature shows up in Yahweh's warning to Adam about the consequences of eating the fruit of *that* tree: *Eat it, you die. Don't eat it, you live. Your call.* While most English translations read, "the tree of the knowledge of good and evil," the JPS reads, "the tree of knowledge of good and bad." Why the change? In his *Commentary on the Torah*, Richard Elliott Friedman also translates the Hebrew word as "bad," because

> "evil" suggests that this is strictly moral knowledge. But the Hebrew word (*ra'*) has a much wider range of meaning than that. This may mean knowledge of what is morally good and bad, or it may mean qualities of good and bad in all realms: morality, aesthetics, utility, pleasure and pain, and so on. It may also mean that things are good and bad in themselves and that when one eats from the tree one acquires the ability to see these qualities; or it may mean that when one eats from the tree one acquires the ability to make *judgments* of good and bad. Perhaps the meaning was clear to the ancient reader who knew the immediate connotation of the words. It is not clear to us in the text of the story as it has survived. The only immediate consequence of eating from the tree that the story names is that before eating from the tree the humans are not embarrassed over their nudity and

after eating from it they are. This is not sufficient information to tell us what limits of "good and bad" are meant, nor does it tell us if absolute good and bad are implied or if it is the more relative concept of making judgments of good and bad.[6]

So, as much as we might *want* to know, and *think* we know, about what J meant by his use of "good and bad," we can't know. We can study the writings of the interpreters, but even the earliest of these, those closest to J's own time, *began* writing because they didn't know, either.

7

ENTER THE SERPENT, CHOICES,
AND CONSEQUENCES

The word *serpent* is from Latin and means "creeping," an activity we asso ciate with legs of some sort, as opposed to slithering—a fate the serpent might have avoided had he kept the conversation to a light banter. Ironically, the conversation the serpent did initiate with Eve, one of the more familiar fragments in Western literature, begins with what appears to be no more than an innocent request for clarification:

"Did God really say: You shall not eat of any tree of the garden"?
"We may eat of the fruit of the other trees in the garden."
"It is only about the fruit of the tree in the middle of the garden that God said: 'You shall not eat of it or touch* it lest you die.'"
"You are not going to die, but God knows that as soon as you eat of it your eyes will be opened and you will be like divine beings who know good and bad."

The serpent knew the answer before he asked the question, didn't he? Already, J has warned the reader that the serpent is "the shrewdest of all the wild beasts that the Lord God had made." His instantaneous and brilliantly outrageous comeback is a giveaway that the question was a setup, a ploy to elicit an answer that he was prepared to annihilate—and that Eve, given that she offered no resistance to the serpent's argument, was willing to see annihilated.

---

*Actually, the admonition, in chapter 2, verse 17, is only against *eating* the fruit. The addition of *touching*, according to some interpreters, came from Adam. Others suggest that Eve added it.

Unlike the traditional image of the serpent plucking the fruit and offering it to Eve, in J's story he never touches it. Likewise, he does not suggest that she eat it, not directly. Instead he entices, seduces with intimacy ("*your* eyes will be opened, and *you* will be like Gods"), subtly implies that the real motive driving Yahweh's admonition is power, keeping the franchise on divine knowledge for himself, and away from her. Then, "When the woman saw that the tree was good for eating and a delight to the eyes, and that the tree was desirable as a source of wisdom, she took of its fruit and ate. She also gave some to her husband, and he ate. Then the eyes of both of them were opened and they perceived that they were naked; and they sewed together fig leaves and made themselves loincloths."

Sometime later, on hearing Yahweh moving about in the garden, they hid from him. When asked why, Adam said, "I heard the sound of you in the garden, and I was afraid because I was naked, so I hid."

"Who told you that you were naked?" Yahweh replied. "Did you eat of the tree from which I had forbidden you to eat?"

They'd been naked all along, of course, judging it neither as good nor bad, living in a state of innocence akin to the toddler who has no opinion about whether he and his family should go to the mall naked, in clown costumes, or drag. Anyone who has raised a child from infancy knows that when an infant is hungry, has a loaded diaper, an irritating rash, or an upset tummy, he'll scream until you fix it. But the child won't judge you as *bad* if you don't fix it, or as *good* if you do. Neither will he care whether you're fat or skinny, liberal or conservative, religious or atheist, gay or straight, good-looking or plain, rich or poor, bald or hairy, or whether you've succeeded in pre-enrolling him in the right preschool.

But, in time, he will. Think of the bite of the fruit as a force-feeding, an apt metaphor for the child's brain crossing inevitable developmental thresholds, growing the capacity for abstract thought, including the first inklings of subject (I, me) and object (you, they, it), including the capacity for making moral and ethical judgments. This latter higher, even *noble* function comes with a dark side. Without meaning to, at least, not at first, he will begin assuming the *good* to be what he likes, the *bad* to be what he doesn't like, and, of course, assume that he is right. This is not an evil process, but an *organic* process that comes with being human. Once started—and it always starts—it can't be stopped. But it *can* be reined in. With time he can learn to step back, to make sober observations—yes, *judgments*—about his behavior, learning to recognize when judgment becomes judgmentalness, then choosing to stop—that is, to stop it *that* time. Then there's the next time.

Looked at from this point of view, the Fall is not a onetime occurrence, but an ongoing process in a life, a product of the fault lines in human nature and human choosing. In other words—and though I claim to speak only for myself here, I suspect I am not alone—those times I notice my judgmentalness coming on, when I *could* choose to *just say no*, but I don't, it's because I just don't want to. In the moment, I'd rather be right than wise.

So, Yahweh's questions are rhetorical. The single avenue provided by the story to knowing shame, a higher function, is the fruit of *that* tree. Eating the fruit, they'd become self-aware, crossed over into an understanding of the duality of right and wrong, good and bad. The first thing they did with their new toy was to make themselves wrong for being naked.

On the subject of punishment, Yahweh, like other ancient gods, was not one to say, *Okay, this one time I'll let it slide.* In fact, what came next was less punishment than a reckoning. For his part, the serpent was told,

> *"Because you did this,*
> *More cursed shall you be*
> *Than all cattle*
> *And all the wild beasts:*
> *On your belly shall you crawl*
> *And dirt shall you eat all the days of your life.*
> *I will put enmity*
> *Between you and the woman,*
> *And between your offspring and hers;*
> *They shall strike at your head,*
> *And you shall strike at their heel."*

To Eve he said,

> *"I will make most severe*
> *your pangs in childbearing;*
> *In pain shall you bear children.*
> *Yet your urge shall be for your husband,*
> *And he shall rule over you."*

Then, to Adam, he said, *"Because you did as your wife said and ate of the tree about which I commanded you, 'You shall not eat of it,'*

> *"Cursed be the ground because of you;*
> *By toil shall you eat of it*
> *All the days of your life:*

Thorns and thistles shall it sprout for you.
But your food shall be the grasses of the field;
By the sweat of your brow
Shall you get bread to eat,
Until you return to the ground—
For from it you were taken.
For dust you are,
And to dust you shall return."

8

EVE TAKES THE RAP

Having studied the passage, some interpreters concluded that the fault for Israel's defeat by the Babylonians and the exile that followed belonged, at least in part, with Adam and Eve, who, by their disobedience, had condemned not only themselves but all subsequent generations. Moreover, among the perpetrators, they saw an obvious order of guilt. First place went to the serpent, of course. Although either of the human beings could have just said no, the woman could have said it first, so second place went to her. Later interpreters, Jews and Christians, would pile on with the likes of "From a woman sin had its beginning, and because of her, we all die" (Sirach 25:24) and "I permit no woman to teach or have authority over men [because] Adam was not deceived, but the woman was deceived and became a transgressor" (St. Paul, 1 Timothy 2:13–14). St. Paul seems to be saying that Adam knew what he was doing when he ate the fruit, but that Eve had been under the spell of the serpent. The text, however, says nothing about a spell, and if Adam was *not* deceived, and did eat the fruit, then either he knew what he was doing, making him equally culpable, or too weak-willed to resist, or was too stupid to realize what Eve was offering. Then there's the text itself, in which J writes, "Eve gave Adam the fruit and he ate it"—an act of free will.

If you're ever in Rome, go to the Sistine Chapel, look up into that magnificent vault, and follow the panels along the central axis until you find the one containing the incident at the tree. Here, in this panel, titled *Original Sin*, Michelangelo has followed an old medieval tradition of depicting the serpent as a woman with a snake's lower body. Look closely and you'll see that the serpent-woman has plucked a piece of the fruit and is holding it out to Eve, while Adam is plucking his own.

9

ANOTHER EVE

Had early interpreters been content to say that scripture proved Eve to be an inferior creation to Adam, and leave it at that, there'd have been little about her to capture the imagination. Guilt made her infamous. This image, of the *Inferior-Guilty Eve* as the woman who brought us all down, would define her and her sex for the next twenty-five hundred years, right up to the modern era, when fluid attitudes about religion and morality would be used to transmogrify her guilt into naughtiness and take her into pop culture. In the decades following World War II, secular interpreters—creators of imagery in advertising, for instance—began tinkering with Eve's likeness, taking liberties that most would not dare with the Virgin Mary.

You've seen her, the barefoot hottie from TV commercials and magazine ads, proudly holding up that apple with the missing bite, wearing minimalist cave-girl couture, a wicked *come-on-down-and-get-some* smile, a hooker selling the promise of sex—which also comes with food, wine, a car, or a trip to Vegas. This iteration of the biblical character in *Hooker Eve* attempts to represent a modern, hip, liberated view of women but in fact is simply another expression of the same, millennia-old ideas about women and their value and place in society—*Inferior-Guilty Eve*.

Taken as metaphor, the incident at the tree is not about right versus wrong but about the consequences of becoming fully human. Taken as historical fact, however, it became the flashpoint for a nasty idea about the nature of humanity that remains at the doctrinal core of Western Christianity.

10

JUST IN CASE YOU ARE WONDERING WHAT
THIS HAS TO DO WITH YOU: ORIGINAL SIN,
MY GRANDMOTHER, ME, AND THEE

Judaism has no doctrine of Original Sin. A construct of early Christians after Jesus's death, it originates not with Jesus, but with Paul, specifically from allusions he made in two of his letters, both written about the same time. In Romans, chapter 5, verse 12, he writes that "sin came into the world through one man [Adam]," and in verse 19, "by one man's disobedience, many were made sinners." Likewise, in First Corinthians, chapter

15, verse 22, he writes that "in Adam all die." Paul refers, of course, to J's account of the incident at the tree, in which Yahweh says nothing about a blanket condemnation. So where did Paul get such an idea? A well-educated Pharisee who'd studied the postexilic interpreters, he'd have known their teaching:

> Adam and Eve were punished by becoming mortal . . . Some interpreters clearly did believe that Adam and Eve's punishment had been transmitted to all subsequent generations . . . Others . . . came to the conclusion that it was not their punishment, but their *sinfulness,* that was passed on . . . [that] if we, their descendants, also are mortal, it is because we, in some fundamental way, are just like Adam and Eve . . . given over to sinning, and it is for that reason that we will die like them . . . So, thanks in part to the problem raised by God's threatened punishment, "on the day you eat of it you shall die," interpreters came to see the true significance of the story as relating to human mortality and, perhaps, a human predisposition to sinfulness.[7]

The idea gained traction with the Christians in the second and third centuries C.E., through the writings of Justin Martyr, Irenaeus, Origen, and Tertullian, who needed theological ammunition in the battle against the so-called heresies. In the fifth century, Augustine, bishop of Hippo (North Africa), answering yet another heresy, Pelagianism, formulated the doctrine of Original Sin *and* sold it, securing its place in the theological mainstream of the church.

Pelagius, an ascetic monk and a contemporary of Augustine, had gained followers by taking the position that, because sin is an act of free will, when free will is not present there can be no sin. The idea that Adam's disobedience "transmitted neither sin nor death to his posterity"[8] threatened orthodoxy because if mankind was not fundamentally corrupt, from what did it need to be saved? Indeed, without Original Sin as the corruption into which all humans are born, the logic at the root of orthodoxy, *that Christ had died on the Cross in order to atone for the sins of all mankind,* would evaporate. This would never do. Starting from Paul's notion of how sin entered the world, and influenced by Tertullian (who'd coined the phrase "Original Sin"), Augustine claimed that the taint of Adam's sin *is* hereditary, transmitted through procreation, and that since all humans are born corrupted, even an infant who dies without baptism will spend eternity in the fires of hell. But even *after* baptism, the desire to go on sinning remains, expressing itself particularly in "concupiscence," lust, *sex.* Promiscuity, adultery, and incest—these were long-standing sexual taboos, but with Augustine's triumph over Pelagianism, in time, most Christians would be taught that the sex act itself, except within the bonds of marriage and for the single purpose of procreation, was an offense in the eyes of God.

To summarize, some of the postexilic interpreters decided that the incident at the tree was *the* reason for the Fall, that Adam's and Eve's punishment was mortality and that, since all humans are mortal, it must be true that we all share in their sinful nature. St. Paul carried this idea over into Christianity, where it lay dormant until the early church, defending orthodoxy, used it to formulate the doctrine of Original Sin, a malignant idea about human nature that has survived to shape the nature of Christianity, fuel its darkness (the Inquisition), and color Western civilization's idea of itself and the world for about 1,600 years—so far.

Nowhere in the Bible, in the Tanakh, or the New Testament are the words "Original Sin" to be found. Yet religious doctrine still blames Adam and Eve, and still attributes more blame to her, an imbalance that religion's darker side has done its best to maintain despite the collateral damage.

My grandmother's life, for instance.

Mount Pleasant, Texas, 1910, 1913, 1932

Emma was born in 1892 into the upper middle class of northeastern Texas white society, a reality so different from ours today that it seems a parallel universe. Every moment of life there was colored by religion, by the certainty that God—a thunderous, demanding, unforgiving tyrant—was everywhere, hearing one's every thought, seeing one's every action, remembering every transgression, and keeping score for Judgment Day. Other eyes were watching, too: God's self-appointed surrogates, women with little else to do but watch others—especially young women—interpret what they observed, and pass it along in whispers. Like the generations of women before them, they believed that Satan was in every desire, and his most powerful temptation was sex. Sexual intercourse, therefore, was to be practiced *only* within the bonds of marriage, *only* for procreation, and *never* for pleasure. Decent Christian women considered sex disgusting, so, while a man might have no choice but to reach orgasm if he were to impregnate his wife, for a woman to take even the smallest pleasure from the act was reason for the deepest, most private shame. Having earned a master's degree, my grandmother may have known something of Augustine, though of her acquaintances, men as well as women, I doubt that more than a few had ever heard his name.

John, my grandfather, was a handsome young man, a fast talker, and just a bit roguish. Emma was a tall, willowy, quiet beauty. When she discovered that she was pregnant, their wedding plans were already under way. They were in love, they married straightaway, Neil's birth certificate was marked "Legitimate," and none of it mattered, because when Neil died at age three, they, their families, and their community interpreted his death as retribution for his parents' sin, especially his mother's: God had taken the child. Nineteen years later, when my mother's twin sister died of rheumatic fever, it was assumed that God, having reconsidered the original punishment, had found it insufficient. Even the milieu in which my grandmother lived was deeply influenced by invasion and exile half a world away and two and a half millennia before her birth, by the returning exiles who, in their need to understand the tragedy in the life of their nation, wrote interpretations of the incident at the tree that in turn influenced Paul, who influenced Augustine, who defined a doctrine that would reach across 1,600 years of history to tell her, just as if it were true, that the deaths of two of her children were her punishment for having had sex before marriage. Most of us raised in Christian households also received some of this indoctrination, even if as individuals we rejected it and our parents deemed Original Sin to be nonsense. Even non-Christians in Western culture are subjected to it when, for instance, Christian leaders from the far right blame the active sexuality of modern-day Eves and feminists—as well as homosexuals—for events ranging from Hurricane Katrina to 9/11 to economic recession.

11

A FEW FINAL IRONIES.
ADAM AND EVE GET THE BOOT

In the southeastern Texas Protestantism of my youth, *Hooker Eve* may have been the star of every good Christian boy's late-night fantasies, but *Inferior-Guilty Eve* was the girl he brought home to Mom. Past the religious and secular interpretations is the original, *Genesis Eve*, the woman as the writers, and particularly J, imagined her: strong, vulnerable, neither apologetic about her womanhood nor tempted to cheapen it. She is carnal, neither *afraid* of sex nor only *about* sex. Her partner never says or implies that her sex is inferior to his own, or that she bears more, or less, responsibility for the incident at the tree, or for the consequences that enveloped their lives as a result. Good thing, too, because following the confrontation, Yahweh, in a fit of divine pique, drives Adam and Eve from the garden and into the world.

By law, *Hooker Eve*'s parts must always be covered. By cultural expectation, *Inferior-Guilty Eve*'s body must be mostly covered. However, *Genesis Eve*—the character in the story—is unburdened by Bible-based standards and so is naked as a jaybird right up to the moment before she and the man are busted. If there *is* life after death, I hope my grandmother got the joke, had a good laugh, and that she and my grandfather had some long-awaited fun.

Most anyone you might ask will know the Adam and Eve story at least in outline. Some will regard it as the history of the world, *and* they'll say these three chapters were written by a single hand. Others will regard all of it as a silly story with naked people and a talking snake, a fairy tale with all the real-world credibility of Santa Claus and the Easter Bunny. A third way, taken here, is to read the story as myth and metaphor, a medium for study but also for self-reflection. This is the most difficult of the paths as it pins the blame for the Fall—aka, the sorry state we humans seem, collectively, to prefer—on us, and in particular, on the face each one of us sees in the mirror. The creation narratives now continue with the story of Cain and Abel, one of the more tragic and poignant tales in the Bible.

Cain and Abel, but Mostly Cain

12

THE FIRST BIRTH IS A CO-CREATION. SO IS THE
FIRST MURDER—THEN AGAIN, MAYBE NOT

Have you ever offered an idea that you thought worthy of consideration, only to have it dismissed out of hand? Or given a gift that was snubbed? Or have your accomplishments been ignored when the kudos were given out? A yes to any of these opens a portal between Cain's story and your own, even if you didn't kill anybody.

The account of Cain and his brother, Abel, is J's recasting of a "widespread culture-founding story of rivalry between herdsmen and farmers . . . into . . . a pattern that will dominate Genesis—the displacement of the firstborn by the younger son."[9] But in this, the first occurrence of the pattern, the focus is on the older son, whose story begins with his conception, which, in the JPS translation, reads, "Now the man knew [had intercourse with] his wife, Eve, and she conceived and bore Cain, saying, 'I have gained a male child with the help of the Lord.'" However, Friedman, Alter, and Everett Fox read "man," not "man child." As in the account of the creation of Eve, lost in the translation from Hebrew to English is the mischief J stirs up simply by way of the particular word he uses to describe exactly *what* Eve and Yahweh had created. "The [Hebrew] word 'man,'" Kugel writes, "does not simply mean 'male person,' [or] 'male child'—there are other words for that. Man means man, a grown-up male."[10] It's no surprise, then, that the ancient interpreters asked themselves, *Why that word?* Opinions were varied, some arguing that, due to Yahweh's direct intervention, Cain must have been born with special abilities, while others, "in view of the wicked turn that his life was to take . . . thought Cain might have been *evil from birth*, in fact, an offspring of the devil or some wicked angel."[11] Still others, these to be joined by some of the early Christians, speculated that "Adam did not know his wife in the biblical sense, he knew something *about* her."[12] Tertullian, the same second-century Christian apologist who coined the term "Original Sin," wrote, "Having been made pregnant by the seed of the devil . . . she brought forth a son."[13] In other words, Eve—*Inferior-Guilty Eve*—had done the horizontal boogie with Satan, which is why Cain was weird at birth, and the reason he was such a dastardly fellow. What the story itself tells us is that Cain (Qayin, meaning "smith," as in blacksmith) is the first human in the Genesis narrative to be born. He is the first child, the first human with a belly button, the first big brother. And he will be the first murderer.

Here's how the story develops: Eve gives birth to another son, Abel (Hevel, meaning "impermanent," "fleeting," "vaporous"), and the next thing we know of them is that "Abel became a keeper of sheep, and Cain became a tiller of the soil." Then, for reasons not given, "In the course of time, Cain brought an offering to the Lord from the fruit of the soil; and Abel, for his part, brought the choicest of the firstlings of his flock." Right away Yahweh acknowledges Abel's offering, but ignores Cain's. Why? The text doesn't say, so the interpreters once again went spelunking.

One theory was that Yahweh had a "preference for the shepherd's offering over the farmer's [that] may really have reflected something of the differences involved in the two professions."[14] Philo, a Hellenistic Jewish philosopher, and primarily a Platonist, in *Questions and Answers in Genesis* wrote, "One of them labors and takes care of living beings . . . which is preparatory to rulership and kingship. But the other occupies himself with earthly and inanimate things."[15] Likewise, Ambrose, fourth-century bishop of Milan, wrote in *Cain and Abel* that "plowing the earth . . . is inferior to pasturing sheep."[16] This statement reflects "the high regard for shepherds and the pastoral life manifest, for example, in the early life of national heroes such as Joseph, Moses, and David."[17] The simplest answer, then, to why Abel's offering was preferred is that J's audience held shepherds in greater esteem than farmers. Indeed, Ambrose and his Christian contemporaries might have pointed out that it was a band of shepherds, not farmers, to whom the angel had announced the birth of the Christ child (Luke 2:8ff.) *and* that Jesus had said of himself that "I am the good shepherd" (John 10:11), not "the good farmer."

Also, the interpreters noticed that Abel's offering was of the *choicest* of the newborn lambs while the text offered no such superlative for the fruit offered by Cain. Was this a subtle hint that Cain's offering had not been the best from his harvest? One interpreter, Ephraim, in his *Commentary on Genesis*, wrote, "Abel chose and brought for sacrifice from the firstborn and the fattest, but Cain brought [merely] the fruits he found at the time."[18] Another speculated that Cain's offering had been "from the leftovers."[19] Still another wrote that the "fruit of the ground [implied] ordinary fruit [rather than the first fruits reserved for God]."[20] Philo, in *The Sacrifices of Cain and Abel*, suggested an additional problem with Cain's offering: "There are here two indictments of this self-lover [Cain]. One is that he made an offering to God 'after some days' and not right away; the other that it was 'of the fruit' but not 'of the first fruit'"[21] —though he seems to have missed the irony in the first part of his indictment, that, since the brothers made their offerings at the same time, by condemning Cain for tardiness he condemned Abel as well. A few interpreters even assumed a past, not recorded in Genesis, in which Cain had proved himself unworthy, and in which Abel had proved himself to be worthy. The problem with that approach, Kugel tells us, is that "in Genesis, Abel is neither good nor bad—in fact, we really know nothing about him. He seems to be little more than a prop, the victim of his brother's rage. As for Cain, if he ends up being bad, he certainly did not start out that way; it was only the incident of the sacrifices that drove him to murder."[22] Because of explanations such as these, "the whole character of the story was altered by ancient interpreters . . . [who] subtly turned the story into an elemental conflict between good and evil."[23]

13

SWIMMING IN ABEL'S POND

When I was growing up, my family was Southern Baptist, so, as much through osmosis as anyone telling me, I learned early on that "Bible" meant the King James Bible (1611) and that every jot and tittle of "The Word" (an informal moniker) and of Baptist doctrine was to be regarded as "Truth" straight from God's lips to our right-believing ears. Beyond that, there was little else worth knowing, not really—certainly nothing else to know about the Bible. Our Sunday school teachers had little idea that the Bible had been translated from ancient Hebrew and Greek texts, or that the doctrine they taught followed the lead of Israelite interpreters. The angle they pushed in class, just as if it had been God's intention, was that Abel was the good boy whose behavior we should want to emulate.

But we didn't like him. Right away we shoved Abel into a paradigm we understood, imagining him to be like those goody-goody kids who never chewed gum in school, threw spitballs, passed notes, or cussed, the sort who would rat us out for no more than a nod and a smile from a teacher, and who actually liked Sunday school and even vacation Bible school, that grinding banality that wasted the first two weeks of every summer vacation. His would be the name at the top of the chart in the Sunday school classroom and from it would flow a constellation of golden stars earned through recitations of Bible verses and from memorizing the names of the books of the Bible, Genesis through Revelation. Sooner or later one of the tough kids would beat him up, even if, like the Abel of the story, he'd not actually *done* anything one could point to.

Cain, our teachers said, was the bad boy, like those "licentious juvenile delinquents" who combed their long hair into ducktails, smoked cigarettes, drank whiskey, carried switchblade knives, and got themselves expelled from school. But even we were beginning to notice the rise of rock 'n' roll, and the new sort of bad boy showing up in films like *Rebel Without a Cause*. Now, more than a half century later, it's clear that these were signals of a culture in transition, whose shadow was beginning to boil up through the cracks, superheated by years of that strangest of couplings, the postwar, shotgun marriage of naïve innocence with blacklist suppression. The Earth may have trembled with wars and rumors of war, with the threat of nuclear annihilation, but Americans seemed sure in those days that if anyone was allowed to say the f- or s-word on television or in the movies, the world as we knew it would end. Such things were, indeed, a symptom of the end of their world, but to most of us kids the rock 'n' rollers and the new character types in the movies and even on television were a lot more interesting than the Mouseketeers and the Beav.

Taken as metaphor, the Cain and Abel we'd received through the interpreters were flip sides of the same coin, expressions of duality—Abel, the good boy who stands in and for the light, and Cain, his shadow, the bad boy who stands in and for the darkness—each representing part of ourselves. Abel's long rule was waning. Now it was Cain's turn.

14

IRONICALLY, CAIN'S RULE DOES
BRING A TOUCH OF CLARITY

When the culture at large began its rightward shift in the 1970s, the subcurrents already deconstructing the old authority structures hardly missed a beat. Beneath the conservative political and religious surfaces of the eighties, nineties, and the early years of the new century, the old, steady, patriarchal imagery of *Father Knows Best* was completely upended within the world of pop culture. In the minidramas of television advertising, the image of the man of entitlement who'd said, "My wife—I think I'll keep her," gave way to the hapless, emasculated dope. Likewise, the father who'd known best in television sitcoms gave way to the boy-men of *Seinfeld* and *Friends*, to *Everybody Loves Raymond*, where, reminiscent of Prometheus, whose liver was torn out each day only to grow back each night, the eponymous Raymond would lose his testicles, these torn out not by an eagle but by the women in his life. In TV dramas such as *Desperate Housewives* and *Grey's Anatomy*, the mother who'd been stuck at home, who did housework with a smile, and wearing her pearls, is modernized to become the harried modern working woman, living in a world of professionally competent but otherwise clueless men. The mother's role is to be understanding and tolerant of her demanding children, for whom she does not have enough time and who regard both her and their father with little, if any, respect (though, on occasion, one of these children will show uncommon maturity and wisdom). In other words, the adults have lost their grip: the kids, with their unformed, undisciplined energies, needs, and wants, rule the house.

It *is* empowering and, to a point, necessary for a child to see the godlike adults in his life fold like tacos beneath the weight of defiance. Later we'll see that Cain, having taken a defiant attitude, will leave Yahweh helpless, unable to reach him—even the Creator of the Universe could not force the lad to change his attitude. It's a manipulation used by children to feel powerful in the world, but without necessarily bearing responsibility for the result. However, J's text seems to hint that self-inflation and *power without responsibility* can, in time, become a narcotic. We can see this in the "extended adolescence" that began in the postwar years, the postponing of maturity in order to remain indefinitely in a self-centered, inflated stage of development.

Gerhard von Rad, in his commentary on Genesis, would seem to suggest that J was well aware that even those who finally escape adolescence return to its self-importance and narcissism. "The narrative," he writes, "sees man's fall . . . occurring again and again in *this* area . . . in what we call Titanism, man's *hubris*."[24] As defined by the *Oxford English Dictionary*, *Titanism* is "revolt against the order of the universe." Hubris, of course, is false pride, arrogance, the human conceit that in Greek tragedy was the bringer of Nemesis, the goddess who served as the agent of one's downfall. In Cain's story, Yahweh played the role of agent, but it was Cain's own actions that set his downfall in motion.

So there it is—hubris, or if you like, Titanism, a primal, *first* sin that, according to J, comes from within our humanity. We can't entirely escape this consequence of being human though we can, for the most part, teach it how to grow up.

Back in junior high, however, I *was* a Titan. I may even have saved the universe.

15

WITH THE UNIVERSE AS MY CAUSE, I LEAD
A QUIET, VERY SMALL INSURRECTION

Pasadena, Texas, late 1950s

We had a Saturday night ritual in those years. Following a light supper, usually sandwiches and a bowl of canned soup, we'd gather in the living room around our television, one of those cabinet-style sets with its twelve-inch black-and-white screen. First was *The Lawrence Welk Show* from seven-thirty to eight-thirty. No one but our mother enjoyed it, but we'd sit with her because she wanted company and because she'd bribe us with large bowls of Neapolitan mellorine (an inexpensive low-fat ice cream) and chocolate sauce.

From the first, I thought the show boring, but palatable. In time, though, I felt a growing dislike that was, in part, the necessary rebellion against parental tastes. But the larger part was what I'd begun to think of as the show's air of Sunday school, an hour each Saturday night of trying to breathe in the same thin, desiccating atmospheres of goodness and virtue that I'd be facing the next morning. It gave me the creeps. In spite of good, clean American values on parade, the life portrayed was juiceless, uninteresting. There was something insidious there, I was sure of it. I couldn't identify exactly what I was afraid of, but I trusted my gut feeling that I was being drowned in cloying virtue. So I began my secret resistance.

Each week, during one of the Welk show's commercial breaks, I'd dash off to my room, close the door, and, in a sort of hiss-shout, say every dirty word I could think of. I regarded the utterance as a verbal force field, a dam against the flood of bland goodness pouring through the television screen. I thought of these weekly harangues not only as acts of resistance, but as deliberate offerings—as *sacrifice*—needed to restore balance to the universe. That may explain why *Have Gun, Will Travel*, the Arthurian-like western that followed the *Welk* show, was my favorite half hour of the week. Paladin, the protagonist, was a mythic hero whose virtue was anchored in the harmonious balance of light and darkness. Knight and gunfighter, gentleman and thug, scholar and killer, he was dangerous but never cruel, compassionate but never bland, moral but not moralistic. On a line between *Cain-the-brother-killer* and *Abel-the-prig*, his was a textured, flawed, gloriously human presence that, after the previous hour, seemed downright transcendent.

16

THE PLAYWRIGHT TAKES A SHOT

All we know of the story of Cain and Abel is how it begins and how it ends. Absent is anything that might provide insight into either of them, leaving present-day interpreters, like those of the postexilic period, to imagine how their story could have come to such an end. In his play *The Creation of the World and Other Business*, Arthur Miller portrays Abel as a thoroughly nonoffensive lad who does not lord his better place over his brother, and who, ironically, is killed at the very moment he is attempting to include his brother in a family event. Miller's Cain lives along the edges of his family, put there through the unconscious, dissonant subtleties of family dynamics that make it seem that he has excluded himself. When, through Cain's narrowing field of vision, God appears also to have put him at a distance, he seems to be left with no other avenue than to regard himself as unwanted, an exile. The irony, of course, is that fueled by that belief he behaves in a manner that will in time bring about that very consequence.

It's rather easy for the tragedy-loving adolescent mind to arrive at such a conclusion and, once there, to find real or imagined evidence to support it, putting into motion a cycle that, feeding on itself, maintains a misery-loving separation. One might even observe that, in Miller's play, the payoff Cain derives from clinging to that idea is that he is free to go on with his rants about the unfairness of things, which, though tiresome, is not all that unusual in adolescent behavior. With Cain, however, his resentment becomes obsessive and in the end grants him permission to do murder.

17

CAIN'S ALL-TOO-FAMILIAR BEHAVIOR.
YAHWEH AS THERAPIST. A CHANCE NOT TAKEN.
SIN AS A *THING* WITH ITS OWN EXISTENCE

It's a fair guess that Cain's strong reaction to Yahweh's disregard for his offering was part of a pattern, that this was not the first time the lad had experienced alienation, real or imagined, followed by anger. Imagine Cain standing there, watching, listening, his mood shifting, darkening, familiar, a silent scream building, wanting release, to shout *What is this? Am I invisible? I was here first!* And yet, what could he do about it? Take a swing at Yahweh? Probably not. But Abel, his little brother—now, he was another matter.

We've all done it. With too much frustration at work, at school, too much traffic, too much heat, we give a taste of our darker side to whoever's down the food chain and handy—subordinates, the kids, younger siblings, the dog, the cat.

Finally, Yahweh turns to Cain and, as if he didn't know the answer already, asks,

> *Why are you distressed,*
> *And why is your face fallen?*

I'd have gone in with something confrontive like *Look, you and I both know you can do better than this. If you're going to bring an offering to me, make it a valuable one. If not, why bother?* Yahweh, however, despite the short fuse he will demonstrate time and again, is gentle, compassionate, creating an opening through which he can say,

> *Surely, if you do right,*
> *There is uplift.*
> *But if you do not do right*
> *Sin crouches at the door;*
> *Its urge is toward you,*
> *Yet you can be his master.*
> —Genesis 4.6b–7

Subtle, life-altering advice—or it would be if Cain were open to it. But Cain does not want enlightenment—he wants Yahweh to acknowledge his offering with the same regard he'd given to Abel's.

I'm always a little embarrassed when someone gives me a gift; I feel awkward, clumsy, never quite convinced I'm worthy. I'll go grasping about for something to say that might express my gratitude; *thank you* has such a flat ring coming from my mouth. And when the gift is especially tender and thoughtful, I might get teary and wordless. On the other hand, when a gift appears to be the product of the giver's afterthought, his obligation—something "half-assed," as my father would have said—whatever the price tag, I don't count it as worth much. According to the rabbis, this was precisely Yahweh's issue with Cain's offering. If so, his response to Cain was the best he had, the very thing Cain needed to hear. But Cain was not willing to hear it.

It's not unusual for someone with an anger problem to deny it exists. One method for helping him overcome the denial, in a therapeutic environment, is to do something that brings the anger to the surface. It's tricky, but in the hands of a skilled practitioner it can work, and when it does the client has an insight into himself, a foothold, a place to begin addressing his problem. When it doesn't work he may become sullen, silent, and begin to stonewall all attempts at interaction. Or, like Cain, he may blow his top and, with blustery self-pity, walk out. In fact, I'd bet the bank that the family's home movies would have shown little Cain, lower lip puckered, demonstrating the same tactics when he didn't get his way.

Let's return to the moment of confrontation: Yahweh asks Cain, essentially, *Why are you so worked up? This is a chance to clean up your act. Why not take it?* Then during a heavy silence Cain looks at the ground, the sky, at his offering, at Abel's, anywhere but into Yahweh's steady gaze. Finally, Yahweh says in a soft voice, "Sin crouches at the door, and its desire is for you, yet you can be its master."

This is a powerful image. To see it clearly, let go of the idea of "sin" as the invention of priggish, humorless, puritanical types determined to put an end to everything that gives pleasure. Here "sin" is personified. It is a thing with its own existence, an internal beast from the darkest corners of human nature. With infinite patience it waits, and its "desire is for you."

Therapeutically speaking, what Yahweh delivers here is a fight-ending knockout punch. But in an ironic twist on the metaphor, the one who decides whether the punch will land at all is the one at whom it is aimed—in this case Cain. Now we see the conundrum in which Cain finds himself even before the murder. If he avoids the punch he walks away, but the jealousy, the anger, the wounded pride—the *beast*—gnaws away at his belly until it consumes him. If he allows it to land squarely, however, the risk is not that he will go unconscious—both psychologically and spiritually, he is *already* unconscious—but that he will wake up to the truth about his life, the mind-sets that dominate it, the behavior that flows from them, and the all-too-familiar consequences of that behavior. This latter prospect can be so frightening that, time and again, I (and everyone I've known well) have walked away to the rhythms of some aphoristic twaddle like "the enemy you know is better than the one you don't know."

But wait! you might say. *This story isn't about what might happen in therapy. It's about a human encounter with the divine! The punch thrown at Cain was a divine punch!* Well, so was Yahweh's admonition about *the Fruit of the Tree of the Knowledge of Good and Evil. What is happening?* First of all, *free will* is part and parcel of creation, which means that we humans get to *choose* between stupidity and wisdom—even Yahweh doesn't get to decide what we will or won't do. "I had no choice," one of the more hackneyed phrases in television and in the movies, is usually said by a character who'd just made a choice to do *this* rather than *that*—for instance, a choice to shoot the other guy rather than choosing to *be* shot. Already we've seen that Eve and Adam could have chosen not to eat the fruit. Indeed they could have wanted it, craved it, *needed* it more than they needed sex, and still walked away. Likewise Cain could have chosen to say no to his tantrum and *listen* to Yahweh instead.

Second, keep in mind that we're only in the fourth chapter of Genesis. Yahweh was still new at all this. J's iteration of the deity is anthropomorphic, *earthy*; if he walks, talks, eats, and so forth, then surely he *learns*. So maybe he made a mistake? Pushed the lad too far? In the moment just before Cain attacked Abel was there a cosmic oops?

But even that would not change the fact that it was Cain who walked away, Cain who indulged his own rage, and Cain who did the killing. Did he think no one would notice? Did he think at all? *How could he do such a thing?*

18

THE BEAST AND I COME NEAR TO TOUCHING,
OR, HOW ONE CAN DO SUCH A THING

Houston, Texas, Summer 1996

Though we are quite close now, the relationship between my daughter, Jenny, and I was breaking apart when she was in her middle teens. She was sixteen, and during the previous three years, as she'd passed through an increasingly nightmarish adolescence, I'd passed through understanding, to frustration, to anger, to rage, to bitterness. A week or so before the day in question, her mother—we'd divorced ten years earlier—had called to say that the bill for the cell phone she'd given Jenny, which was to be used only in emergencies (these were the days before unlimited minutes), was some six hundred dollars for the previous month. That afternoon, as I drove Jenny to her summer job, I told her that not only would the phone bill be paid out of the money set aside for her first car, but that we wouldn't be replenishing those funds until we saw a great deal more willingness to be responsible. Her comeback was particularly nasty. Already angry, now I was shaking. Minutes later, as we drove into the parking lot, I reminded her that I would pick her up at that same spot after work. She said she might not be there, that she might go and stay with her boyfriend. I told her that was unacceptable. She said she didn't care whether I liked it or not. I said that she'd better care, because she was sixteen and he was eighteen, and if she went there to spend the night, I'd have him arrested. Saying nothing, she opened the car door and was about to step out when I grabbed her forearm and said, "Tell me what you're going to do." She said—shouted, really, for the benefit of fellow workers waiting for the shift to start—that I was hurting her. I told her I wanted an answer. She yelled, "Let me go," and tried to pull away. Just then, I heard a male voice shout, "Hey!" I looked up to see several young men, looking rather menacing, now walking toward the car. She saw them too, smiled, and said I'd better let go before they got there. I reached under my seat, took out a two-foot length of hickory, and in a voice I remember as surprisingly even, said, "I'll let go when you tell me what you're gonna do. And if one of 'em so much as touches you, or me, somebody's gonna be going to the hospital, and somebody's going to jail. And I don't really give a damn who goes where."

I know, I know—strictly B-movie, both plot and dialogue, especially that last bit. But I said it just like that, and I meant it (though I want to buffer that by saying *he* meant it, that version of myself who was running the show). To be sure, I'd been blazing angry in the minutes leading up to that moment. Then, quite suddenly, the heat was gone, and in its place was a cold and vacant calm—a place without outcomes, consequences, or anything identifiably human. Mind you, this was no Zen-like serenity—I know the difference. Then she relented, agreed that I would pick her up after work, and the moment passed.

19

ANOTHER SORT OF DEATH

Cain lured his brother into a field and killed him. In the end, whatever motivations or mitigating circumstances we might dream up, the fact remains that Cain did it. But was it *premeditated* murder? It seems doubtful, given that premeditation requires the ability to form intent, which, in part, requires a reasonable understanding of the consequences of one's actions. Within the boundaries of the story, Cain's tiny universe had no experience of human death, until now. They were not strangers to death— Abel *had* just sacrificed one of his flock. But the death of a human being was wholly outside their experience. Yahweh had introduced Adam to the idea of human death, but regardless of what was meant by "on the day you eat the fruit of that, you'll die," given that both Adam and Eve had eaten the fruit and were still alive, it was certainly not that spooky draining away of life force they'd witnessed when a plant withered or, later, when Abel had slit the throat of a lamb. It was another sort of death, and it had to do with separation, a matter Adam and Eve had come to know intimately. Now it was Cain's turn.

20

CAIN'S QUESTION, RICHARD WRIGHT,
AND A MATTER OF LUCK

"The Lord said to Cain, 'Where is your brother, Abel?'

"And he said, 'I do not know. Am I my brother's keeper?'"

That question, which for centuries has left untold numbers of questioning people all weak-kneed, is arguably Cain being a defensive wiseass. And foolish. While there's no indication in the text that he had options, some interpreters have speculated that had he confessed, his punishment might not have been so severe. As it was, however, Yahweh was not amused.

"What have you done? Hark [Listen], your brother's blood cries out to Me from the ground! Therefore, you shall be more cursed than the ground . . . If you till the soil, it shall no longer yield its strength to you. You shall become a ceaseless wanderer on earth."

To which Cain replies, "My punishment is too great to bear."

"My sin is too great to forgive," an alternate translation of the Hebrew, would seem to suggest that Cain's outcry is from remorse. Kugel, however, argues that this "is clearly *not* what Cain was saying. But ancient interpreters, who were fond of preaching the virtues of repentance, seized on this opportunity to claim that the world's first murderer was overcome with his own guilt after the deed was done."[25] Gerhard von Rad points out that while Cain does fall apart, it is not because of what he has done. "The 'awon of which Cain speaks and which he thinks himself unable to bear is the *punishment* for sin. It is a cry of horror at the prospect of such a life of unrest and harassment without peace."[26] Finally, Cain's fear that, without divine protection, "anyone who meets me may kill me" is met by Yahweh giving him a mark of protection, which is in fact a warning to anyone who would dare to do him harm.

In Richard Wright's groundbreaking novel, *Native Son* (1940), the protagonist, Bigger Thomas, an African-American, goes to work as a driver for a wealthy white family that, for its time, is remarkably enlightened in its attitudes about race. Part of the tragedy in this story is that, given enough time, Bigger's near total mistrust of white society might have been diminished by their kindness, but that first night, overwhelmed with fear, and without intending to, he killed the daughter. It is the end to an afternoon and evening during which white people had attempted to treat him as a social equal—at least, that was how it must have seemed from their perspective. To Bigger, however, who had no foundation of experience to provide some glimmer of perspective on what they were attempting to do, their behavior had been not only confusing but also terrifying, humiliating. Attempting to escape, he killed again. Just at the end, having been captured, tried, and found guilty, his bravado and anger now incinerated by the reality of his impending execution, and in a voice Wright describes as "full of frenzied anguish," Bigger says, "What I killed for must've been good. . . . When a man kills, it's for something."

He's right, isn't he? In any peak moment of rage, or fear, it will seem to the person that whatever he or she is about to do will be in the service of something "good." I wonder what Cain might have identified as the "good" at the root of his actions. I can't say for sure that I would have gone after those young men to which my daughter was appealing that day, but I might have. Over the years, in my memory, I've returned to the scene. I know that at the root of my anger was the certainty that I'd been betrayed by my daughter, this child who had once been so loving, whom I'd loved beyond all reason and who'd become this unpleasant, *ungrateful* stranger who lived in my house. But *that* is only a piece of the truth, isn't it—self-pity wrapped in reasonableness, self-justification wrapped in the cloth of insight and confession. The fuller truth is that I'd been feeling increasingly sorry for myself and wanted to get even. My something "good," then, was revenge for hurt feelings.

Being "my brother's keeper" had always been a role that, despite my having held it in varying degrees of regard, had never disappeared from my personal radar. Then, in a moment, it was gone, the "I" who'd cared about such things pushed aside in favor of that crouching beast who was ready to drive the train right off the tracks. My daughter giving in may have saved us all that day. I got lucky. Cain didn't.

21

GRIEF

Years ago, during a seminar I was leading, a man told a story about what had happened ten years earlier. I don't recall his name, and only the sketchiest image of his face remains, but I do remember that he was recounting the beginning of the holiday season, and his daughters were expected home that afternoon from university. They knew to call before they left, but he'd not heard from them and was growing quite anxious when, finally, his oldest daughter called to say that she and her sister were about to start the drive. Without waiting for him to say it, she assured him they would be careful, then reminded him that it was the holidays, so if the trip took longer than normal, he shouldn't worry. A number of us were listening to him, many of us parents, and when he said that they'd never reached home, that they'd been killed in a car crash, the group moaned in a single voice that was eerily primal. Both children gone in a moment. The man said he'd died that day. *Of course you did*, I thought.

Adam and Eve had two children, both gone in a moment. Did *they* grieve? The text is silent. However, the experience of that one man, and that of the group on hearing it, says they must have. Whether one regards Adam and Eve as real people or as characters from ancient literature, they are a template of sorts for human experience. Their creator, whether a divine being or a human author, set out to make human beings, creatures who begin grieving for their children at the moment of their birth—or even before.

Spring 1975, Pasadena, Texas

When I interviewed for the job of associate pastor at Church of the Holy Spirit, a parish in west Houston, they'd all but offered me the job on the spot, and I'd all but said yes. During my four years of grad school in northern Virginia, and a two-year posting in Tyler, in east Texas, after graduation and ordination, my wife and I had not seen much of our families. At my parents' house for the night, when I told them that we'd soon be living only half an hour away, Mom had gushed, bounced, hugged me, then ran to the phone to tell her friends. Dad had looked up from his paper, smiled, and said, "That's great, Son."

After supper, Mom left for a church function, so for a few hours it was just Dad and me, sitting as we had so many times at the red Formica-topped kitchen table. What happened next was ritual. Within an hour, we had put away the better part of a bottle of Scotch. It was a thing we did once, maybe twice, a year, usually around a family birthday, and always for the boozy warmth and connection we could never seem to manage otherwise. Sometimes one or more of his friends would be present, or one of mine. Had my brothers not been off at college, Frank at the University of Texas at Austin, Ralph at A&M, they'd have been sitting with us. Part of the ritual was Dad telling the same jokes and college stories we'd all heard so many times. He knew we'd heard them, but it was a house rule that you didn't mention it. Besides, he enjoyed recounting the stories of his youth and telling his jokes, and if you were inside the peculiar zeitgeist of being his son (which meant that you recognized these moments as in-house liturgy, as *communion*, you being the acolyte, him the celebrant) and if you were a bit sloshed, it could be a hoot. Just after he'd finished the story about throwing the bucket of ice water on the upperclassman, I decided to jump in and tell him about one of the wilder things *I'd* done in college, the basic elements of which were a lot of alcohol, a drunk fraternity brother, the .45 automatic he'd brought back from Vietnam, and the local police chief. I thought it was hilarious, but it was clear from the look on his face that he'd just as soon never have known about it, so I shut up and we had one of our awkward silences.

Then, "I love you, Son."

Huh? I glanced up to see him looking right at me. Not just in my direction, mind you, but with that California, group therapy, touchy-feely, eye contact sort of staring. I looked away. When I looked back, he was still staring, so I tried looking at his forehead. It's a dodge I learned from a guy during an encounter-group weekend at my seminary. If you're, say, five or more feet away, the person you're supposed to be making eye contact with can't tell the difference and it makes the whole thing less tedious. But with my father, even *that* was too intense, so I looked over his head, to the built-in bookshelves against the wall of the breakfast nook. *Heeey*, I think, *there's that* Encyclopaedia Britannica *we've had since, what, '54? Oh yeah! I remember that report on Burma I did in the seventh grade. Dad and I sat right here with the B volume. Maybe we could talk about that!*

I opened my mouth to speak, but when I looked at him he was still staring. *Christ, what's he doing?* We were supposed to be funny when we drank. Sure, we got a little maudlin at times—half hugs, manly slaps to the back, sappy grins, that sort of thing—but never this! I went back to the bookshelves.

"Urrmp-*UGHMMM!*" It was one of those throaty, phlegm-clearing sounds, a Dad sound. It was time to say something. This was one of those *moments*.

"I love you, too, Dad." It sounded pretty thin.

"No," he said. "I mean, I *really* love you."

I looked away. I'd never, *never*, felt so awkward with him, and that's saying something. "I, ah . . ." My throat clogged. I tried to clear it, but no luck, so "I really love you, too" came out sounding like Wolfman Jack.

"You don't know what the hell I'm talking about."

"Okay."

He paused, his eyes now on the ceiling, his elbows on the table. He

rubbed the top of one hand with the palm of the other. Another house rule was that, when you saw these things in combination, you shut your mouth and paid attention, because he was thinking something through and was about to speak. Then, sure enough, "See, someday I'm gonna die, and you and your brothers and your sister will miss me, right?"

"Yessir."

"But you'll get over it. You'll move on. That's the way it's supposed to be, right? You have kids, you grow old and die, and your kids move on. Right?"

"Right. But . . ."

"Don't interrupt me."

"Yessir."

"But if one of you kids were to die first, I don't think I could ever get over it." He went quiet and looked away, his eyes watery now, his face and body slumped as though even to say it drained his life force. "You don't know what the hell I'm talking about." Tears were welling over, collecting on his lips, so he pulled a wadded handkerchief from his pocket and wiped his face. "And you won't know 'til you have a kid of your own. See, when your kids are born, a place opens up in you that's just for them, that just isn't available to anyone or anything else." He looked back at me. "See what I mean?"

"Yessir."

"No you don't."

"Nosir."

We were silent for a while, suspended in a quiet, awkward wonder. Then the moment passed and we went on talking, but of other things. Four years later, when I first held my baby daughter and looked into her eyes, my very first thought was *This is what you meant, Dad.* In a moment, *in the twinkling of an eye,* as if through the touch of this six-pound, eleven-ounce magician, I was made new, the world was new. The love I felt for her was strangely intense, rich, and frightening.

I would have survived her death, but would have been changed, as her birth changed me. If we are to imagine Adam and Eve as characters with human qualities, then we're left to imagine their grief as well, which, ironically, would have been unimaginable, except to those parents who've experienced the death of a child. About Yahweh, and whether he grieved, we're left to imagine that as well.

22

THE MATTER OF CAIN'S WIFE, THEIR SON,
AND THE FOUNDING OF URBAN CULTURE

Cain had a *wife*? Right there in chapter 4, verse 17, we're told that "Cain knew his wife . . ." Where did she come from? Nahum Sarna notes the tradition found in the Book of Jubilees *and* in the Talmud that "Cain married his sister."[27] Cain had a *sister*? Yep. More than one, so we're told, and brothers, all of whom were yet to be born when he "left the presence of the Lord and settled in the land of Nod, east of Eden." As for how they eventually met and married, the author doesn't say, only that they did, that she conceived, and that their son was named Enoch. Since Cain's punishment, in part—and this is reminiscent of Adam's punishment—was that the ground would no longer grow anything for him, in lieu of farming, he founded the first city, naming it after his son. Thus urban culture was born. About the origin of this myth of the first city, Robert Alter suggests that the coincidence of its founder also being the first murderer is "a possible reflection of the antiurban bias in Genesis."[28] Likewise, in his commentary on Genesis for *The Jewish Study Bible*, Jon Levenson suggests that this account of city founding may originate in "well-known legends that have not survived."[29]

23

ADAM AND EVE HAVE MORE CHILDREN,
A GREAT-GREAT-GREAT-GREAT-GRANDSON WHO DOES
NOT DIE, WHOSE GREAT-GRANDSON WAS NOAH

Chapter 5, called the "Book of Records," is not a creation of J, E, or P, but is from a source designated as *other*. Biblical scholar J. P. Fokkelman (1987) "has noted [that] the genealogical lists or 'begats' (*toledot*) in Genesis are carefully placed compositional units that mark off one large narrative unit from another."[30] The function of chapter 5, then, is to mark the end of the creation narratives and provide a genealogical segue into the story of Noah. It begins with a recapitulation of creation through the death of Adam that, curiously, mentions neither Cain nor Abel (though the reason may be that we've already read of Cain's descendants, and Abel had none):

> This is the record of Adam's line—When God created man, He made him in the likeness of God; male and female He created them. And when they were created, He blessed them and called them Man [read, *humans*].—

When Adam had lived 130 years, he begot a son in his likeness after his image, and he named him Seth. After the birth of Seth, Adam lived 800 years and begot sons and daughters. All the days that Adam lived came to 930 years; then he died. (Genesis 5:1–5)

Adam and Eve go on to have more sons and daughters; none of these is named in the text. Adam's great-great-great-great-grandson was Enoch (not Cain's Enoch).

When Enoch had lived 65 years, he begot Methuselah. After the birth of Methuselah, Enoch walked with God 300 years; and he begot sons and daughters. All the years of Enoch came to 365 years. Enoch walked with God; then he was no more, for God took him.

Imagine the interpreters, their eyes widening, whispering, *Enoch walked with God— twice? And talked with God? Then God took him?* Enoch was a loose end in need of serious pondering, which he received—in shiploads. In point of fact, the lengths to which interpreters were willing to go in their pursuit of loose ends are evidenced in their speculations about this one character, who comes and goes from Genesis in the span of four verses. Below are the four categories of speculation about him as identified by James Kugel in *Traditions of the Bible.* Each is followed by a representative source.

The Immortal Enoch, based on the theory that Enoch did not die: "He [Enoch] was 'transferred,' that is he changed his abode and journeyed as an emigrant from the mortal life to the immortal."
—Philo, *Change of Names* 38

The Heavenly Scribe, based on the theory that he was living in Heaven, writing down the heavenly knowledge, and giving it out to the humans through the writings of certain interpreters: "And he was therefore with the angels of God six jubilees of years; and they showed him everything which is on earth and in the heavens, and the rule of the sun, and he wrote down everything."
—Jubilees 10:17

Enoch the Sage, based on the theory that he must have been wise and, moreover, an astronomer: "And he [Enoch] wrote in a book the signs of the heavens according to the order of their months, so that the sons of man might know the [appointed] times of the years according to their order."
—Jubilees 4:17

Enoch the Penitent, based on the theory that, since it was only after the birth of Methuselah that Enoch had walked with God, and not before, Enoch must have won divine favor by repenting for some evil deed performed earlier in his life: "Enoch pleased the Lord, and was taken up; he was an example of repentance to all generations."

—Sirach (Greek) 44:16

So, Enoch was the father of Methuselah, who was the father of Lamech, who was the father of Noah.

24

A MATTER OF EVIL?

Now we've come to the end of the creation narratives, and have examined Adam, Eve, and Cain, to whom much evil has been ascribed and guilt levied, with a contemporary eye and with the help of traditional and modern scholars and thinkers. In a nutshell, we find the following in the text:

Adam shows up, names the animals, plants, et cetera, takes the tour, gets instructions on the dos and the one don't, gets a mate, joins her in eating the fruit, makes a loincloth, gets caught, blames his mate, joins his mate in being tossed out of the Garden, fathers two sons, fathers more children, one of whom is named Seth, lives 930 years, and dies.

Eve shows up, has a conversation with the serpent, takes a bite of the fruit, offers some to her mate and, ditto on the loincloth and getting caught, blames the serpent, likewise gets tossed, gives birth to two sons, claims the first one was a co-creation with the Lord, gives birth to Seth and other children she and Adam have together.

Cain is born, becomes a farmer, makes an offering, gets angry when it is ignored, ignores divine advice, kills his brother in anger, prevaricates when confronted, is banished, finds a wife, has children, founds a city.

Are these profiles of inherently evil people? Adam and Eve were guilty of eating the fruit, by which they gained the *knowledge* of good and bad, of duality, but does that make them *evil*? Cain did kill his brother, which makes him guilty of murder, an evil act, but does it then follow that *he* is evil? If Abel's offering had been ignored instead of Cain's, might he have been the murderer? Did the interpreters who condemned Cain see the same potential for evil in themselves? What about Augustine? What about St. Paul? (After all, in Acts 26:10 he confesses that "I not only shut up many of the saints [Christians] in prison . . . but when they were put to death I cast my vote against them.") What about you? Me?

Haunting the West in the decades following World War II was the question of how it was possible that so many average Germans had been willing participants in mass murder. In the early 1960s, the Milgram experiments conducted at Yale tested the lengths to which average people would go in blind obedience to authority. While no one was actually harmed, during a three-year period, 65 percent of volunteers proved willing to obey the instructions of the "experimenter" and inflict what appeared to be painful electric shocks, even potentially fatal shocks. Variations on the original experiment conducted around the world had similar results. In the same period, Philip Zimbardo conducted his now infamous "prison experiment" at Stanford University. Twelve volunteers, each with a strong mental health profile, were randomly divided into groups of six "guards" and six "prisoners." Designed to be conducted over a two-week period, the experiment had to be terminated after six days because the guards were becoming increasingly sadistic, and all the prisoners were showing signs of extreme mental distress. Solomon Asch's experiments in the 1950s proved that, when pressured, most individuals will abandon an opinion they know to be true and align themselves with a group opinion they know to be false. The results of each of these experiments would seem to prove that a capacity for evil is present in every one of us. Zimbardo, in a lecture given at the Technology, Entertainment, and Design conference in 2008, said that the capacity for evil exists alongside an equal capacity for what he calls heroism, and "that's a decision that you have to make."[31] Again, free will.

The difficulties thus far in Genesis result from the exercise of free will, by which humans make choices to do this or to do that—to eat the fruit or not eat the fruit, to listen to sage advice—"you can be its master"—or walk away and nurse your anger. Adam and Eve did what they did, but to claim that I'd be a better man were it not for their actions would be a lie, and more than a little cowardly. At the same time, it seems only appropriate to put a few questions to the divine actor in the story. For instance, "if you wanted obedience, why give the humans free will?" and "Since you *did* give the humans free will, why get upset when they used it?" and, finally "Wasn't this whole thing *your* idea?"

Thirty-five years ago, a dear friend, the wife of a seminary classmate, was killed in a car crash. That night I found myself standing in the rain, screaming all sorts of things toward the sky—an unkind assessment of the divine character, an invitation to fight, along with several questions that began with *Why*. The only answer that night as well as on other nights I wanted answers to similar questions was *Because*, which, in time, has come to make more sense than all the theological tomes put together.

What comes next is not forty days and nights of rain that fill up the earth as if it were a bathtub, but a deluge of such violence that the fabric of space/time itself is threatened.

NOAH

IN THREE ACTS,
A STORY FAR MORE INVOLVED
THAN YOU MIGHT THINK

ACT ONE

Before the Flood*

25

GODLINGS AND WOMEN MAKE GIANTS IN THE EARTH.
PLANS ARE SET FOR A MAKEOVER

Ten generations have passed since the death of the original humans, and the world is in a sorry state. In fact,

> The Lord saw how great was man's wickedness on earth, and how every plan devised in his heart was but evil all the time. And the Lord regretted that He had made man on earth and His heart was saddened. And the Lord said, "I will blot out from the earth the men whom I created—men together with beasts, creeping things, and birds of the sky, for I regret that I made them."

Not only is a do-over in order, it's on the calendar: a deluge is coming. First, however, a bit of evidence is needed to justify such a radical step. Otherwise, drowning most every man, woman, child, aardvark, bird, bug, cat, dog, lion, lizard, etc., on the earth might seem excessive. J begins chapter 6 of Genesis by offering, apparently as evidence of how low humankind had fallen, one of the strangest stories in the Bible.

> When men began to increase on earth and daughters were born to them the divine beings [Nephilim] saw how beautiful the daughters of men were and took wives from among those that pleased them—The Lord said, "My breath shall not abide in man forever, since he too is flesh; let the days

---

*While *deluge* would be the more accurate term, for the most part I will be using the familiar *flood*.

allowed him be one hundred and twenty years."—It was then, and later too, that the Nephilim appeared on earth—when the divine beings cohabited with the daughters of men, who bore offspring. They were the heroes of old, the men of renown.

It's an odd, sore thumb of a story, reading less like a biblical tale than a plot line for one of those campy 1950s sci-fi flicks. The interpreters were troubled by the mythological and polytheistic overtones of the story, which "reads like a condensation of a much longer, well-known myth."[32] Certainly, the motif of gods mating with mortals does ring of Greek mythology— Achilles is the son of Peleus, a mortal, and Thetis, a sea nymph. But "whatever the ancient roots of this story," writes Nahum Sarna, "no Jewish commentator accepts the notion of a sexual union between divine beings and mortals, giving rise to a semidivine race."[33]

In an interesting twist, the editors of *The Chumash*, Stone Edition,* interpret the story as a commentary on social justice, translating the Hebrew not as "Nephilim" but as "the sons of the princes and judges," and stating that the women they pursued were daughters of the powerless who "did not have the power to resist their superiors. Thus the Torah begins the narrative of the tragedy of the flood by speaking of the subjugation of the weak by the powerful."[34] Both they and the editors of *The Soncino Chumash* tell us that Maimonides† believed Adam, Eve, Seth, and his son Enosh to be the "Sons of God" and the Nephilim to be their inferior, though in appearance quite impressive, children. Still other sources say they were angels who fell to earth.

What a headache this odd, one-of-a-kind story must have presented to the interpreters. Though at first blush it seems that little, if anything, would be lost if this small bit of Genesis were excised, modern scholars say it is part of a thread connecting this story with that of those Israelite scouts sent out by Moses and, finally, with the story of David and Goliath (the Philistine giant). "Such widely distributed stories are there," writes Richard Elliott Friedman, "because the Bible is not a loose collection of stories. It is an intricate, elegant, exquisite, long work with continuity and coherence."[35] Long and intricate, yes, and often elegant, even beautiful. But continuous and coherent?

It's a point of view shared by scholars of Friedman's caliber and experience, whose decades of immersion in biblical studies grant certain insights—in his book *Outliers*, Malcolm Gladwell writes of the finding

---

Chumash is the Torah with supporting passages from the Prophets.
†A twelfth-century rabbinic scholar, and author of *Guide for the Perplexed*.

by neurologist Daniel Levitin that world-class expertise in a given field is acquired after ten thousand hours of study and practice. Our Old Testament and Hebrew language professor at Virginia Theological Seminary, James Ross, would sit across the broad wooden table in our seminar room looking every bit the skinny, younger Moses in a suit, with a Marlboro between the first two fingers of his right hand, and in a deep, gravelly voice, he would read the biblical Hebrew with the same effort, speed, and comprehension with which I might read a newspaper. His depth of learning allowed a penetration into the texts, into the connective tissues of continuity and coherence that we, his students, there to become priests, not scholars, would likely never have. But he did tell us about them, and we believed him.

While a surface read of the story of the Nephilim might leave a first-time reader to wonder why in the world such a bizarre story was there, the reader already familiar with the texts will know that this story gives background for a later account of Nephilim-spotting, in Numbers 13:33, when the Israelite scouts sent by Moses to reconnoiter the Promised Land reported having seen men so large that "we looked like grasshoppers to ourselves, and so we must have looked to them," and again with the story of David and Goliath. Loaded with that connection, the Nephilim found in Genesis 6 must have seemed to the interpreters to be a double threat—not only demigods who lure human women into the sack, but really large warriors who were downright dangerous.

From a purely mercenary point of view, if one *were* looking to make a case for obliterating everything but the fish, this sort of thing would be a prosecutor's dream. You've got your hanky-panky between godlings and human women, *plus* whatever else those wicked, evil, corrupt humans were doing when they thought no one was looking. Before you know it, you might find yourself lining up with the decision to *Drown 'em! Drown 'em all!*

26

ON REFLECTION, I BEGIN TO SUSPECT THAT
MADE-IN-THE-IMAGE-OF MAY WELL BE
AN ONTOLOGICAL TRAP

You may have wondered from time to time about the sanity of the decision to wipe out most of humanity. Then again, you've probably had days in which you said "Amen" to the sentiment behind it. When I was young, my *I-give-up-on-humanity* moodiness was over wars, genocides, and the like.

Now I'm used to hearing of such things, sadly, and although my outrage at them continues, my cynicism might come over me at more mundane, ordinary moments. For instance, I'll be at the local mall, one of the river of bodies on cell phones flowing in and out of stores, caught in the gravitational vortex of consumer frenzy, and I'll be seized by the fear that we're never going to "get it," me included. Giving up can seem so logical.

Fourteen years ago, I arrived in South Africa, where I planned to lead a series of workshops. On the afternoon of my arrival, while relaxing at my host's house, I watched news footage of a massacre. The chieftain of one of the tribal homelands along South Africa's northern border, under the guise of common cause against Nelson Mandela, had invited a white supremacist group from the Orange Free State to send representatives to meet with him. As they stepped from their helicopter, the chieftain stepped back, and his soldiers killed them all. I'd been in country three times previously, each time for about a month, and knew the South Africans to be rather inured to the violence—not uncaring, just used to it. But now, the wife of the couple with whom I was staying, said, "This is very bad," then asked if the American embassy knew where I was staying. When I asked why, she said, "In case things go wrong, and your government orders an evacuation." Mandela's election as president was less than two months away. The impossible was about to happen—a native black African was about to become president of a nation once divided by a policy of state-enforced segregation—and the hope had been that the transition would be relatively bloodless. Always present, however, was a sense that just the right incident at just the right place and time could spark a flood of violence. *So close*, I thought, *and now this. Same song, zillionth verse. Human history in a nutshell. What in hell are we doing here? What's the point?*

Such moments are gloriously depressing, even darkly fascinating—we and the news media cannot get our fill of mass tragedy. Just the other day, on pondering all this, I asked myself why *any* deity, especially one with Yahweh's heightened sense of irony, would bother to destroy us when he could just sit back and watch us do ourselves in. As my years accumulate, and the shiny surface of my cynical self wears away, I find that the satisfaction of moments of high cynicism, especially those shared with like-minded friends, is just not what it used to be. My and their underlying conceit poke through and into my awareness, reminding me that I'm not all that different from most people. This growing revelation about the nature of my own cynicism has left me to wonder whether this human penchant for playing the *know-it-all*—a fine example of the hubris that regularly brought punishment from the gods on ancient people—might have been an item on some antediluvian list of divine complaints: "Things Humans Do That Really Annoy Me!"

While geological evidence of great floods does exist, none of it supports a worldwide immersion of the continents in the time since *Homo sapiens* first appeared. Besides, the story of the flood is *not* about a flood, but about consequences brought on by human behavior. In the story, all that water—and violence—is merely the divine means to a desired end.

27

MUSING ON SAID TRAP, I DISCOVER THAT MAKING THE PERFECT HUMAN BEING AND BUILDING THE PERFECT MODEL AIRPLANE ARE ENTERPRISES WITH SURPRISING PARALLELS

In *Answer to Job*, Carl Jung observes that "Yahweh is no friend of critical thoughts which in any way diminish the tribute of recognition he demands."[36] If Jung is correct, then the simplest answer to the obvious question of conscience, *Why does everyone have to die in the Flood (or, indeed, at all)?* might be that humanity, that divine experiment, simply was not playing ball to divine standards—that is, behaving itself, doing what it was told, and giving said tribute. Even though humanity had been born in the divine imagination, the creator now uses that same imagination to form the manner of its destruction. It does seem unfair—even unjust—since no divine law had yet been handed down to tell them what was and was not "wicked" in Yahweh's mind. In fact, it could be argued that humanity was sentenced to death for interpreting free will a bit too freely for divine tastes. That said, however, I may have had a glimpse into the divine motivation, though of course on a smaller scale.

When I was a boy, I was fascinated by World War II aircraft, especially the single-seat fighters. About twice a year, having saved part of my allowance, I'd buy a plastic model kit: a P-40 Flying Tiger; a P-51 Mustang; a P-38 Lightning; a Japanese Zero. In every box was a diagram showing how the parts fit together, and where to place the decals. What could be easier? Creating the world, perhaps. For instance, the plastic parts didn't always fit just so, and even when they did, the slightest excess of airplane glue would gob out along the seams, leaving an unsightly smear no matter how carefully I removed it. Then came the decals. First, each had to be scissored from the sheet, then soaked in a shallow dish until the decal itself could be slipped from its backing. Too long in the water meant too much water in the glue, making for too long a drying time during which the decal might—*would*—slip out of position. Too little time in the water, however, and the glue would be a mucus-like goo that resisted all attempts at smoothing out its wrinkles before drying. Most of the imperfections in a finished model resulted from my lack of skill or patience. Then again, given the time and effort I would invest in building it, it seemed to me that the model—*the thing I was trying to bring to life*—could have met me at least part of the way. So I would find myself angry at the model, as if its flaws were in part the product of its own willfulness. Having granted sentience to molded plastic, I might, at the first sign of obstinacy, decide that if it didn't want to be perfect, I didn't want it. After warning several models of the consequences, I took one of them, a real disaster, into the backyard and blew it up with a cherry bomb. More would follow.

Painters have destroyed their canvases, sculptors their clays and marbles, and writers their pages, when the thing that emerged was not the thing imagined. Thomas Moore, Jungian analyst and author of *Care of the Soul*, commenting on the work of James Hillman, also a Jungian analyst and the originator of post-Jungian archetypal psychology, writes that "he [Hillman] says that of its nature the soul pathologizes. That is to say, it gets us into trouble . . . makes us see perversely."[37] Later in the same book, Hillman writes,

> The soul sees by means of affliction . . . The crazy artist, the daft poet and the mad professor are metaphors for the intimate relation between pathologizing and imagination. Pathologizing processes are a source of imaginative work, and the work provides a container for the pathologizing processes. The two are inextricably interwoven in the work of Sophocles and Euripides, Webster and Shakespeare, Goya and Picasso, Swift and Baudelaire, O'Neill and Strindberg, Mann and Beckett—these but an evident few . . . Pathologizing is itself a way of seeing.[38]

That *imagined thing*—it can arrive like an occupying force, inviting *itself* in, giving *itself* leave to gestate in the mind, to haunt, to whisper mantra-like, "Give me life or I'll haunt your dreams." So one begins creating the *thing*, the *it*—a painting, a poem, a garden, a house, a sculpture, a book, a play, a new pattern for the kitchen tile, restoring the beauty of something old and neglected—pushing and pushing until this *thing*, recognized by now as an expression of *self* (aka, *made in the image of*), arrives fully in the world! Yet despite everything you've given, *it* has the gall, the *temerity*, to not be the perfect physical reflection of the imagined thing, but of failure, always personal and at times bitter. It's only natural, then, that we'd want to loose the *creator*'s flip side, the *destroyer*, to blow it up, burn it, smash it, shred it, or otherwise remove it not just from our sight, but from existence.

So, if we're all *made-in-the-image-of*, and if we're a bit overinvolved, hypercritical, and overwrought, at least in regard to our creations, we may find there's an argument to be made that we've come by it honestly.

28

WHO IS NOAH? IT'S A QUESTION OF CHARACTER. OR SANITY. OR BOTH. BUT *WHOSE*?

The decision to do away with most of the life on earth is followed by not simply lots of heavy rain, but by a deluge, an inundation from above and below. Noah is the one human being deemed worthy of saving—his family seems to have come in on his coattails—and the first to receive a divine commission.

Like the story of Jonah (of "Jonah and the Whale" fame), the story of a cleansing flood is archetypal. It leads to a character's transformation. For example, the Epic of Gilgamesh recounts the Sumerian/Babylonian version of the flood, but where the characters in Gilgamesh are fully drawn, the biblical writers don't say much about Noah. What they do say in this first part of Noah's story is just enough to leave us, and the one hundred or so generations before us, confused, and asking questions. In chapter 6, verse 9, J writes that Noah "found favor in Yahweh's eyes" (his name, in Hebrew, is "favor" spelled backwards[39])—and in the next verse, depending on which translation we follow, P describes Noah as "righteous, blameless in his time" (Alter), "virtuous, unblemished in his generations" (Friedman), or "a righteous, wholehearted man in his generation" (Fox). This seems rather straightforward, the sort of language one would expect to describe a biblical hero, and some of the postexilic and later interpreters wholeheartedly supported that image:

> When the earth was flooded . . . wisdom again saved it, steering the righteous man by a paltry piece of wood.
>
> —Wisdom 10:4

> Noah alone among us all was most upright and true, a most trustworthy man concerned for noble deeds.
>
> —*Sybylline Oracles* 1:125

Other interpreters, on reading chapter 7, verse 1, perceived a rather glaring problem: "Then the Lord said to Noah, 'Go into the ark, with all your household, for you alone have I found righteous before Me in this generation.'" The trouble lay in that last phrase—"in this generation." While the righteousness and virtuousness declared in chapter 6, verse 9 may be character traits, more than that they are value judgments that, without context, tell us nothing. In other words, would Noah have been a standout in any generation, or only "in this [his] generation"? Was he just the best of a sorry lot? Some said yes.

> However, having praised that man [Noah] with regard to these virtues, [the text] adds that he was "perfect in his generation," indicating that he was good not in absolute terms, but in comparison with the people who were living at that time.
>
> —Philo, *On Abraham* 36

> It says specifically "in his generation" so as to show that he was not just according to perfect justice, but that by the standards of justice of his generation was he just.
>
> —Jerome, *Jerome's Hebrew Questions on Genesis* 6:9

Most of the interpreters took the former position. Origen, a third-century Christian apologist, reflecting the position of mainstream Christianity then and now, wrote that "God used a most righteous man to be the father of all born after the flood." As for what the author intended to reveal about the character of the man, we know only that Noah is singled out, told what to do, and, obediently, faithfully, without protest or question, he sets about doing it.

This being the Bible, and Genesis, you wouldn't think that an act of such blind obedience would present yet another problem, but it does. The difficulty lies in the picture drawn for us by the author, that of a man who so far is without dimension, who seems more mechanical than human—switch off, switch on, build the ark. The questions asked again and again over the millennia have been, essentially, *What sort of man warns no one? Pleads for no one? Why does he not offer up at least some word of protest? Why does he not ask the most obvious of questions—Is there no other way?* and *Why me?*

All in all, what little is in the text, taken with what is *not* there (and, so, left to the imagination), makes it easy not only to paint Noah as a true believer with a heart of stone, but Yahweh as spiteful and murderous. Given the importance of the story of the flood to Genesis, indeed to the whole of the biblical narrative and the foundation of Western psychology, and the danger inherent in allowing the story's hero to look like a schmuck—to say nothing of the divine looking a bit psychotic—does it not make sense that interpreters would have used their skills to fill in the blank spots, and to spin the same facts in another direction, to interpret them in such a way that they appear to mean something else? One midrash suggests that Noah was commanded to build the ark "So that others might see him at his labor and be moved to repent . . . but they paid no attention to Noah's urgings."[40] Josephus, the Roman historian and author of *Jewish Antiquities*, wrote that Noah tried to persuade his contemporaries to adopt "a better way of thinking and to change their ways."[41] Both Clement, the third bishop of Rome, *and* Clement of Alexandria, a Christian theologian and interpreter, claimed that "Noah preached repentance."[42]

Not a word of this is supported by the text, however. So we'd be free to judge these interpretations as an outrageous taking of license were it not for the fact that what the theologians did—here and with other parts of the Bible—is little different from what we see, hear, and do every day. They just wrote it down and formalized it. To paraphrase the familiar punch line from a story in the Gospel of Luke, "If there's anyone who, *in the last week*, has *not* spun the facts of a story in his or her own favor, or in support of a desired outcome, or to bolster a favored point of view, let him, or her, cast the first stone!"

As for Noah, he is a man about to find himself in the midst of nothing less than a cosmic reckoning, caught in a vortex of energies so immeasurably violent that they strain the fabric of the universe. It's not in the text, but wouldn't a guy in that situation wonder how he'd brought this on himself? Wouldn't you?

The Flood

29

FIRST, ABOUT THE ARK, WHICH IS
DEFINITELY *NOT* A BOAT

Noah is told to build an ark three hundred cubits long and fifty cubits wide. The word *cubit*, according to the *Oxford American Dictionary*, comes from the Latin *cubitum*, meaning "elbow" or "forearm," though the actual measure was considered to be the distance from the tip of the middle finger to the elbow. But *whose* hand and forearm? If you're wondering why that matters, ask yourself this: "If I were facing an undetermined amount of time in a craft with my parents, my siblings, thousands of bugs, snakes, and animals that, by the way, had no place to, er, *go*—that is, except on the floor—would I rather be in a craft measuring 300 by 50 of Truman Capote's cubits, or of Michael Jordan's?" The measurement was eventually standardized, sort of, into short and long cubits, about 18 and 21 inches, respectively, which would've made the ark either about 150 yards long, and 25 yards wide, or 175 by 29 and some change. Whatever the length of the cubit in Noah's time, Richard Friedman points out that these are not measurements for a boat, but a box—*tebah*, in Hebrew. Other than the fact that it floats, nothing about it is boatlike.

30

ABOUT THE FLOOD, WHICH IS
DEFINITELY *NOT* A FLOOD

We know the Earth to be a planet, one of several that orbit the sun, a star, one of billions of stars in the Milky Way galaxy, itself one of an untold number of galaxies. However, six hundred years ago, our ancestors believed the Earth to be the center point of the entire cosmos, a disk around which the sun, the planets, and the stars rotated. Several thousand years before that, the authors of the story of Noah had yet another picture in mind. In order to grasp how they understood the biblical flood, it's necessary to draw a picture of exactly what, to them, was being flooded. For that let's go back to the creation narratives, to the second day, when, according to the King James

Bible, "God said, 'Let there be a firmament in the midst of the waters and let it divide the waters from the waters.' And God made the firmament, and divided the waters which were under the firmament from the waters which were above the firmament: and it was so." The word *firmament* is the key. Friedman translates the same Hebrew word as "space," Robert Alter and others as "vault." Whatever the translation, the *meaning* is that of a living space with an arched dome, "a habitable bubble, with land and seas at its base, surrounded by a mass of water."[43] The blue of the sky, they believed, was indicative of the presence of cosmic waters that, like the waters below, were held at bay by the firmament, or vault, in which they lived. Also, the vault had doors above and below, which so far had remained closed.

Once Noah's preparations were complete and everyone was aboard, the J source interjects a single sentence to tell us that Yahweh closed the door to the ark. Then, E writes, Yahweh opened the doors in the heavens and released the waters from below the vault, bringing about *not* a flood but rather "a cosmic crisis in which the very structure of the universe is endangered."[44] So, stuffed into a huge box, the whole of what remained of life now finds itself in the midst of a catastrophe of such magnitude that existence itself is threatened with nonexistence.

Human and other beings, along with the whole of creation, reduced to nonbeing. *Can they do that?*

Not so long ago, a team of extraordinary people asked themselves if their success might bring about that very end. When Robert Oppenheimer and his colleagues at Los Alamos, New Mexico, had developed the first atomic bomb, they knew the result would be no ordinary explosion—would not, in fact, *be* an explosion by any conventional definition. What they did not know, at least not for certain, was whether, once begun, the process of nuclear fission—atom splitting—would contain itself to the six-tenths of a gram of uranium 235 in the bomb's core or continue beyond that tiny mass and deconstruct the universe. The biblical flood, this *deluge*, was perceived by E as an event containing, as possibility, an end every bit as final.

Let's stop to appreciate the moment from a passenger's point of view. Imagine that you are on the ark, a supersized cargo container with "neither a keel nor a rudder nor a sail . . . [and in which] the humans and animals are utterly helpless, cast about in the waters without any control over their fate."[45]* With the animals, insects, provisions, and family now aboard, the

---

*The familiar, and by contrast, gentle image of rain lasting forty days and forty nights—forty being a symbolic number for cleansing—is but a single sentence from the J source, dropped in the midst of all that violence of the E account by the redactor-editor.

door is closed and sealed. Now you wait. It is nearly pitch dark, the air already thick, stale. In the quiet you hear yourself breathing, those around you sighing, shifting. Restless animals mew and growl, others erupt into quick, violent combat. Others screech. *You* want to scream. Then, sudden, overwhelming violence. In the same moment, the doors in the dome of the vault are thrown open, the fountains below are unleashed, and the waters held back since the second day of creation come crashing into the world all at once, and everything is caught in a surreal maelstrom of destruction.

Later, to describe the experience, you reach for a simile, some experience we humans hold in common, but everything pales.

Isn't the author of the story telling us that there *is* no crossover experience, that we *can't* know, that we can't imagine our way into that experience? (Though Yeats may have touched on it when he wrote, "Things fall apart, the centre cannot hold; mere anarchy is loosed upon the world."[46]) Nor can we know how long that part went on. But it did stop, and whether the end came in a gradual tapering off or all at once, there must have been a moment when the beings in the dark knew the worst was over. The astonishment they must have felt at being alive—the sheer, giddy joy of it!

Soon it settles on them that they are *still* enclosed in a massive crate, with one window, with each other, with all those animals and insects, and for *who knows how long.* How did they cope? Did they talk about, obsess about, see in their day and night dreams an end time, when the door would open, when they would escape back into the world—when things would again be *normal?* Of course they did. Wouldn't *we?* In fact, we would. Viktor Frankl, in *Man's Search for Meaning,* and Bruno Bettelheim, in *The Informed Heart,* each writing of his experience in the Nazi concentration camps, observed that the prisoner who could not visualize a time in the future when he would regain his freedom might very well experience what Frankl calls "an existential loss of structure," a state of mind so dangerous that one could literally die of it.

Finally, after a year, it was time to leave the ark. The swell of euphoria they surely knew at being alive and *out,* however, would soon have given way to "Okay, *now* what?" Given what had just happened, however—and by that I mean both the external events and the psychological/spiritual trauma inevitably suffered by survivors of catastrophic events—and the depleted world into which they now emerged, it's a safe bet that they soon lost any lingering hope of a return to normalcy. The life they'd known and the milieu in which they'd lived it had vanished.

After the Flood

31

THE FIRST COVENANT. NOAH PLANTS
A VINEYARD, MAKES WINE, GETS DRUNK,
AND IS (FIGURATIVELY) MURDERED

Instead of what one might expect to see in the aftermath of a flood—oceans of mud, uprooted vegetation, human and animal dead, and the detritus of civilization—the world they step into is rich and verdant. Then "Noah built an altar to the Lord and, taking one of every clean animal and of every clean bird, he offered burnt offerings on the altar." Yes, right there in chapter 6, he *is* told to put only two of each species, a male and a female, on the ark, but in chapter 7 he's told to load up *seven* pairs of each. Ironically, the first number, the one we remember, is from J, the second from P, whose version forms the spine of the flood story and includes the sacrifice. After the sacrifice comes the promise "Never again will I doom the earth because of man," followed by the details of the covenant with Noah, which is to be symbolized by the rainbow.

Noah's already dark tale now goes beyond the ark and toward an event that, like the first part of his story, leaves the reader to wonder what really happened, to question his character yet again, and to ask how, after surviving so much, his life and that of his family could take such a tragic turn. Here is the sequence of events as reported in the text: After the making of the covenant, Noah plants a vineyard, harvests the grapes, makes wine, and drinks himself into a stupor—a first in the biblical narrative. Passing out in his tent, he "uncovered himself," meaning that, whether by accident or on purpose, his genitals were uncovered. At some point Ham, Noah's son, enters the tent, sees his father lying there exposed, then goes to tell his brothers what he's seen. You might not think that seeing the genitals of a six-hundred-year-old man would be all that special, but in that culture to see one's father naked was absolutely forbidden. Yet how could Ham be held liable for seeing what was right in front of him as he walked in? At first blush, the problem seems to be less in the accidental *seeing* than in Ham's failure to cover his father followed by his going back out to tell his brothers. Again it seems pretty straightforward, but the story we have in Genesis may be only a fragment of an earlier, more detailed account, without which "no one has ever figured out exactly what it is that Ham does to Noah."[47] Pointing out that the biblical text itself reads "Noah woke up from his wine and learned what his younger son had done to him," James Kugel writes,

> [T]he Bible itself seems to suggest that Ham had done something *to* his father . . . What is more, if Noah could tell as soon as he awoke that something had been done to him, it only seemed reasonable to suppose that the thing in question had left some physical mark. Some sources seem to have understood that Ham committed a homosexual act: three later translations of the Bible into Greek . . . all replace the word "see" in Gen. 9:22 with a Greek word sometimes used to denote homosexual relations . . . From the second century C.E. on, however, another motif appears, according to which Ham castrated his father (to which various mythological parallels have been adduced).[48]

In regard to the mythological parallels, Alter writes, "Some, as early as the classical Midrash, have glimpsed here a Zeus-Chronos story in which the son castrates the father or, alternately, penetrates him sexually."[49] The latter possibility is reinforced by the fact that "to see the nakedness of" frequently means "to copulate with."[50] In other words, the ancient interpreters saw the possibility that in some older, more complete version of the tale, Ham had raped or even castrated his father. What happens next will lend credence to that possibility.

After Ham tells his brothers what he's done, they go to their father's tent, take a cloth, and, walking backward so as to not look on their father, cover him. When Noah wakes up and realizes what had been done to him as he slept, he says,

> *"Cursed be Canaan;*
> *The lowest of . . ."*

Notice the dissonance? Didn't the narrator just tell us that *Ham* did it? Didn't Ham's brothers just tell their father that *Ham* did it? Then, again, maybe Canaan, Ham's son, did do it—that is, in another version of the story.

Interpreters speculated that in a more expansive version, Canaan may have been a part of whatever his father did. Perhaps he'd even instigated the action by having been the first to see his grandfather naked, then going right away to tell his father. Whether Ham acted alone, or Ham and

Canaan acted together, and regardless of what he or they did—shaming Noah by one or another form of violation—the story becomes archetypal: it is the murder (in this case by neutering) of *Father* by the son.

So there are three possible scenarios, any of which may have included Canaan's participation. Each ends in tragedy. First, the story as we have it in the text, that Ham saw his father uncovered and ran to tell his brothers. Second, that Ham, seeing his father uncovered, either raped or castrated him, then told his brothers. Even if Ham, having seen that his father was uncovered, did no more than run off to tell his brothers, the act, especially in that time and place, would have signaled profound disrespect for Noah's authority, a symbolic fratricide. The irony, and the tragedy, in such a reading of Ham lies in the fact that while he is not a child, he behaved as a child might have behaved. By that I don't mean childish—we all have our moments of that—but as one who *is* a child, in Ham's case, a man who has reached adult *years* but not adult*hood*. Certainly, in our own time, this very image has become iconic as the pop-culture notion of manhood, the ubiquitous boy-man content to be a living irony, that is, growing old while not growing up, matured in body but not in character, arrested at the developmental stage at which, in order for him to separate from his father, his priority becomes the killing of the father and everything that smacks of *Father*.

Biblical scholar Karen Armstrong suggests a third perspective, that "damaged by his experience [of the flood], he [Noah] abused himself, his children and the gift of the vine. When he awoke, he refused to take responsibility for his state but immediately projected his guilt and self-disgust onto an innocent party, his grandson Canaan, the son of Ham."[51] If she's correct, and I think she is, we're left to wonder how the pre-flood Noah, a character so buttoned-up, so lacking in dimension or nuance that interpreters were free to invent him as they pleased, became this seeming madman. All we can know is that enough time had passed for Noah's vines to mature, and for the grapes to be made into wine; the event in question could not have taken place until several years after their leaving the ark, giving the trauma from that experience ample time to fester. Remember what they'd been through: The world they'd known before the ark was gone; everyone but family was dead; and while inside the ark, and for an indefinite length of time, they'd experienced an event so violent that it seemed to threaten not only their lives but existence itself. Is the author (P) suggesting that Noah, Ham, and even Canaan were now victims of yet another near total destruction, this one *after* the flood, yet rooted *in* it? Are we seeing in these characters the aftereffects of traumatic shock, something like the emotional free-fall experienced by soldiers returning from combat, like that often seen in some disaster survivors? Perhaps. In the aftermath of significant trauma, some of us are able to find our footing, some are not. Why would we not expect the same to have been true of our most distant *Homo sapiens* ancestors?

Where my own tendency would be to focus on the cause of Noah's behavior toward Ham, Armstrong's focus is on the behavior itself, on making a case for how this very sort of scapegoating—"when we blame others for our own crimes and inadequacies"[52]—has led to some of the greatest tragedies in history. Yes, and to personal tragedies as well.

32

SEARCHING FOR NOAH, I TAKE A SIDE TRIP
TO THE FIRST BOOK OF SAMUEL AND COME
TO TERMS WITH AN OLD HATRED

Can the Bible make a good shrink? I'm all for using what works, and for me the Bible works well as a resource for mental health—that is, in its role as a repository of human stories that continue to aid my understanding of my own story, the world, and my relationships with others. As I pondered the strangeness of the Noah-Ham-Canaan story, particularly the unfairness of Noah's behavior toward his son and grandson, I felt an old, stale anger begin to rise. So I got curious. A bit more digging brought to mind yet another similarly difficult biblical relationship, this one between Samuel, the prophet, and Saul, Israel's first king. Theirs was a relationship that for decades had left me troubled, agitated, though I didn't know why. I wondered if another story lay hidden beneath the story on the page, one that could be reached only by wrestling with this one, particularly with Samuel, the old man whose neck I'd wanted to wring for more than three decades.   .

At the beginning of the 1st Book of Samuel,* Israel was a loose confederation of tribes ruled over by Judges, men and women whose role was a mix of prophet, priest, and arbiter, as well as political and military leaders. This arrangement was supposed to be reflective of God's kingship over his chosen people, of the covenant struck between their ancestors and their God.

---

*When the Tanakh was translated into Greek (the Septuagint), the Greek letters being larger than Hebrew letters, the entire book would not fit onto a single scroll. Thus 1st and 2nd Samuel.

But what had sustained their ancestors was not enough to meet the perils of the present day. No, this generation, the generation before David, was certain that they needed a king.

Actually, what they needed was *unification,* and monarchy was the reigning model for achieving that. Located as they were along the region's primary invasion corridor, a loose confederation of twelve tribes would appear far tastier to invaders than the same twelve united under a king. Even so, it would take an internal crisis of leadership to finally force the question. Samuel, who'd been Judge over the tribes for decades, had stepped down, appointing his sons to succeed him, but they'd turned out to be bums bent on personal gain, and despite complaints and appeals from the people, Samuel had done nothing about it.

The result was chaos, but Samuel, still the most powerful figure among the tribes, considered the idea of a monarchy to rule over Israel to be apostasy and Saul, whom Yahweh had made known to be his chosen, as the embodiment of this apostasy. When the people would not relent and Yahweh gave the go-ahead, Samuel essentially told the people, "You want a king, you'll get a king. Just don't come crying to me or Yahweh when he uses the power you give him to take everything you've got." With a king forced on him, this frightened and resentful old man saw the world dissolving. There are parallels between Saul and the pre-flood Noah—their passive acceptance of what was about to happen, their incuriosity, the trancelike state that each seemed to occupy, the final crack-up. But the sharpest similarities are between Samuel, the man whose world was slipping away, and the post-flood Noah, the man whose world had slipped away.

From what we've learned in the last century and a half of the workings of the human psyche, we could make the argument that each of these characters began to regard himself as one who'd been abandoned—Noah by Yahweh, Samuel by his family and possibly by Yahweh, and Saul by Samuel and Yahweh. Noah, chosen by God, had survived the violence of the deluge only to emerge from the ark into an unrecognizable, foreign world from which God seemed absent for him. Samuel's birth had been the result of a bargain between his mother, Hannah, and Yahweh: if he would give her a son, she would "dedicate him to the Lord for all the days of his life and no razor shall ever touch his head." In other words, as soon as Samuel was weaned, she'd give him over to be raised by the priests of the Temple at Shiloh. Since he *was* still a boy when he received a divine revelation, signifying him as a prophet, we *could* argue that, like the haloed Christ child of medieval art, the infant Samuel was born with foreknowledge that his mother would one day leave him with the priests. Or we could regard him as a fully human character, a child who understood only that his mother had handed him over to strangers and walked away. That the psychological awareness of our time was not part of their culture, that neither Hannah nor the priests seemed to regard her actions as abandonment—these factors have no bearing on how the child himself might have interpreted the moment, or the subsequent and unconscious psychological and spiritual framework he may have built around it. In my work as a seminar leader, I heard hundreds of people tell stories of childhood abandonment. Yes, these were modern people from Western cultures, whereas Samuel was born in the Middle East of some three thousand years ago. But unless we assume that a child's precognitive brain functioned differently then, we can use their experience as guide for the emotional trauma that Samuel would have experienced and the standard mental constructs he'd almost certainly have put in place—*I can't trust anyone; people will always leave me, so I'll leave them first (or drive them away), blah, blah.* Given these early experiences, it's no surprise that he became an unpleasant adult, or that he will so easily and pitilessly abandon Saul. Understanding him doesn't make him likable, mind you; I've never liked him, but I find that I dislike him less now that I myself am older and have applied a broader perspective to his actions and words.

Even in the early Iron Age, nothing boosted a leader's image like a well-managed crisis, and no sooner had Saul assumed the throne than the Ammonites, an ancient tribe east of the Jordan Rivers, laid siege to Jabesh-Gilead, a city along the Jordan River, midway between the Sea of Galilee and the Dead Sea, and part of Saul's kingdom. Flexing his kingly muscles by promising death and dismemberment to all who refused to follow him, Saul organized an army, defeated the Ammonites, and rescued the city's inhabitants. He was a hero. But not for long.

Following a successful raid, the opening shot in a revolt against Saul, the Philistines brought up an army "as numerous as the sand on the seashore." Seeing their numbers, Saul's army, more a ragtag, undisciplined gathering of men than professional troops, "hid in caves, among thorns, among rocks, and in cisterns," or simply ran for it. To their minds, they needed Yahweh's help, and to secure it a sacrificial offering had to be made. But sacrifice was a priestly function that required Samuel, who was due to arrive sometime within the next seven days. There was nothing for Saul to do but wait. At the end of the seven days, however, no Samuel. Saul, his strategic situation grave, his army dissolving, decided to perform the ritual, with himself in the priestly role. Just as he was finishing, Samuel arrived, and was outraged, even though Saul had taken what appeared to be admirable initiative in a desperate circumstance: "You acted foolishly," he said, "[so] the Lord will seek out a man after his own heart . . . and appoint him ruler over his people." Already (though he doesn't know it), and as if his function all along had been to keep the throne warm for David, his successor, Saul is being pushed aside.

Each time I read it, just at this point in the story, feeling outrage at the injustice, I want Saul to step up to Samuel, knock his block off, and shout, *Look! You didn't show up! I did what had to be done!* Since the author of 1st Samuel has yet to ask my opinion on this matter, but always rolls on without pause, I, annoyed, have always rolled with him. After I read it the last time, however, the encounter stayed with me, nagging like an itch in the mind, so I kept returning to it, scratching around for anything that might help to make sense of what had happened.

First, I wondered if the problem lay in the fundamental difference between religious and secular interpretations of events. For Samuel, priest and prophet, Israel's fortunes rose and fell according to its faithfulness, not the size and readiness of its army. But Saul was a king, and kings, historically, despite their religious mantles, have been secular, military leaders. Looking out over the plains in front of him, Saul would have seen a well-organized force with superior numbers and weaponry. Behind him, his army—what was left of it—was a collection of ragged, frightened men. When Samuel failed to arrive as promised, Saul's decision to proceed with the blessing, with himself in the role of priest, may well have been directed less by religious concerns than by strategic exigencies. Some scholars suggest this episode is a later addition by an antimonarchist redactor making the point that kings must be subordinate to prophets. By itself, however, this is too easy an explanation for Samuel's reaction, hardly more than the sort of predictable conflict endemic to any period of profound transition. No, more was at work, and this trouble, I suspected, was to be found not in Samuel the priest but in Samuel the *man*. Angry with the foul-tempered old priest, I'd failed to consider the *man* whose ground of being had been so thoroughly disrupted, whose rage at Saul in large part might well have stemmed from that disruption. Nor had I asked why I'd taken Samuel's behavior toward Saul so personally. As these considerations were necessary to reach a deeper understanding of Samuel, they were necessary to understand Noah as well.

The third story, the one I sensed in the shadows behind Samuel, was one from my own life, and it harbored a knot of resentment more than thirty-five years old.

Alexandria, Virginia

In late January 1973, four months short of graduation from Virginia Theological Seminary, I was summoned to the dean's office. It had just come to his attention that for months I'd not been attending morning chapel. This left him with no choice, he said, but to recommend to the faculty that I be expelled. He felt just awful about it, with graduation so close, but I *had* known all along that chapel was mandatory, so I *had* brought this on myself, had I not?

The reasonable answer would have been "Well, yes and no," but having heard the words *expel* and *you* in the same sentence, the best I could manage was a flippant observation that if he were to expel every student similarly guilty, he'd need army trucks to carry us all away! He didn't appreciate my attitude, he told me. I apologized, tried to explain why I'd not been in chapel (a lame excuse, at best), argued my merits, restated the fact that many students didn't attend chapel, and, finally, promised to attend chapel for the rest of the academic year. But I could see that none of it mattered, that this meeting was no more than a courtesy. The decision had been made.

But it made no sense! Given that others, equally guilty of the same offense, would not be punished, it followed that the issue of chapel attendance was misdirection. The real issue lay elsewhere, in something that was not being said, and at such a volume that I could hear little else.

Between my second and final academic years, I'd taken a full-time internship with the innovative Episcopal parish, St. Mark's in Washington, D.C., and worked with Dr. John C. Fletcher at the Interfaith Metropolitan Theological Association, an alternative, interfaith seminary he'd founded the year before in Washington. A former faculty member of my seminary, Fletcher had resigned and, when asked to state the reason for his resignation from the faculty, had replied, "I refuse any longer to be part of a school that takes men and turns them into boys." In short, the dean and many on the faculty hadn't cared for St. Mark's, Fletcher, or my decision to work with them. Now, or so I suspected, as an apostate from tradition, I would be served up as an example (a martyrdom that appealed to my youthful grandiosity). That agenda hovered in the air, unsaid—and unsayable, without the risk of escalating the situation beyond all recovery.

But was even that the dean's real agenda? Then, and for years, I was certain of it. Now I wonder if it was but the mask of something deeper at work in him that day, as it may have been in Samuel, in Noah, and now, in these late-middle years, in me.

*   *   *

Look once again at Samuel: not the prophet but the man who'd spent his life in the service of a single idea—that Israel and Yahweh were bound together by the covenant with Abraham. To his mind, the choice for monarchy was a rejection of that relationship, and Saul, remember, as king, was the incarnation of that new, distressing reality. Now look at Noah: not the man chosen by God to build the ark but the man we see after the flood, whose pre-flood life had been deleted, who'd survived catastrophe to find himself in a world all but emptied of people, and for whom this incident with Ham, some years later, may simply have been the tipping point into madness, however temporary or permanent. Again, whether we look at these biblical characters as historical or literary creations, if we're to allow them their humanity—a necessary allowance even for fictional characters—then, just as a harried parent's sudden outburst may be the result of more than his child having dropped a dinner plate on the floor, Samuel's rant may have been about far more than what Saul did that day, and Noah's about more than whatever Ham did, or failed to do. Certainly, we can't say of either man that what pushed his outrage was the fear of losing what he'd had because, for each, it was already gone.

No matter how many billions have gone ahead of us, I can say from my own experience of aging that, like the rest of one's life, growing old is a very personal journey through an uncharted wilderness. The perspectives of age that can lend deep satisfaction to the journey, however, will give up their secrets only when one is willing, finally, to look straight into the eyes of one's own mortality. Think of it as Life itself saying, "Repeat after me, 'I, *say your name*, will die one day.'" Now, imagine how much more difficult that would be if one's external world with its familiar pathways had also become a wilderness. I am reminded of the opening lines of Canto I of Dante's *Inferno*: "When I had journeyed half of our life's way / I found myself within a shadowed forest / for I had lost the path that does not stray."[53]

As it was with Noah and Samuel, just so, perhaps, with my dean. Formal, reserved, handsome, with the aristocratic bearing and impeccable manners of a gentleman of the Deep South, he was the picture of the high-collared, low-church Anglican clergyman. The Episcopal church he'd known throughout his life had made little substantive change to its Book of Common Prayer in five hundred years, giving it and its liturgies a steadfastness rarely found in the accelerating atmospheres of postwar America. Now the very architecture of that beloved icon was undergoing massive revision. As if that were not enough, women were pounding down cathedral doors, demanding ordination to the priesthood, and gays and lesbians were beginning to find their own voices. A new worldview was breaking loose in the church, and everything I'd done that previous year was representative of it. After years of despising, then dismissing him, I wonder now if the deepest level of what was left unsaid that day was that, like Samuel, like Noah, the changes were leaving him more than a little undone.

"Getting old," said Mae West, "ain't for sissies." Older now than my dean was then, I find myself in a psychological-spiritual crisis of sorts, one similar in nature to what his might have been. Having grown up in the predigital world of typewriters, of record players and rotary telephones, advances in technology in the last twenty or so years have left me not so much technophobic as concerned that their negative impact on individual health *and* on the social fabric is not enough on the national agenda. Besides that larger concern, I have of course a quite personal one. Throughout human history, the knowledge, skills, and wisdom that I've spent a lifetime gathering have been considered valuable to any society, but at times these days I fear that these attributes are to the early twenty-first century what buggy whips were to the early twentieth, and that I, and others like me, will become irrelevant.

One day a few years back, having called for tech support, I spent a half hour or so on the phone with a young man who, unable or unwilling to fathom my technical insufficiency, continued to instruct me in how to go from, say, step five to step six despite my protests that I needed to begin at step one. When his sighs and tones of condescension had sufficiently encouraged my darker side, his supervisor intervened, apologized, and put me with another tech who, though polite enough, may as well have been speaking in Klingon. Afterward I indulged a daydream in which my hand rested on the master cutoff switch of the digital world, an image that would be far more amusing were it not for the self-pity hidden behind the curtain of self-justification. In this way, I think, Noah, Samuel, the dean, and I are mates.

While I have not yet descended into cursing those who annoy me, Noah says *three* times that Canaan will be the slave of his brothers. Modern scholars suggest the entire episode may have been invented in order to show the sort of pervo-creep the Canaanites had descended from, thus painting all Canaanites with the same brush and providing justification for Israel's having taken the promised land from them.

At the end of the story and the speculation about both it and him, we are left with three possible images of Noah: the hero, the scapegoater, and the one whose post-traumatic self, over time, became a shadowy, even ridiculous reflection of who he'd been. And how *human* is it to have been a hero, and to have been small, and even pathetic, all within the same lifetime—

perhaps again and again? Anyone who can say he or she has not experienced all three at least once—yes, including the third, which comes in varying degrees of intensity—is likely not paying attention.

33

TOWER OF BABEL, OR, OUR GIFT FOR
MISSING THE MEANING IN WORDS

How often have you stopped for directions, written down exactly what the guy said, followed them impeccably, only to find yourself on Mars? It's one of my very favorite things to whine about, and I love telling the story about the night, in 1982, when I'd agreed to do a presentation for a colleague who'd fallen ill. The location was out in the sticks of northern California, but I wasn't worried—I had directions: *Follow "Route A" to "FM B." Turn left, then right onto "C."* Easy as it gets, I thought, assuming that "left, then right" meant "C" would come up right away. Nope. "C" was twenty-five miles down "FM B," a country road with no streetlamps to light the road signs. And it was raining. There was no GPS then, not for the masses, and no cell phones. I was *real* late.

You've heard the World War II slogan "Loose lips sink ships!" How many times have you wished you'd just kept your mouth shut? Or at least employed it more judiciously, perhaps using different words altogether, or the same words, but strung together in a different order, like, say, one that did *not* bring *that* response? Or, maybe they were the right words in the right order, but your tone conveyed a meaning you'd not intended—not consciously, anyway. Or the words and the tone you'd used had been fine; the problem lay elsewhere, at the other end of the conversation. This may have happened to you: You say "x" but he or she hears "y," the very thing you should have known *not* to say in *that* situation. Now, just as if you'd set out to be offensive, hurtful, and insensitive, as if you'd actually said "y," he or she is angry, hurt, weepy because you've been intentionally nasty, hurtful, insensitive. From your end, he or she seems to have been in another conversation altogether. The problem? By the time your words had made it through his or her ears, passed through that part of the mind that assigns a meaning to *everything* one hears or sees, the chasm between what you'd said and what he or she had *heard you say* is vast.

In the fable of the Tower of Babel, one of J's contributions, humans once again are at odds with Yahweh. Migrating eastward, and coming upon "a valley in the land of Shinar," they decided to settle there and, with their new construction technology, build a city and "a tower with its top in the sky" in order to make a name for themselves and to prevent humans from eventually scattering all over the world. J "never tells what they will do when they finish the tower, what is meant by 'make ourselves a name,' or why they fear being scattered if they do not have this tower."[54] We are told, however that Yahweh, on seeing the tower, assumed the worst, that these post-flood humans were as uppity and rebellious as the pre-flood humans—Adam and Eve, Cain and Abel, and the generations he'd drowned.

What to do? He can't kill them all—he'd promised never to do that again. What about divide and conquer? It's so simple. Make communication impossible by giving them different languages *and* by separating them from one another. J's Yahweh being *so* like us in his emotional makeup, it's not all that surprising that rather than *asking* them what they're up to, he simply goes with his assumptions.

Since the humans, as a species with free will, would not come around, it was time for a new plan and a wholly new strategy. Why not start with just one human, focus on him, and see what happened next?

PART II

THE WANDERERS

CALLING

34

MUSINGS ON "BEING COMMISSIONED,"
AKA DRAFTED, HIJACKED, SHANGHAIED

You'd think that a seventy-five-year-old man "of a well-to-do social class"[1] like Abraham would have his best days behind him. Not even close. And not that he had much to say about his destiny; the very first verse of his story reads, "The Lord said to Abram, 'Go forth [*Lek Lekah*] from your native land and your father's house to the land that I will show you.'" In English, this has the ring of a Realtor's invitation to view a piece of prime acreage, but the meaning of *Lek Lekah* is "to take leave of, separate."[2] In other words, what Abraham* hears is neither an offer nor a request, but a command: "Pack up. Your life in this place is over." Like the others who will be similarly drafted into divine service, if Abraham had other plans for the rest of his life, those were abandoned.

The relationship that Yahweh had with Adam, Eve, Cain, and Abel was different from all that would follow. Beginning with Noah, individuals are singled out by God for a task. Sometimes the task is specific—Noah is told to build an ark, how to build it, and what to put in it. Sometimes the task is open-ended—Abraham is told, essentially, to start walking. This interplay between *caller* and *called* drives the biblical narrative and gives it its power, so, before moving further into Abraham's story, it may be useful to ask, *What is a calling?*

By and large, we are a people of the great middle way. When one of our own becomes obsessed—that is, with something outside the box of the normal obsessions of money, career and, to a point, sex and religion—it throws our normative world out of balance. We don't like imbalance, or those oddballs who create it. Therefore, *if* at some point in your life, be it early, midlife, or late, you begin to hear the whisperings of a *new* voice, and *if*, God forbid, that voice will not be ignored or diminished, but only grows stronger, manifesting itself in your life as, say, some gravitational or magnetic force that is tugging you toward *another* life from the one you're living, or the one you've planned, or the one planned *for* you and expected

---

*Although "Abram" and "Sarai" are not renamed until chapter 17, verse 5, and only in the P source, following the lead of many modern and ancient interpreters I will use the familiar "Abraham" and "Sarah."

of you, and *if* you begin to imagine that *other* life as the *only* life worth *your* life, *then* you and the people in your life could be in big trouble.

Whatever numinous, ethereal, wispy, airy-fairy, or otherwise meaningful cloth we wrap *Calling* in, it is a noun that, not so long ago, referred to the singling out of an individual who'd been chosen for divine service. That has changed of course, and rightly so. *Calling* has to do with *spirit*, and both in biblical Hebrew and Greek, the word *spirit* can be rendered as "breath" or "breath of life," the breathing in and breathing out of that which inspires (from Latin, *inspirare*), and in human experience, that sort of transaction overflows the confines of what we've come to think of as religion. For instance, if you asked someone to explain what he meant by "Medicine (or teaching, or law, or music, et cetera) is my *calling*," he might say that he was drawn by an interest in the field, but more than that, he had had a very definite sense of being *compelled*, even to the degree that nothing else has mattered nearly so much.

From that, we might say that *calling* is a name we give to that *need*, that *hunger*, that *longing* that, as if it were something acting from outside the self and apart from the ego, urges one's life toward a greater clarity, even toward *the* larger purpose for one's life. James Hillman, in *The Soul's Code: In Search of Character and Calling*, writes, "Sooner or later something seems to call us onto a particular path . . . Despite early injury and all the slings and arrows of outrageous fortune, we bear from the start the image of a definite individual character with some enduring traits . . . Each person enters the world called."[3] Hillman draws his "Acorn" theory from Plato's Myth of Er, found at the end of *The Republic*. "In a nutshell," he writes, "[Plato tells us that] the soul of each of us is given a unique daimon before we are born, and it has selected an image or pattern that we live on earth . . . [and it] remembers what is your image and belongs to your pattern, and therefore your daimon is the carrier of your destiny."[4] What the Greeks called the *daimon* was known to the Romans as one's *genius*, and to us, variously, as *guide, soul companion*, and *guardian angel*. To make the acquaintance of this image bearer, then, is to perceive at least the outlines of one's *calling*, to recognize what all along may have been the missing piece needed to sustain one's life. That has been my experience, which stems from a single moment over fifty years ago, about which I will tell you presently. I will say, with Hillman, that recognition is but the first step. "Unpacking the image," he writes, "takes a lifetime. It may be perceived all at once, but understood only slowly."[5]

The "image" or "pattern" of one's *calling* may reveal itself early in life through actual accomplishments, or remain encoded within a fabled self born in the youthful imagination. "[F]or fifteen years or more," writes George Orwell, "I was . . . making up . . . a continuous 'story' about myself, a sort of diary existing only in the mind. I believe this is a common habit of children and adolescents."[6]

My own fabled self was the product of truly outrageous invention—that is to say, entirely normal. By the time *I* was seventeen, I had imagined that I had caught the game-winning, last-second Hail Mary pass that won the Texas 4-A football championship, and hit the grand slam home run that brought home the Texas 4-A baseball championship. I'd also spent a summer in the majors where, at short stop, I'd executed a triple play that would be talked about as long as the game of baseball endures. And as a lover, I'd satisfied Marilyn Monroe, Elizabeth Taylor, and others, too many to mention.

What accounts for such grandiosity? In his book *Evolution's End*, Joseph Chilton Pearce points out that adolescence is in fact a recent historical construct, a sort of holding pattern that, however natural it may seem to us, goes entirely against our genetic encoding. Throughout most of human history, "children were children until their early teens wherein, through some rite of passage, they were ushered into and took their place in adult society."[7] Remnants of that encoding, he tells us, remain in the early adolescent's "idealistic image of life," in the expectation "that something tremendous is supposed to happen." "Adolescents," he writes, "sense a secret, unique greatness in themselves that seeks expression. They gesture toward the heart when trying to express any of this, a significant clue to the whole affair."[8]

Those events from my imaginary life *were* compensation for what was happening, and not happening, on the outside, but more than that they were attempts at expressing that "secret, unique greatness." Even now I remember each of them with a clarity equal to or greater than events that took place in normal time and space. I can say with certainty that they were sustaining during those difficult years, providing the image of another self from the loser I perceived in the mirror each morning. This fabled self, Hillman suggests, bears the imprint of the *daimon*, the *guide*, the *guardian angel* that, when it speaks, says, "The stories I tell [about my history] *are* the facts. The fables I tell more truly tell who I am."[9]

When my parents' friends would ask questions such as *Well, young man, what will you do with your life?* I had no idea that the correct answer would prove to be, "Well, I have this really weird, sort of sensual, even erotic, though nonsexual, urge that's been bugging me for *years*! First, I'll spend three or four decades doing work that won't really satisfy that urge but *will* prove to be important steps on the way to understanding what it is *and* to finding what, finally, *will* satisfy it. Then, I'll do that. Of course, I might be pretty old by then." A calling can, and often does, work just that way.

35

SCHOOL CHUMS DISCOVER WHAT THE POET
KNEW. THE SHRINK, HIS A-BOMB, AND LIMITS

Once in a while, toward the end of an otherwise typical Sunday morning service, our pastor would invite a young man from the congregation to join him on the dais. There, with the two of them facing the congregation, the pastor would announce that this "fine young man" had been called by the Lord into the Baptist ministry. The pastor would be glowing, the young man would be glowing, his parents, most of the congregation—a veritable light show of pleasure. And why not? Here, incarnate, was a triumph of their faith, a saver of souls for a new generation! Had the guy joining the pastor on the dais been a middle-aged lawyer, a CPA, or a plant foreman, with three kids, two cars, and a mortgage, proclaiming that he was ditching *that* life because God had called him into the ministry, I doubt so many would've been beaming. In fact, the few middle-aged members of my seminary class, each of whom had left a successful career in order to follow a voice bidding him toward another path, reported a range of negative reactions, from skepticism to utter disbelief. Each said he'd tried to satisfy the urge through more involvement in his parish or another type of service, but couldn't. It was *all-in* or nothing.

Actually, it was *all-in* or the funny farm. Each had found himself tangled in a rather splendid web of catch-22 irony: While total commitment practically guaranteed that most friends, family, and colleagues would assume he *had*, indeed, lost his mind, each had discovered that to do anything else guaranteed that he *would* lose it. While I knew that what they were saying was true, I couldn't say why until I heard it from a poet.

In 1904, the poet Rainer Maria Rilke, writing to a younger man who'd sought his advice, suggested that the genuineness of one's calling can be found only inside oneself. "[A]sk yourself this: Must I write? Dig deep into yourself for a true answer. And . . . if you can confidently meet this serious question with a simple, 'I must,' then build your life upon it. It has become your necessity."[10] Substitute work with the poor, religion, forestry, medicine, law enforcement, the stage, the military, painting, banking, coaching, law, politics, teaching, or another pursuit, and the answer remains the same: If you can live a full, satisfying life without doing it, it's not "your necessity," it's not a calling—at least not *your* calling. Not even if you're really good at it. Not even if your parents, their friends, your teachers, religious leaders, your friends, all *want* you to do it, think you *ought* to do it, and would be nuts *not* to do it—would be *wrong* not to do it. Not even if *you* think you should want to do it, but, in fact, don't. Indeed, Rilke might agree that the presence of any language of obligation would be all the evidence you would need to differentiate the true calling from the false. To say *I must because I should* implies an obligation, not a calling. *I must because, if I don't, I'll die inside* is quite another matter.

How do you find your own calling? You don't. It finds you. As it was for Rilke and so many others, *necessity* is the only measure I've ever found useful. There is the adage, "Do what you love and the money will follow," but ask the ghost of van Gogh—his paintings may be worth tens of millions, but he never saw a dime—or contemporary starving writers and painters, who might tell you that to follow your calling may require that you make your money elsewhere. Of course, even should you discover, then follow, your calling, and even get rich, you may from time to time find yourself wishing that you'd been called to do something else. You have to appreciate the irony in that.

There remains the question of just *what* and/or *whose* voice is doing the calling. "God does the calling," my childhood pastor might have said, then backed it up with something biblical, such as, "Trust unto God and He shall direct your path." Yes, but *which* God? When he used the name, he meant the Christian God, Southern Baptist version, that vengeful score-keeper, the arbiter of damnation and salvation. The author of the proverb he'd used as backup, however, would have had a different idea.

In the Tanakh are many names by which the Holy is called: Elohim, El Shaddai, Hashem. Called the Tetragrammaton (from Greek, *tetra-* "four," and *gramma-* "letter"), the name "Yahweh" (also "Jahweh" or simply "YHWH" or "JHWH") is an anagram constructed from the initial sounds of the words spoken to Moses from the burning bush, which, in English translation, are "I AM WHAT (or WHO, or THAT) I AM." Then, and in some places even now, it was considered a sound so holy that it was not to be written but represented in the biblical text by four dots. Nor was it to be spoken aloud or even in the silence of one's own thoughts. This was hardly the recognition of one's buddy, or pal, but of the holy, the unknowable, the *awe-full* presence of unfathomable mystery.

Carl Jung, in an interview just days before his death, said, "To this day God is the name by which I designate all things which cross my willful path violently and recklessly, all things which upset my subjective views, plans and intentions and change the course of my life for better or worse"[11]— sort of the A-bomb version of *If you want to make God laugh, tell him your plans*. I particularly appreciate how he avoids both anthropomorphism and reductionism while at the same time managing to communicate the reality of the limits that confront the ego—that is, the moment-by-moment confrontation of the *ego* by the *Is*, the collision of *The Way I Want It* with *The Way It Is*, with the *"I AM (WHAT I AM)."*

Also, I like Jung's definition because it fits so nicely with what's coming up next.

36

NOAH, ABRAHAM, JONAH, TEXAS IN THE FIFTIES,
AND HOW A CALLING MIGHT SOUND

Throughout the creation narratives (Genesis 1–5), the characters come into being, live their lives, and pass on. Along the way, but for a few dos and don'ts, little is asked of them. Beginning with Noah, however, the reader encounters characters whose lives, already under way, are interrupted by a divine command that not only comes from out of the blue but does so without so much as a word of divine foreplay—no *How are you? Nice to see you. How's your mother?* to soften the message of *Oh, by the way, your life as you've known it is over.* Moreover, there is the expectation that, without question or pause, the character will say, "Sure, I'll just drop everything I'm doing or ever hoped to do because you want me to do this other thing." And each of them does: Noah starts building; Abraham starts wandering.

When asked "Why'd Noah and Abraham do that?" the preachers and Sunday school teachers of my youth basically answered *Because God told them to.* Then they explained that blind obedience "is how all of us who truly love the Lord *should* behave." I'd lay odds that most of the preachers and teachers back then would've actually felt it was better to disobey than to have the wife asking, *What's with all the lumber in the front yard?* Or to have her come home to find the household being loaded into a truck, because *God told me that we were to go wandering. We'll be told where, later. Okay? So, could'ja help me load this table, then go upstairs and give the kids a hand?* But the biblical men did obey. Moreover, generation after generation, others who were singled out repeated that same, immediate *yes.* All but one, that is—Jonah. *His* response, especially his initial response, most clearly resonates with me, because it is so very human. If we were to imagine a backstory for Jonah, it might be that of an ordinary man living an ordinary life when "The word of the Lord came to Jonah son of Amittai: Go at once to Nineveh, that great city, and proclaim judgment upon it; for their wickedness has come before Me" [or, "become known to me"]. Although others who heard God's orders dropped everything and got to work, Jonah dropped everything and headed in the opposite direction from Nineveh, toward Joppa, a seaport, where he found a boat bound for the farthest reaches of the earth. *That* I understand. Blind obedience I don't. While I do find the zealousness of Noah and Abraham admirable, even enviable, it is mostly foreign to me, and by that I don't mean just the broad strokes of historical time, place, culture, and religion.

I am shaped in part by the ethos of Texas in the 1950s, with its peculiar iteration of the American ideal of the primacy of self housed within a protean structure of fundamentalist Christian morality. It is a curious symbiosis, this relationship of Texas culture—and other parts of America—to Christianity. While Christianity has molded the region, as surely as if Jesus had been born in Abilene, Christianity has *been* molded to fit the frontier ideal of self-reliance and the darker ambitions of self-interest (of which astonishing excesses have been tolerated, justified, or simply overlooked, provided they were dressed in garments of religious, moralistic, sentimental patriotism, "making it appear identical with the common good"[12]). While I've never been entirely at home with the brittle certainties of that ethos, nevertheless I am sufficiently *of* it that, along with my admiration, I've always felt uneasy with the biblical characters and their seeming readiness to be brought to heel. Especially in my rebellious teen years, I wanted somebody to do what a man was supposed to do—*to stand up!* This is what Jonah did, or so it might seem. It depends on the definition of "stand up."

In the jingoistic, Cold War atmospheres of my youth, the greatest virtue was courage that a man might display in battle. World War II veterans, still young, many with physical and psychic scars, were everywhere. Just down the street, Mike's dad's gaping, wine-red scars on his right leg and torso still held shrapnel from a German land mine. Once, when a piece had worked its way to the surface, and just before heading off to the veterans' hospital to have it removed, he invited us to feel the lump just below the skin. Here was an American-style Achilles, at times an ordinary man, other times—and especially after the release of the film version of Audie Murphy's *To Hell and Back*—elevated in our minds to the near-mythic *warrior* who had heard the clarion call and, like the biblical prophet Isaiah, had answered "Here am I. Send me!" It was considered the only answer that any "real man" could give. By this measure, however, it was the likes of Noah and Abraham who'd stood up, not Jonah. His was a coward's answer.

But was it? Pascal wrote, "To deny, to believe, and to doubt absolutely— this is for man what running is for a horse." Doubt is self-preservation. It is an instinct that ensures physical survival as well as spiritual survival—the will, the *need*, to choose one's own life. Jonah's behavior might be perceived as a declaration of "I," as in "This is *my* life, and *that's* not what

'I' wish to do with it." (It's the sort of question my seminary mates and I would toss about late into the night through clouds of tobacco smoke and over bottles of cheap wine.) This urge to individuate, to break free from the "parent," especially the "father," is archetypal, so the author of Jonah's story might have wanted his audience to assume this desire for liberation was the fuel for Jonah's desire to run, but I doubt it. Jonah's story goes on to reveal a man not especially troubled by depth, which *is* a prerequisite for any such pursuit.

Am I, a man living long after the authors of Genesis, with ideas and mind-sets made possible by twenty-five hundred additional years in the development of human consciousness, using these as tools to better understand these ancient texts, or am I ascribing meanings that are simply echoes of my own time and my own life? That is always the risk. Awaiting any attempt at biblical interpretation is the conscious and unconscious imposition of norms prevalent in one's own time and place, these having become so ordinary, so natural, so *obvious*, that surely they must have been typical of human culture at all times and in all places. "Perspective," writes Harold Bloom, "governs our response to everything we read, but most crucially with the Bible. Learning from scholars, whether Christian or Jewish, one still questions their conditioning, which too frequently overdetermines their presentation. Obviously that caution applies to me as well . . ."[13] And to me, and to you. Indeed, any one of us attempting to come to grips with the Bible would do well to consider the multiple factors that influence perspective: family, religion, education, where one was born, and even *when* one was born. For instance, the archetypal impulse toward "individuation," which we see in the Bible and throughout ancient literature and, perhaps, in the story of Jonah, is a far cry from the American ideal of "individualism." While the former is the natural process of learning to distinguish oneself first from parents and then from others in the same group, of discovering one's "I" while remaining part of the whole, the latter is what Tocqueville, in *Democracy in America*, noted more than a century and a half ago: the idea of the "American" as the strong, quiet, simple, virtuous individual who heels for no one, needs no one, who stands entirely alone, gazing at some far horizon. The Texas version is the same, only turbocharged with frontier images and what can be, especially of late, a near-to-smothering sentimentalism. Neither is an idea likely to find legs in any tribal culture such as the ancient Israelites. Yet, ironically, a biblical calling in Genesis is always to an individual. Though Noah's family is invited to go with him on the ark, it is Noah who is called and expected to act. Likewise, while Jonah could have invited a friend or two to accompany him, he is expected to go to Nineveh—*now!*

37

THE QUESTION NEVER ASKED

Whether we regard Noah and Abraham as historical or as literary charac-ters—and, so, as metaphor—we still don't know whether either of them actually wants to fulfill his commission. We do know, however, that Jonah did not want that life, that he made a run for it, away from Yahweh and toward something else, an extraordinary act in the biblical narratives.

A lot of good it did him. Hiding from the gods was a familiar motif in the ancient world, so the story's original audience would have known right away that escape was impossible. Sure enough, Yahweh arranges for a violent storm that threatens to sink the boat. The crew, at Jonah's sug-gestion, throws him overboard, where a big fish (not a whale) was waiting to swallow him. Finding himself in the belly of the fish, having just faced death by drowning, and now, for all he knows, by digestion, his options nar-rowing, Jonah begins sucking up to Yahweh, using a literary form called a lament. Modern biblical scholars, however, tell us that the lament was not part of the original story, but added centuries later by some redactor *cum* spinmeister. Without it, Yahweh would come off as a big bully, and Jonah's motivation for going to Nineveh would not be religious zeal but rather fear that, if he didn't, Yahweh would kill him! Then again, given that Nineveh was the capital of the Persian Empire, and that he would be yelling not only at citizens, soldiers, and the like, but also at the Persian king, *the most powerful human being on the known earth*, it must have crossed Jonah's mind that to go *there* to do *that* could also get a guy killed.

But he wouldn't die before looking really stupid, as Noah must have the moment he started gathering materials. Right away, people must have started in on him with questions like *What're you gonna do with all that stuff? Make a what? And you're gonna put the wife and kids in there with all those bugs and snakes and . . . Are you kidding?* Jonah is told, "Go to Nineveh and proclaim my judgment." Okay, but how, I ask you, does one go about doing that? Long ago, pondering that very question, I conjured up a Woody Allen–like scene in which this frightened, reluctant fellow walks into a bustling marketplace, muttering (to the divine presence no one else can hear or see), "Where, *here*? No? Over there? By the fruit stand? Yes? No? *What?* Yes, I remember what to say! Just gimme a second, will you?" Finally, he stands on a box, and in a timid voice, says, "Excuse me . . . Might I . . . *uh* . . . Hello? Might I have your . . . *uh* . . . attention f-for a, uh . . . ?"

This has nothing to do with a fear of public speaking—I've been doing that off and on for decades—nor of being perceived as a bit odd. But even when I account for the historical and cultural differences between Noah's or Jonah's *there-and-then* and my *here-and-now*, I can't come up with a single scenario for either situation in which I would not look like a fool. My extremities go cold at the prospect. Given my high regard for personal dignity, and, yes, its sometimes doppelganger, vanity, if I'm to do something that risks public humiliation, I want it to be *my* idea—at least that. I doubt that I'd have followed Noah's or Jonah's example.

38

AT TWELVE, AN ECSTATIC EXPERIENCE, OR AN ALLERGIC REACTION TO INCENSE, DISRUPTS, THEN REDIRECTS, MY LIFE

But how can following a divine calling not be my idea? Aren't *yes* or *no* mine to say, the product of a free will? Well, yes, and no. Imagine that you've mapped out a life plan, one that is goal-oriented, sensible, and moving along quite swimmingly, when, like a secret lover, that (aforementioned) voice begins whispering, beckoning, seducing, stripping away the layers until, like St. Paul on the road to Damascus, that *necessity* flashes with such intensity that it knocks you flat on your keester, leaving you blind and hearing voices. Wouldn't that be fun?

Religious people call these *ecstatic* or *mystical* experiences, and speak of them as transcendent—that is, *outside* the realm of the normal, day-to-day experience of life. I've had a few, one of them a real blockbuster, and I can tell you that they come in a variety of shapes and sizes, that they happen when they happen, and that you have little to say about any of it. One of these muggings happened in Paris. I was wandering through the Jeu de Paume, the Impressionist museum in the Tuileries, when, quite suddenly, and without expecting it, I was face-to-face with a painting that had haunted me since I'd first seen it in a magazine many years before. It was Van Gogh's self-portrait, the one in which he is without a hat, in which his craziness seems to radiate off him like rays from the sun. As if it had its own gravity, I felt myself caught, then drawn into that mad beauty, into a terrible, wonderful, transcendent unknown.

The big one, however, was in the fall of 1958, a few months after my twelfth birthday, less than a mile from my home, and in a place as foreign to my experience as Pluto. Accustomed to low-church Protestant-ism, plain architecture, and minimalist sanctuaries, except in movies, I'd never seen anything like the silken, embroidered altar cloths at St. Paul's

Roman Catholic church, or the golden candelabra, or the statuary, especially Mary, or what struck me as the rather miserable-looking Jesus on
the cross above the altar. And there was a faint fragrance in the air, something *of* the place itself, spicy, old, remnantlike, haunting, and mysterious.
My family and I were there for a nuptial mass. I'd been angry when we'd
arrived; it was, after all, the first cold Saturday of autumn, a day for playing
football with my buddies, not sitting in church. But all the beauty had surprised me, and I was calmer now, even peaceful. When the music swelled,
people stood, half turning toward the back, straining their necks to see, like
people waiting for a parade. Curious, I turned with them, and through the
adults, saw a boy about my age holding what appeared to be a brass cross
mounted atop a varnished broomstick, and in front of that was another boy,
this one swinging a smoking pot. As they passed, a bit of the smoke wafted
toward me, and it was the same scent.

It was like a scene from an old movie when someone remembers the
past and the picture dissolves into wavy lines, but this was only in one spot,
sort of oval-shaped, and just above and in front of the cross. Then, like a
camera shutter, it blinked, and in the same moment I had the sense of
something hitting me in the belly, but not hard. With that, it—whatever it
was—was over. I felt a heaviness now, like the heartache I'd felt when my
dog had died, and again when one of my best friends had moved across the
country. I have a dreamy memory of the service, of the priest's murmur-
ings in Latin, the bride and groom, more of the incense, and the presence
of something I could not name. That night, drifting toward sleep, as if
the fabric of space had opened a hole beneath me, I felt as though I were
falling, tumbling, into some other place where I was surrounded by stars.

Then, *Who am I?*

The voice was soft, intimate, but *whose?* Was it my voice? That presence
I'd sensed? Was the question about me? Or about *it?* I was more curious
than frightened. The tumbling continued, the question repeating every
ten or fifteen seconds until I fell asleep. The next night was the same at
first, then a second question: *Who am I asking the question? Who am I?*

Every night it was the same. Something, I knew, was different about
me, shifting. Even so, I was still a twelve-year-old boy awash in the cultural
zeitgeist of southeast Texas in the late 1950s, where boys were supposed to
play football, learn to shoot things, and grow up to be like their daddies,
where low-church Protestantism reigned supreme and it was not unusual
to hear absurdist statements such as *Catholics don't even believe in Jesus;
they think the pope is God.* So, exactly what was I supposed to do with a
peculiar experience I'd had in, of all places, a Roman Catholic church,
one that wouldn't go away, and, depending on the day, was making me

a little crazy? Talk to someone, right? Almost certainly, my nonreligious father would've half listened, rolled his eyes, and said *Go talk to your mother.* My mother would have listened, then dragged me down the street to the pastor's house; or called together church members for a full-throttle gang-save; or phoned my grandfather, who might well have boarded the next train with the intention of saving me from eternity in hell.

The tumbling and the questions repeated each night for months, then several times a week for years. The questions were never intrusive, but more like koans, satisfied to *be* rather than demanding answers—a relief, since I had none. Though it was a single moment, a split second in my sixty-plus years, the man I've become, all that I've done in my professional life—parish priest, speaker and trainer, management consultant, writer— can be traced to the experience. Yet it remains a mystery. I've tried saying it was "of God," but the name arrives like a king and his court; there is simply too much baggage and too many extras for my small house. Other names present the same. I've come to prefer the mystery, the lack of logic in the fact that I understand it far better when I don't try to understand it.

Besides, understanding has its own timetable and comes when I'm not looking for it. While still a teenager, the word *milieu* arrived as a welcome guest because that was the sense of it for me that Saturday afternoon—an immersion, a *surrounding* too vast ever to say, "It's here, but not there" or "under this roof, but not that one." Later I would stumble across the Latin, *Mysterium Tremendum*, and know its meaning without asking, and the vast experience to which it pointed. Then I came across the German mystic Meister Eckhart, who wrote, centuries ago, "That which one says is God, he is not; that which one does not say, he is more truly that than that which one says he is."[14] I've loved the image inherent there, of the definition of the *infinite* existing only in the spaces between the words, whether written or spoken.

Was it a *call*? It did act like one, although it had no "Go there, do that," or anything else specific—which bugged me to no end—but its effect was undeniable, a personal earthquake that took what had been the familiar, planned landscape of my future and wrecked it, leaving me disoriented, often lost, but always with the sense that it was carrying me somewhere. Or leading me. *Where? When?* It would be a decade before I had a clue, and another forty years, so far, spent in the unpacking. I've likened the process to Jacob's wrestling all night with the angel (Genesis 32), refusing to let go until it tells me its name, or gives me a new name.

I continue to be surprised at the number of biblical characters, who, like most people in my life—like *me*, for that matter—have qualities I like and qualities I dislike. I admire both Noah and Abraham for what my grandparents would have called their cussedness, that stubborn certainty of being in the right. And I even admire Jonah for having the chutzpah to run, and for his moment of sterling character during that storm when he tells the crew to save themselves by throwing him into the sea. But in the end, Jonah is whiny and small, the sort I'd rather be dead than be like. A good shrink might say that each is a mirror reflecting those bits of my own character that I'd just as soon keep on a leash and out of sight. In fact, I've found most of the major, and even the minor, biblical characters to be rather relentless in their mirroring. Also, I have a hunch that a few of them, when that *necessity* began to emerge, were as clueless as I was—as I remain, some days, these fifty years later.

ABRAHAM

ACT ONE

A New Approach

39

AFTER PLANS A AND B, ONCE AGAIN
TO THE DRAWING BOARD

So far, the creation, with respect to the humans—who, after all, were the *point*—has been pretty much of a bust. Adam and Eve, having failed to measure up, were cursed, then expelled from the garden. The promise their children represented died with Abel's murder and Cain's expulsion from God's presence. Before the flood, Noah may have been a genuinely righteous man, or just the best of a bad lot, but in the years *after* the flood he and at least one of his sons had arguably begun to unravel. Next came that monument to hubris, the Tower of Babel, proof that "the new world order planned by God after the Flood had come to nothing. If anything, humanity was now in a worse state."[15] Plan A, the man and the woman in the garden, *should* have worked, and if not for *free will*, that catch-22 put in place at creation, *would* have worked. Plan B, the flood, starting over with Noah, his family, and the creatures carried on the ark, must have seemed like a slam dunk. But the divine had been angry at what had become of his creation. Certainly, all of us know the disappointment and frustration of failed plans. Any one of us who has managed even small projects at work, at home, or at church or temple has probably learned the hard way that the unforeseen and unintended consequences that always follow in the wake of a strategic move can be surprisingly explosive when the planning and execution are done in anger.

40

A MATTER OF RESPONSIBILITY

So, the divine had an idea that, in practice, had failed rather spectacularly—twice. Imagine J's anthropomorphic Yahweh grumbling, to no one in particular, about what a bunch of willful screwups he'd created—and who could argue? We humans have passed the twenty-five centuries since Genesis was written trying to make up our minds whether to go for progress or self-annihilation. What thoughtful observer of the nuclear arms race over the past sixty years has not marveled at our continued existence? While conservatives and liberals might differ in the details as to who is responsible for this mutually assured destruction, it's likely that they'd agree that *we* are responsible, we *humans*, for our sorry state. But, biblically speaking, who is responsible?

If the helmsman of a U.S. naval vessel runs his ship aground, it is the ship's captain who bears the final responsibility. How unfair that seemed to me when I first learned of it, at sixteen, from a navy pilot, one of the men accompanying our YMCA group on a wilderness trip into Ontario in the summer of 1961. But, fairness aside, where was the sense in holding the captain at fault because some dimwit failed to watch where he was going? The pilot explained "command responsibility," the idea that the guy with the final authority had to be the guy with the final responsibility. I didn't get it—not then.

When I was thirty-two, and vicar of a parish in the Diocese of California, I noticed that when things went right, everybody—my bishop, my parishoners, my colleagues—gave me the credit. And I got the credit when things went south, even when the pressures taking things in that direction seemed to have little if anything to do with me or my leadership. I still didn't get it. Four years later, after having joined a training organization and qualifying as a senior trainer, I'd begun leading intensive two day seminars, each with variables far more numerous and complicated than anything I'd encountered in parish work. In the beginning, the task of delivering the material, conducting the maze of interactions, staying sharp hour after hour, could be nearly overwhelming. The idea that I was responsible for the final outcome of every training assigned to me, however, proved the hardest to grasp. If the results were substandard, I could expect a morning-after phone call, and the question "So, what happened?" It may have been that the support team had been lacking in some way, or the trainees that weekend had been particularly surly and uncooperative, but *how*, I would argue, could any of that have been my fault? Well, none of it was. In fact, if that morning-after inquiry had been looking for fault instead of cause, I'd have been in the clear. Turns out, however, that for someone in my position, there was no such place.

The logic was simple enough, and not unlike what that navy pilot had described all those years before: *If* the effectiveness of the training material was proven, and it was; and *if* the technical skills of every trainer in the organization were not vetted once, but instead were under constant scrutiny, and they were; and *if* the senior trainer had the authority, before and during the training, to order any change in procedure, and to remove anyone—trainee, support team personnel—who proved to be an impediment to the success of the training, and he or she did, *then* how could final responsibility rest anywhere else? *So, if you don't want that sort of heat, don't be in that position!* It was, without question, the most difficult lesson I've ever learned. Learning not to be sanctimonious about it is a close second.

Back to that business of our being "made in the image of." When it came to the creation—biblically speaking, that is—*who was responsible for getting it right?* Well, who had the final word? Maybe that's why he made the choice not to wipe out humanity again.

41

**IT SEEMS, AFTER ALL, THAT THERE ARE
NO NONPECULIAR PEOPLE**[16]

Why is it that the creator of an original vision never finds someone else with quite the same fire in the belly about that vision? The reason may go back to *calling*, to Plato's theory of the *daimon*, that bearer of a unique vision that is so personal, that, while it can be *supported* by others, it can never be *possessed* by another. The owner and founder of a multistate trucking business once told me that no matter how well he compensated his managers, none of them seemed capable of regarding their work as more than a good job. When I asked how he'd started, he said he'd begun with a single used truck, but the glow in his eyes suggested that the genesis of his company was not the truck but rather the vision of what he'd wanted to create, was *compelled* to create. You've seen that haunted glow in the eyes, a touch of madness, of affliction. As long as the vision is kept alive, it remains, but when the vision dies, or, perhaps worse, is corrupted, the madness escapes and the eyes go dead. Most any founder-owner will have that same glow when talking about "back then," and speak of the same frustration in trying to find someone able to grasp his vision with the same clarity.

No, this isn't to slip in one of those reductionist metaphors—you know, "God as CEO"—but there is an analogy to be drawn between the human and the divine as they are represented so far in Genesis, especially by J. That is to say, *if* being human, in part, is to carry a vision that no one else can perceive with the same clarity, and *if* humans are "made in the image

of," *then* the vision of creation carried by J's anthropomorphic deity, likewise, will never be fully grasped by the humans. To stay with the analogy:
as with humans, failure to realize the original vision would have remained
in the divine memory, haunting him with its compelling possibilities, and
of almost making it—*twice*.

42

ADDITIONAL CREATIVITY IS CALLED FOR

Already, by the end of the creation narratives, we've read of two divine
expulsions—Adam and Eve from the garden, and Cain from the divine
presence—each accompanied by a curse. Yahweh says to Adam, "Cursed
be the ground because of you," and tells Cain, "You shall be more cursed
than the ground . . . If you till the soil, it shall no longer yield its strength
to you." While the curses seem arbitrary—the deity's response is immediate, reactive rather than thoughtful—the text is clear that the fault lies not
with the deity but in human behavior. Until the incident at the tree, Adam
had not been required to work the soil. While Cain did have to work the
soil, it yielded abundance until he killed his brother. Neither case is about
the hard life of a farmer, but about the far larger human truth that each
of these men, *through his own behavior,* had made his life and the lives of
those around him harder than they might have been. The same curse had
followed Noah, who, having planted vines in the cursed soil, drank too
much of his own wine, leaving himself vulnerable to the alleged abuses of
his son, Ham, which in turn led to the cursing of Canaan.

Plan A had failed because the humans, employing the free will given
them at creation, ate the fruit. Plan B had not anticipated the human
psyche's fragility in the face of such massive trauma and loss. But faulty
outcomes can say more about the plans than the vision itself. The new
plan would have to allow for some human frailty. Moreover, it could not
include the fallback of giving up on humanity. Following the flood, and
before the Noah-Ham incident, Yahweh had promised himself, "Never
again will I doom the earth because of man . . ." Plan C, the one that
would work, that would change the world, was hovering, unwritten, a
veritable blank canvas awaiting the artist's first stroke. In fact, with a little
imagination, if one were to put one's ear to the text and listen closely, one
just might hear the divine wheels turning, whirring, pondering.

43

A CHANGE IN THE DIVINE APPROACH.
THEN, AS IF THE IRONY IN PLAN C WERE NOT
QUITE THICK ENOUGH . . .

That biblical imagination now preoccupies itself with moving out of exile
and toward promise. We see Yahweh in greater relief as, like his humans,
he learns, adapts, bestowing blessings now instead of curses. While Plan
B did require a human agent to build the ark and see to the gathering
of the creatures, a wholly new divine-human relationship now enters the
narrative, one in which the divine intention will, to a point, be carried
out through those he chooses. Twenty-five hundred years of interpreters
agree there is no clear answer to the question of why he picked Abraham.
Thomas Aquinas, in his *Summa Theologiae*, writes, "And if you press the
question . . . then Augustine's answer will have to do: *why he attracts this
one rather than that don't try to decide—you will only make mistakes.*"[17]

Even without reasons, you've got to appreciate the avalanche of irony
that enters the story along with Abraham: a people who gave birth to a
new religion and a new nation of believers, who survived the foolishness
of spiritual leaders and the corruption of kings, who survived exile *and*
the degradation and destruction of the Romans, who were *the* formative
influence on Christianity, and through that prism, and in their own right,
profoundly influenced the shape of Western civilization—traces its origins
to a seventy-five-year-old man with no résumé and apparently nothing else
to do, and whose sanity will come into question as his story progresses.
With his wife, Sarah, Abraham will play a very dangerous game we might
call "Can You Hustle a King (and Live to Tell About It?)." His son Isaac
will try the very same thing, and his grandson Jacob will hustle his own
family. Given that I'm more at ease with the self-seeking, the duplicitous,
the sneaks and liars of the world—my closest friends have always been
the odd ducks who tilt a little away from virtuousness—I find Abraham's
idiosyncrasies, if not always admirable, to be familiar, trustworthy in their
humanness, oddly soothing.

It is this multidimensional Abraham, not the cardboard character from
Sunday school, who enters the narrative at the beginning of chapter 12,
when he is told,

> *"Go forth from your native land
> and from your father's house
> to the land that I will show you.*

I will make of you a great nation,
And I will bless you;
I will make your name great,
And you shall be a blessing.
I will bless those who bless you,
And curse those who curse you;
And all the families of the earth
Shall bless themselves by you."

Abraham went forth as the Lord had commanded him. And there you have Plan C. Where Noah's commission had been quite specific—build an ark with these dimensions, use these materials, then load two of every living thing—Abraham's is no more than a command to start walking. Armed with only the sketchiest of promises, he packed his wealth and with his wife, nephew, and their slaves started walking toward Canaan, the land named for the grandson cursed by Noah, and which Abraham's descendants would call Israel.

44

"YAHWEH'S PICK TO LEAD NEW PLAN— A CAUSE FOR CONCERN IN THE MARKETS?"

Or so a modern headline might read. Yahweh is about to launch a new plan, and we know that there will be no escape clause, which is to say that it had better work, because he and the humans are stuck with it. Which leads to my speculation about the headline. If we look at the story through the norms of our twenty-first-century youth culture, it seems incredulous that a seventy-five-year-old man would be chosen to execute the plan. The argument might be made that while old men have *been* there, their accomplishments were yesterday, when they had the vibrant, creative, even reckless adventuresomeness we associate with youth. *And* when they had the strength and virility of youth. The journey would be physically demanding: Abraham and his entourage begin walking south from the city of Haran, in what is now southeastern Turkey, toward Canaan, through what is now Syria and Lebanon, a journey of some four hundred miles over terrain that can be difficult and in a climate that, depending on the time of year, can be quite hot and humid. The divine plans, whatever they were, depended on this one old man. Don't people go to court to stop their dotty parents from getting away with just this sort of thing—you know, from screwing up the estate, the *future?*

Abraham, with no idea where it all will lead, jumps at the chance. If asked why, might he have answered with something like *Comfort is overrated* or *Old age, as in, "waiting to die," is too bloody tedious* or some Early Iron Age equivalent of *Better to burn out than rust out*? Perhaps the reckless adventuresomeness of youth still resided in that old body.

45

I BECOME AN AGEIST

It started pretty early, around age four or five, during long summer stays with my maternal grandparents in far northeast Texas. Every few weeks we'd set out to visit older relatives or friends housed in one or another of the region's nursing homes. There was at least one in every small town, each given its form by the almost identical school of architectural banality: a one-story, white- or red-brick structure that, even when embellished with a faux colonial façade and a sweeping, circular drive, managed to appear compressed and dull. Inside, the usual admixture of pine cleaner and incontinence gave even the air in the foyer the sweet-rotten stench of a bus station toilet. Behind the Formica-topped reception counter would be the same fat, humorless, compassionless, middle-aged woman, her hair teased into a beehive and sprayed into a solid mass. One or two inmates might be parked in their wheelchairs next to the entrance, gazing out, as though waiting for the chance to make a run for it. Other specterlike creatures would be stumbling about on walkers, or sitting in the recreation room, staring at a soap opera or a game show on the black-and-white television. Others would be in their beds, a wide leather strap across the chest, leather cuffs anchoring their wrists and ankles, bits of food clinging to chins and clothing, mumbling at the ceiling, calling out the same name to everyone who walked into the room or past the door.

Relatives, heavy with obligation, worry, boredom, and guilt at the shared though unmentionable wish that the loved one would just die, prowled the halls or just sat in a resident's room. Most every word they or the nursing staff uttered to these elderly folk, even those still quite lucid, was in that insipid, syrupy, infantilizing tone that sometimes gave way to the grief and fatigue and hostility hovering just beneath its surface—"Mother, will you *please* just eat the damn Jell-O?" Then silence.

As a child, I was certain of it: old age was a horror and the old worse than useless. But even if I could have imagined myself as an old man, it would have seemed a million years in the future. Even as a young and then a middle-aged man, though my rational mind accepted it, I'm sure I never quite believed I would ever grow old, much less be regarded with the same contempt I'd felt and witnessed all those years before. Then, in the early summer of 2002, this view, now embedded in the culture, was illuminated in one of those rare moments of perfect, startling clarity.

46

THE VIEW THROUGH A CERTAIN LOOKING GLASS

In June 2002, my wife, Pam, and I moved to a bungalow in the Heights, a century-old area on the northwestern edge of downtown Houston. About a week after the move-in, the following encounter took place at the pastry counter of the local grocery store. Because I went straight home and wrote it down, it is nearly verbatim.

"You want a cup of coffee?"

"Hmm?"

"Coffee."

The woman behind the pastry counter pointed to the coin-operated coffee machine mounted next to the register.

"Sure," I said, and pushed my hand into my pocket for change.

"You're over fifty-five, aren't you?"

"Yes. Why?"

"Seniors get free coffee."

"Seniors?"

"Over fifty-five."

"Oh . . . Great."

"And you get a cookie, too," she said, pointing to a plastic tray that must have started the day full but now had only picked-over remnants—small children had been at them as well—that brought to mind a magazine article about fecal matter being found in bowls of unwrapped mints in restaurants from people who'd failed to wash their hands after using the toilet.

"I think I'll pass on the . . ."

"That pink icing is *reeeally* yummy," she said with a broad, crinkly smile. "But first I need to show you how to use the machine. So, pay attention, o-*kaay*?"

Her voice was louder now, its cadence slower, more singsong, the idiomatic southeast Texas slurring of speech giving way to deliberate spacing as though she'd plucked each word from a basket before carefully placing it in front of me.

Now she took a brass token from the register, reached for the stack of small paper cups, and said, "Okay, the *first* thing you do [she held up her index finger] is take a cup [she held up the cup] and place it under the spout [she pointed to the spout] where the coffee comes out. Just like this. O-*kaay?*"

Nod.

"And the token goes right here," she said, placing the token in the coin slot and holding it there. "*Seee?*"

Nod.

"Now, *sir*, this token [she held up the token] is good only for a *small* cup," she said, pointing to the small-cup icon, her tone just a bit dark, sort of a pre-sin admonition. Then, sliding her finger to the large-cup icon and shaking her head, she said, "But not a large one. Under-*staand?*" Then she held out her index finger, pushing it toward me like an ophthalmologist testing my eyes.

Nod.

"And you only get *one* token per day. O-*kaay?* Just one," she said. Back came the finger. "And just *one* cookie," she said, now pointing to the plastic tray. "O-*kaay?*" Again with the finger, but so close that I think my eyes crossed.

Nod.

"O-*kaay!*" she said, sort of cheerleader-like, and dropped in the coin. Then, pushing the small cup icon, she said, "I'll make it for you the first time, but you've got to do it for yourself from now on. O-*kaay?*"

Nod.

I tell you, it was *hypnotic!* I wanted to do something to stop her, but what? I felt utterly helpless, as if the senses with which I normally made my way through the world had suddenly dulled.

Together we stared as the coffee machine glugged through its machinations. An excited notice (*lots of exclamation points!!!*) on the machine's outer shell invited fans to watch the brewing process through the clear plastic front. But there was nothing to watch. *Some interior light must have gone out*, I thought. *How appropriate.*

Out came the coffee.

"*Theeere* you are," she said, taking the cup, expanding the first syllable to match the sweep of the cup from the machine to my hand. It was beautiful.

I took the cup and smiled back. Then her smile became a frown. Was I in trouble? Had I lapsed and missed something? *What?* "Thank you," I squeaked. It was more a question. But it was the right answer because her frown turned upside-down.

"You're *welcome!*" She was all crinkly again. Then, pointing to the plastic container, she said, "Now, don't forget your cookie," and with the same practiced sweep of the hand took one and presented it to me, icing side out.

"Thank you."

"Now, I have to get back to work. So, you can do this for yourself next time?"

Nod.

She nodded and walked away.

I was much older now. In one hand was my senior cup of coffee and in the other my senior cookie with its yummy pink icing, dusted with no-see-ums of seniors' and children's scratchings.

At the first hint of condescension, my great-uncle Ralph may well have invited her to have sex with herself. He'd spent most of his life in the Mexican and South American oil fields and, before all that, in 1916, he (and, oddly, my wife's grandfather, who when she describes him sounds like Uncle Ralph) was one of the cavalrymen who rode into Mexico with Black Jack Pershing after Pancho Villa, who'd been raiding Texas border towns.

Now, fast-forward about sixty-five years to a day when a storm off the Gulf of Mexico had dumped enough rain on McAllen, Texas, to overwhelm the storm sewers and flood the streets of his neighborhood. With water now well up into the yards in his neighborhood, a group of thugs began driving up and down the street, making waves that washed into people's homes. When the police didn't respond quickly enough, the neighbors called my seventysomething uncle, who agreed to see what he could do. So he went out, flagged them down, and told them to knock it off. They made some rude reply, and as they drove away for another run down the street, he put a brick through the rear window of their car. They stopped, yelled curses and threats. Uncle Ralph gestured for them to come on back, but after taking a hard look, they drove away. Family legend is that he had tucked in his belt his old cavalry revolver—I remember it as a handheld cannon—and that Great-Aunt Cil, who was watching from behind the screened front door, may also have been carrying.

The image is pure Texas gothic, but I wonder if there's a glimpse of Abraham and Sarah in them—the same raw stuff that transcends the accepted limits of age. If so, it would help me understand why a seventy-five-year-old man agreed to walk away, *for good*, from his comfortable life. Yes, Abraham was called, and yes, there is evidence aplenty that refusal was not an option. But he wasn't stupid, naïve, or robotic. Nor was he a romantic. Most seventy-five-year-olds (and older) whom I've known well have about them a certain savvy that, whether natural or learned (though probably both), had helped them survive. They've learned, for instance, when and how to say *no*, even to power. So why did Abraham say *yes*? The closer I get to official "senior-citizen" status the *curiouser* I get, the more I dig, and the nearer I get to what may be at least part of the answer.

"Old men," wrote T. S. Eliot, "ought to be explorers."[18] *Explorer! Yes!* If there are times in a life for exploring, certainly one of these is the later years when one has had time to learn of life's brevity and of just how little one understands of it. And if ever there has been a society that discourages such exploration—there's no money in it, and it suggests the heretical idea that growing old can be preferable to staying eternally young—it is the one that we Americans have created, beginning with my own baby boomer generation. Given the witness of our founding fathers and mothers— Benjamin Franklin was seventy in 1776—you'd think it wouldn't have come as such a shock to my friends and me that one's late middle years could be so alive.

Abraham's journey, while written as an outward experience, was an inward journey as well. It is not simply a chronicle of *He did this, he did that, he did other things, then he died*. Earlier, I expressed surprise at how Abraham seemed to jump at the chance to leave. That spark of youthful enthusiasm that I infer the old man possessed is one of the bits of his story I like the best. In a touching remembrance of Paul Newman, writer Stephanie Zacharek tells of the moment when, in 2005, she happened to see him in the flesh. He'd turned eighty that year, "but I didn't have to use my imagination to see the young man still alive in the old one. It occurred to me then . . . that while it's impossible to stay young forever, it's entirely possible to carry the best aspects of youth within you."[19] Amen to that.

My oldest friends and I will stand as witness to the fact that there *are* undeniable physical realities in growing older. Nothing catastrophic, mind you, not normally. It's less a tsunami than a slow-rising tide beneath which the human body, by design, will sink one day. If Abraham wondered whether his aging body were up to the task, the only truthful answer would have been *Maybe*. Yet, *maybe*, the prospect of collapsing out there was more appealing than remaining here, counting the days, the aches, the pains, the liver spots, waiting, for that *last* thing. *Maybe*, Abraham is an old man who'd assumed his life was behind him, who, with the prospect of the greatest adventure of his life now suddenly *before* him, remembered his youth and by that resurrected its spark, its—*his*—enthusiasm for life.

47

WRAPPED IN A CONUNDRUM,
MORALITY ENTERS A GRAY ZONE

Before Abraham can start walking south, he, Sarah, his nephew, Lot, and the family slaves have to pack. It is hardly their first time. "The Hebrew vocabulary [in Genesis 12:8] . . . is meticulous in reflecting the procedures of nomadic life. The verb for 'journey' in verse 9 also derives from another term for the pulling up of tent stakes . . . [and indicates] movement through successive encampments."[20] What happens next is a series of events that could be taken as a rough draft of the future. When they finally arrive in Canaan, "There was a famine in the land," leaving them with little option but to continue on to Egypt. As they are about to cross over into Egypt, Abraham sets in motion a paradox that has yet to be resolved.

In my junior or senior year in high school, our history teacher presented us with one of those ethical problems. The dialogue went like this:

"How many of you believe it's wrong to lie?"

Most of us raised our hands.

Pointing to a student, he asked, "Is it always wrong to lie?"

"Yes, sir."

"Always?"

"Yes, sir."

"You can think of no situation in which it is better to lie than tell the truth?"

"No, sir."

He then told us about Dutch families who'd hidden Jews in their homes during World War II, and what happened to those who were caught. When he asked how many of us would take that risk, hands went up, and he called on the same student as before.

"So, why would you do that?"

"It would be the right thing to do."

"Just like always telling the truth is always the right thing to do?"

"Yes, sir."

"Always? You're sure?"

"Yes, sir."

"Okay, then, let's say it's 1942, and your family is one of those Dutch families hiding Jews in the attic of your home. Hearing a knock at your door, you answer it to find a German SS officer standing there. Behind him is a detachment of twenty SS soldiers. 'Are you hiding Jews,' he asks.

You know that if you say yes, you, your family and the people you are hiding will be arrested and sent to a concentration camp where it is almost certain that you will all die. But, just for argument's sake, let's say that, if you tell him no, he'll take your word for it and go away. Understand?"

"Yes, sir."

"So, what would you tell him?"

Beginning at Genesis 12, verse 11, we're told, "As he [Abraham] was about to enter Egypt, he said to his wife, Sarai, 'I know what a beautiful woman you are. If the Egyptians see you, and think, 'She is his wife,' they will kill me and let you live. Please say that you are my sister that it may go well with me because of you, and that I may remain alive thanks to you." Sure enough, they no more get to Egypt than "Pharaoh's courtiers saw her and praised her to Pharaoh, and the woman was taken to Pharaoh's court." Just like that, she was gone. You'd think that Abraham would be broken up about his wife being forcibly carried off to another man's bed, but there's no mention of it. And, the very next verse, 16, tells us that indeed, it *did* go well with Abraham, that "because of her . . . he acquired sheep, oxen, asses, male and female slaves, she-asses, and camels." Again, the modern sensibilities erupt: *Abraham is getting richer while Pharaoh is sleeping with—"using"—his wife!? Who is this guy?*

48

WHAT'S GOING ON HERE?! INTERPRETERS GET CREATIVE, MY PERSONAL FAVORITE, AND YET ANOTHER SURPRISE

Whether it happened right away or after a time, "the Lord afflicted Pharaoh and his household with mighty plagues on account of Sarai, the wife of Abram." Though we're not told the exact nature of the plagues, eleventh-century scholar and rabbi Rashi suggested that they effected some sort of sexual dysfunction. In other words, no one could perform— not even Pharaoh, which must have been awkward, since he was considered a god. Having learned the truth, Pharoah sent for Abraham and demanded to know why he had lied about Sarah being his sister. No answer is recorded. Perhaps he shrugged, or allowed a wide "gotcha" grin to spread across his face—after all, Abraham *was* in the superior position. Or perhaps he simply followed the wisdom of "Quit—as in *shut your mouth*—while you're ahead." And Abraham and his family were ahead, and all were sent on their way unharmed, and with all the booty Pharaoh had given Abraham.

✳ ✳ ✳

Imagine the dilemma of an early biblical interpreter as he tries to extract a greater meaning from the story, but, no matter how many times he reads it, always comes back to Abraham asking Sarah to *Say you're my sister so that it will go well with me*. Though unstated, his logic appears to be *They'll take you, anyway*—which, given the situation as Abraham describes it, is true. The problem lies in the manner of his delivery, as if speaking to something inanimate, say, a piece of artwork, a statue of the sort that Pharaoh is known to collect. From that vantage, the second part of his reasoning—*so why not set it up so that I get something out of it?*—makes perfect sense, in a cold-blooded sort of way. Not that women weren't used as chattel by the men of that time and place, but this was Abraham, conniving how he might profit from his wife's kidnapping. Abraham would be so much more sympathetic if only he'd made some humanizing gesture, an expression of regret or sorrow, or said something like "Gee, I'm really gonna miss you." Already, Abraham is *the* central human figure in the interpreter's world, and right there, in the story, he appears to be a man who is so self-involved that not only is he unconcerned about his wife's well-being, he feels nothing when she is taken from him.

If you're an interpreter—ancient, medieval, or present-day—your options are limited: either go with the facts as they appear in the text or start imagining a different story. Abarbanel, a fifteenth-century philosopher and leader of Spanish Jewry, was of the latter group and explained in his commentary on the Torah that Abraham accepted Pharaoh's gifts because "in the context of Abraham's claim that Sarah was his sister and the implication that he would allow her to marry a suitable person, Abraham had no choice: Had he refused the gifts, he would have aroused Pharaoh's suspicions."[21] Still others assumed parts of the story must have been left out, or deliberately cut out, or lost. Or *added*. Maybe that bit about how they would take her anyway had been invented and inserted in the text, and the part in which Abraham grieves over losing her was surely taken out. As for Abraham's fib about Sarah being his sister, it must have been an invention because "the honesty of the Patriarchs makes it impossible to believe that Abraham would have told an outright lie, which is why the sages wonder: Was she then his sister?"[22] As a matter of fact, she *was*—or so Abraham claims in chapter 20, in the second of these wife-sister incidents.

Others simply reimagined the story. Rashi speculated that Abraham had never seen her face until the moment when, as they were crossing a stream on their way into Egypt, her veil fell away and "he saw the reflection of her beauty in the water like the brilliance of the sun."[23] To prevent the Egyptians from taking her, he hid her in a chest. But she was found, Pharaoh was told, and an armed force was sent to bring her to the palace. There's more (a *lot* more). For instance, in Jubilees, a book that "purports to contain a revelation given to Moses . . . that takes the form of a retelling of the book of Genesis and the first part of the Exodus,"[24] we read, "So Abram went to Egypt [and] lived in Egypt five years before his wife was taken from him by force . . . When Pharaoh took Abram's wife Sarai by force for himself, the Lord punished Pharaoh and his household very severely because of Abram's wife Sarai."[25] James Kugel points out that "not only does this account omit Abraham's words to Sarah, but the words 'take . . . by force' are intended to make it clear that Abraham in no way cooperated with Pharaoh's deed."[26] Philo, in his work *On Abraham*, not only omits the part in which Abraham asks Sarah to say she is his sister, but writes that Pharaoh, once he'd seen her, "paid little regard to decency or the laws enacted to show respect to strangers . . . [He] intended, he said, to take her in marriage, but in reality merely to dishonor her."[27] Other accounts, such as *Midrash Tanhuma*, an early medieval collection of rabbinic commentaries, and *Genesis Apocryphon*, an Aramaic text found among the Dead Sea Scrolls, tell of Sarah being taken by force and of Abraham weeping.

Ramban, a thirteenth-century Spanish scholar, and one of the leading interpreters of the Torah during the Middle Ages, was one of those who took the text as it was, commenting that while it was not unusual for a man to refer to a female relative as a sister, and "though Abraham thought that this ruse would protect Sarah as well as himself . . . it was a 'great sin' for him to put her in danger."[28] But he saw more in Abraham's deception than a man making foolish choices. "Ramban," writes Jon Levenson, "makes a powerful theological criticism of Abram, observing that the patriarch 'committed a great sin inadvertently' by not trusting in God's protection."[29]

I find myself wondering if what we see in this incident is not a man who didn't trust Yahweh's protection, but one who *counted* on it. Had he dreamed up another, more involved—dare we say *tricksterish*—plan of action? Something like *They'll take Sarah, sure, but if we say she's my sister, they pay me a hefty sum. Yahweh sees what's happening, leans on 'em, they let her go, we keep the booty and leave.* It's a scam any movie buff would recognize: A woman, dressed for effect, goes to a bar, selects a mark, hits on him, and takes him to a hotel. Once the two are *in flagrante*, a scary-looking fellow claiming to be her husband or a cop kicks in the door. Then, to avoid a beating, arrest, or his wife finding out, the mark pays up. This reading of the story paints Abraham and Sarah as a pair of grifters—even *extortionists*! However, the fleecing of a power-happy creep who assumes he can do what he wants to whomever he wants leaves the populist in me smiling. Besides, if you read Genesis as a continuous narrative—and the Redactor-editor(s), or those who are called the

R source, did intend it as such—then, given that the nearly identical scenario repeats in chapter 20, this one written by E, it at least begs the question of whether the editor(s) wanted both present and future generations not to miss how Abraham and Sarah had made saps of these mighty kings, especially Pharaoh. Of course, there's nothing concrete in the text to suggest this motive, either. Nor is it my original idea. It's just such a nice thought.

Among the modern interpreters, Jack Miles, in his Pulitzer Prize–winning *God: A Biography*, makes the intriguing argument that Abraham's motive in all this had nothing to do with his trust, or lack of it, in Yahweh's ability to handle the Egyptians. "In Genesis 12," he writes, "and in the remaining chapters of the Book of Genesis, we see the deity in an ongoing struggle with mankind over control of human fertility."[30] He points to the "subtly aggressive meaning" in the first three verses of chapter 12, found both in Yahweh's command to "Go forth" (*Lek lekah*) and the initial statement of promises, the first being, "I will make you a great nation." However, at Genesis 1:28, and again at 9:1, the humans were told, "Be fertile and increase." Though not apparent in translation, the first of these, said just after the man and woman were created, was said in the form of a blessing, while the second, just after the flood, was a command. In each occurrence, says Miles, it is clear that the power over human fertility rests in the hands of the humans. But now, with God's promise to make Abraham fertile, the power over human fertility has been taken back, repossessed. "[I]t is the Lord," writes Miles, "who will give the fertility . . . taking back from mankind a large measure of the gift of life."[31] Abraham, who doesn't care for the new arrangement, goes silent. When he and Sarah reach Egypt, "Abram gives his wife to Pharaoh to act out his displeasure with the Lord . . . giving offspring to Pharaoh by giving Sarai to Pharaoh."[32] Looked at through that particular lens, Abraham's strategy seems to leave Yahweh off-balance, flustered, as if he did not know how to deal with this new expression of willfulness, especially from his chosen one.

Were bits of the story lost or left out? Was Abraham the sort of man who, on appraisal, saw an opportunity both to save himself and to profit from the inevitable loss of his wife? Or was he playing the scam artist, running a grift on Pharaoh? If so, was Sarah part of it, or simply a pawn? Was he more like the man who tried to hide his wife but lost her anyway? Or was he motivated by anger and resentment at Yahweh's reclaiming of the power over human fertility? Without knowing the mind of the author(s), we can't know. But we can make an informed guess, given that the identical scenario will be repeated by Isaac, his son, and because Jacob, his grandson, will prove to be a natural grifter who plays his own marks just as Abraham played Pharaoh.

Like father, like son—like grandson. And Sarah was a willing player. Cool customers, I think—survivors.

It is worth mentioning Richard Elliott Friedman's observation that "there is no evidence in the Bible that the Egyptians or anyone else ever did what Abraham fears they would do."[33] Did J and E know this? Or later editor(s) or their contemporaries? Is it possible that Abraham risked so much—Sarah's life, his own, the credibility of his relationship with Yahweh—against a nonexistent threat?

49

TOO MANY CATTLE

Abraham and Sarah, "very rich with cattle, silver, and gold," left Egypt and went up to the Negeb, accompanied by Lot, his nephew. When they reached Bethel, in Canaan, an area already settled, it was soon clear that they had too many cattle for the available grazing ground. Conflicts begin to break out between their herdsmen, and they needed to separate. Abraham would go to the south, Lot to the north, into the Jordan valley, where he would settle close to Sodom. After Lot departs, Yahweh tells Abraham that everything he sees in every direction was given to him and his offspring. Abraham then "moved his tent" south to Hebron, where he built an altar.

50

ABRAHAM SHOWS A SURPRISING GIFT FOR MILITARY TACTICS, THOUGH IT PROBABLY NEVER HAPPENED

Some time after Abraham and Lot had parted ways, the Jordan valley was invaded, Lot and his household taken hostage, and their possessions confiscated. When Abraham learned of this, "he mustered his retainers, born into his household, numbering three hundred and eighteen, and went in pursuit." Attacking at night, they defeated the invaders, rescued Lot and his household, and recovered their possessions. When the king of Sodom tried to reward him, Abraham, while making it clear that his retainers were free to accept, declined. Heroic, magnanimous, Abraham was the man of the hour.

But something's funny, isn't it? Old men, especially wealthy old men, don't lead commando raids, do they? Nor is it likely that 318 of Abraham's retainers would have prevailed against a force that already had put several armies in the ditch. Was the story never *meant* to be believed? It was not penned by J, E, D, or P but a source designated as "Other," one that reads "like an excerpt from a battle report in an ancient Near Eastern royal inscription."[34] "And some scholars . . . have seen this story as an Israelite adaptation of an old Akkadian literary form . . . meant to glorify kings."[35]

In other words, someone took an existing hero story, filled in the appropriate names and places, then inserted it, whole cloth, into the narrative. This would seem more than a little outrageous if it weren't so normal, if it were not the same sort of mythologizing we humans still do with the larger-than-life characters in our midst. We tell their stories with a mix of history and myth, even epic myth, which also contains and tells aspects of our own stories. In the decades since their deaths, Great-Uncle Ralph stories, stories about our colorful father and mother, these have become family scripture, told in tones of ribald reverence.

Some national and tribal stories are entirely made up, such as the story of how young George Washington, when just a boy, took an axe one day and for no particular reason chopped down a cherry tree, and when asked if he'd done it, young George replied, "I cannot tell a lie." It is a complete fabrication, a fable invented for the purpose of boosting Washington's image. Just so, perhaps the biblical editors perceived a need to add a bit of testosterone and leadership creds to Abraham's profile.

51

YAHWEH REPEATS THE PROMISE—
AGAIN, THEN AGAIN, AND AGAIN

At some point after Abraham had saved the day, Yahweh came to him in a vision and said, "Fear not, Abram, I am a shield to you; you shall be very great." With this *third* time, with more to come, the promise is becoming fuguelike in its multiple expressions of the same theme. This time, however, something shifted in Abraham. Where before he had remained mute, Jack Miles writes, Abraham "seizes the moment of potential embarrassment for the Lord to press his complaint: 'Divine Lord, what use are your gifts? I am still childless, and a slave born in my house will be my heir.'"[36] To which Yahweh said, "That one shall not be your heir; none but your own issue shall be your heir," then "He took him outside and said, 'Look toward heaven and count the stars, if you are able to count them . . . so shall your offspring be.'" Then he added, "I am the Lord who brought you out from Ur of the Chaldeans to assign this land to you as a possession." Yahweh thought Abraham was satisfied. But Abraham asked, "O Lord God, how shall I know that I am to possess it?"

Yahweh told Abraham to bring a heifer, a she-goat, and a ram, each three years old, as well as a turtledove and a young bird, setting in motion the making of a covenant. All but the bird were cut in two, each half placed opposite the other. At sunset, Abraham fell into a deep sleep, "and a dark dread fell upon him." Yahweh then foretold Abraham of the dark times that awaited his ancestors. "As for you, you shall go to your fathers in peace; you shall be buried at a ripe old age." Then, once it was dark, using the elements of a smoking oven, a flaming torch passing between the animal halves, Yahweh bound himself to a covenant with Abraham, stating again the parameters of the land being promised. This is the fifth time Abraham had heard the promise.

"The effect," writes Miles, "of the Lord's four-times-repeated promise of fertility is to inspire not trust but doubt in the reader . . . an effect of mounting unease [because] . . . now it seems that the promise is not being fulfilled."[37] Karen Armstrong writes that "the promise seemed flimsy . . . an enigma; it referred only to the future, leaving the present insecure and unproductive."[38] But *not* unprofitable. Abraham had considerable more wealth than at the start, though that gain, arguably, was due to his own cleverness in orchestrating the wife-sister sideshows, forcing the divine hand to intervene on his behalf, to *save his hide*, as it were, so that God's plan could move forward. However, *increase* had been the bargain, not wealth: he'd been rich already. It was to *that* end that, when called to "Go forth," he'd *gone forth* without question, carrying with him the promise that his seed would become a great nation, that his ancestors would be as numerous as the grains of sand, the stars in the heavens—which promise, so far, had come to nothing. So, what kept him *going forth*?

Abraham's leaving was not like a son or daughter today moving to a distant city. The command to *go forth* from his father's house was a command to *separate* from everything, making him "a breaker of the old law . . . the enemy of the old ruling system, of the old cultural values [so] . . . the midrash [therefore] interprets [the command] as meaning that Abraham is to destroy the gods of his father."[39] With his first step in the new direction, he became an outlaw. The willingness to free-fall through his twilight years, the steely nerve required to play two monarchs like street chumps, these things would seem to indicate a rather remarkable ability to see beyond the moment and an equally remarkable knack for quelling unwarranted self-doubt. Armstrong suggests that Abraham was "a man of vision [with] . . . the imagination to look beneath the unpromising surface of things and to realize that blessing is not always found in the most obvious places."[40]

Yet even visionaries possessed of extraordinary will, imagination, and patience require some foothold in familiar turf, a place to stand and remember. Given that "unpromising surface of things" reflected now in decades of *going forth* toward a promise he could imagine but not touch, what might Abraham's "place" have been? The answer to that question has always been *faith*, a word we've come to associate with an adherence to this or that set of beliefs about this or that god, but "[Abraham] was not allowed to approach his new God with any preconceived ideas. The authors of Genesis do not show Abraham evolving a theology, a set of beliefs."[41] But without a theology, just what was he supposed to have faith *in*? The answer to that is all too obvious for those of us who've been exposed to complex orthodoxies or simplistic interpretations that insult the intelligence. He was to have faith in his *experience*—"[T]hey imagined him responding to events and experiencing the divine in an imperative that broke down old certainties and expectations." In other words, in the same way one's own previously accepted absolutes can be adjusted by actual contact in which one's day-to-day experience breaks down those absolutes, whatever Abraham may have believed about the nature of divinity was to be assaulted by his experience of this *new* deity. In our own day-to-day contact with the people in our lives, we learn from experience whom to put our faith in. "In the ancient world," writes Armstrong, " 'faith' did not mean theological conviction as it does today, but rather a total reliance on another. Having launched himself on this quest for the unknown, Abraham was impelled not by a set of strong, orthodox beliefs in one or another particular god, but by a sense of presence that it was impossible to define or categorize. He is depicted as traveling forward toward the perpetually new, rather than taking his stand on ancestral piety."[42] This can only mean that the relationship between Abraham and Yahweh began on an equal footing. Faith—*trust*—was not a given at the start of the relationship, but had to be earned, over time, through faithful, concrete action.

In the same way that Abraham's faithfulness was being tested, he, in turn, was testing Yahweh's faithfulness. With so much time having passed, surely he had spells of doubt, days of wondering what he'd gotten himself into, and how anything worthwhile could ever come of it.

Families

52

SARAH HAS AN IDEA. THE FIRST SOAP OPERA

Ten *more* years passed, and still no children. Sarah was worried. Though Abraham had been chosen to be the patriarch of the new nation, the matriarch, who was yet to be specified, would certainly not be a woman incapable of bearing children. *What to do?* Then, in a flash of insight, Sarah saw that one solution to the problem was right in front of her in the person of Hagar, her personal slave: Why not send *her* to Abraham's bed, where *she* can get pregnant and have *their* child? This sort of slave-girl/wife-by-proxy arrangement was not unusual. It would, in fact, be used extensively by Jacob's two wives. Also, a slave's child, whether fathered by the master or another servant, belonged to the master, who had naming rights. Abraham agreed, and Hagar entered his tent, in a capacity that is unclear—mistress or slave. Alter tells us that "most English versions, following the logic of the context, render this as 'concubine.' The word used [by J], however, is not *pilgesh*, meaning concubine, but *'ishah*, the same term that identifies Sarai at the beginning of the verse."[43] In other words, she was not Abraham's baby mama, but his wife. Nevertheless, Hagar's place in the household, her value, would finally be determined by Abraham, who could, if he liked, divorce Sarah and make Hagar's children his heirs. Soon Hagar was pregnant, and "given the high estimation of motherhood in biblical culture, the status of Sarai and Hagar now reverses,"[44] or so it must have seemed to Hagar, because she now began to treat Sarah with open disrespect, perhaps giving back some of what she had received from her mistress. But she had misread her status. Infuriated, Sarah went to Abraham and said (*shouted?*), "The wrong done me is your fault." (Yes, she was blaming him for having gone along with her idea.) Abraham's measured response was to say *Look, she's your slave. Do what you want with her.*

With that, Sarah turned on Hagar with a vengeance. Exactly what she did we're not told, but uppity slaves did not fare well in that age: "The Laws of Ur-Nammu prescribe that the insolent concubine-slave have 'her mouth scoured with one quart of salt,' while Hammurabi prescribes that she be reduced to slave status and again bear the slave mark."[45] Whatever Sarah did, it was enough to warrant Ramban's judgment that "the matriarch sinned by such maltreatment, and Abraham too by permitting it,"[46] and enough that Hagar chose to escape into the desert. There she herself would have a strange encounter.

53

A DIVINE MESSENGER (WHO IS *NOT* AN ANGEL!) MAKES A PROMISE TO HAGAR

As she fled Sarah, Hagar paused by a spring on the way to "Shur," which anyone reading the English translation would reasonably assume to be a town or region. In fact, Nahum Sarna tells us that *shur* is the Hebrew word for "wall," which would indicate that Hagar was on her way south, toward the "wall of fortifications built in the eastern Delta along the present-day Isthmus of Suez in order to protect Egypt from the incursions of Asiatics."[47] Then again, "the same word could also be construed as a verb that occurs in poetic texts, 'to see' . . . and may relate to the thematics of seeing in Hagar's story."[48]

Resting by the stream, Hagar was found by a divine "messenger," which appeared in human form. Feigning surprise, the messenger said, essentially, *Well, Hagar, Sarah's slave. What in the world are you doing here?* To which Hagar replied, *I'm running away from Sarah!* To which the messenger replied, *Go on back and take her abuse.* Hagar was dumbfounded. He added, and *I'll see to it that from your offspring will come too many to be counted.* Then he went on to tell her about Ishmael, the son now in her womb.

This was unexpected and no doubt a little confusing: Hagar was a slave one moment, then a wife/slave pregnant with her master/husband's child the next, then driven into the desert where she met a divine messenger who told her that, if she went back to her crazy co-wife/mistress and took her abuse, then she too could count on much the same promises as the mistress's husband. This *can* be read to mean that the wife/slave had just trumped the mistress.

The messenger left, and Hagar gave him a name, "El-roi," meaning "God who sees me." Hagar, the wife/slave, had not only been assured that her children will be beyond counting, like Sarah's, but, in the messenger, she had seen the face of God, an experience thought not to be survivable, one that would be denied even Moses (Exodus 33). She would go back and give birth to Abraham's son, Ishmael, whose name means "God has heard."

While this encounter with the divine demonstrates Hagar's equality to

Sarah's in the eyes of Yahweh, and her pregnancy had bestowed a sort of titular superiority to Sarah, none of it affected her day-to-day reality. Whether she'd been born into slavery, or taken as war plunder, she was *shifhah*, property, a family asset whose principal human value was her ability to bear children. Secondary was her adequacy as Sarah's personal slave or, to use the more gentrified translation, her "handmaiden." Arguably, her actual worth in *their* eyes was demonstrated by Sarah's unconscionable behavior and by Abraham's complete lack of concern for the well-being of this young woman he'd slept with and who now bore his child. Given that Hagar's value to Sarah and Abraham appeared to be measured solely by the services she provided, and their value to her was of no concern to them, and the fact that she could be so easily discarded, the relationship was not lopsided—it was entirely one-way, not unlike the situation in which employees, especially in the larger, impersonal corporations, increasingly find themselves today.

54

A COVENANT, NEW NAMES, A GOOD LAUGH, CIRCUMCISION, PROMISE OF A SON NAMED LAUGHTER, AND *WHY NOT ISHMAEL?*

Sarah's plan to move things along *did* work, just not so much in her and Abraham's favor. At the beginning of chapter 17, P's version of the Abrahamic covenant, Abraham was ninety-nine, Sarah ninety, and still childless. It had been a long, *long* time since their last encounter with the divine, when, suddenly, out of the blue, Abraham heard "I am El Shaddai. Walk in My ways and be blameless. I will make you exceedingly numerous." Abraham must have been startled, because he "threw himself on his face," meaning he hit the ground like a soldier who'd just heard the sounds of *incoming*. As for the use of the divine name, El Shaddai, Friedman tells us that "the issue is not that the sources have different names for God. It is that the sources have different ideas of when God's name was *revealed* to human beings. In J it is known from the early generations of human beings. In E and P it is not revealed until the generation of Moses."[49]

This fifth repetition of the promise of children to Abraham (though the first in the priestly material) has a few new clauses, which are to be enacted immediately. First, Abraham and Sarah are renamed, signifying "a change in destiny" by which "the childless couple will become the ancestors of many nations, including royal dynasties."[50] Next, as a sign of the covenant, all men and boys are to be circumcised, along with each new male child on his eighth day. Finally, within the next year, Abraham and Sarah will have a son who is to be named "Isaac," meaning "he laughs." At this, "Abraham threw himself on his face and laughed, as he said to himself, 'Can a child be born to a man a hundred years old, or can Sarah bear a child at ninety?'" A quarter of a century has now come and gone since the initial promise, and no child. Now, prostrated, "he laughs, wondering whether God is not playing a cruel joke on him in these repeated promises of fertility as time passes and he and his wife approach fabulous old age."[51] Then he goes on to say that "he would be content . . . to have Ishmael carry on his line with God's blessing."[52] God replies that Ishmael will be taken care of: "I hereby bless him. I will make him fertile and exceedingly numerous . . . But my covenant I will maintain with Isaac." Then El Shaddai was gone, and Abraham circumcised himself and all the boys and men.

The introduction of circumcision is significant not because it is a new idea, but because of the meaning it is intended to carry. An ancient widespread practice, "Circumcision is . . . generally linked with puberty and premarital rites. In the ancient Near East, it was observed by many of Israel's neighbors . . . ,"[53] though to Mesopotamians like Abraham it would have been a new practice. Also new is the context for the practice, since "the stipulation of circumcision on the eighth day after birth dissociates it from . . . a puberty rite."[54] Though it is scarification of sorts, a cutting of the body that in many older cultures marks the male's passage into manhood, circumcision is introduced here not as a rite of passage but as a physical sign of belonging to this new nation.

Halfway through the chapter, Abraham appeared to be a man on the edge of giving up—so much time, and so little to show for it. As if recognizing Abraham's desperation, El Shaddai made the promise specific, giving the name, Isaac, and in verse 21 the promise that Sarah will deliver "by this season next year."

55

THREE VISITORS ARRIVE.
NOW IT'S SARAH'S TURN TO LAUGH

One afternoon Abraham was sitting at the entrance to his tent when, suddenly, three men stood near him. Hospitality being foremost in the nomadic culture, he invited them to take refreshment before they moved on. They accepted, and he ran off to make arrangements for a feast. Already, J, a far better writer than either E, D, P, or R, has managed to give these three a mysterious presence, important, regal, ominous, *dangerous*.

So, when Abraham returned and one of them asked, "Where is your wife Sarah?" it was both surprising *and* creepy. *How did they know his wife's name?* Abraham, perhaps because he knows something the reader does not yet know, seemed wholly *un*startled by the question. He told them she was in the tent. "I will return to you next year," one of them said, "and your wife Sarah shall have a son.'" Overhearing this, "Sarah laughed to herself," and the visitor wanted to know why Sarah was laughing. Then, without waiting for an answer, the stranger asked, "Is anything too wondrous for the Lord?" thereby identifying himself.

In our own time, one might be tempted to say aloud what Sarah was thinking, that this is the seventh time we've heard this and, after almost a quarter of a century, it's become a joke. Sarah is of another time, a different worldview, and frightened, so she lies, saying she didn't laugh. That Abraham got away with laughing at the same divine proclamation likely has more to do with the authors, E and J, and far less, if anything, to do with him being a man in a patriarchal culture. Nowhere in the ancient world were the gods big on mortals laughing at them, which may account in part for why the humor in the Bible is so understated and why religious observation can be solemn to the point of oppressive. Certainly human belief in the gods' insistence on being taken seriously has been used as justification for religious people killing one another for perceived blasphemies (the Inquisitions and the Crusades, eighth-century Islamic imperialism, and religious terrorism today) as well as for the violent protests over characterizations of the Prophet Mohammed, and the fatwa ordering the death of the author Salman Rushdie.

56

**THE RELATIONSHIP SOLIDIFIES,
AND ABRAHAM IS MORE THAN HE SEEMS**

Abraham's tent was a stop for the three visitors on their way to Sodom and Gomorrah. Having taken their refreshment, they moved on, and Abraham, like a proper host, walked with them a ways, seeing them off. I take the sense of the text to mean that the four paused just at the place where the land began to fall away, a spot from which one could see the entire plain, including the cities, and these especially after dusk when lamps would be lit and cooking fires started. The four were silent. Yahweh was deep in thought. Asking himself, "Should I tell Abraham what I am about to do?" he set off on an inner dialogue about the full nature of his covenantal relationship with this man he had chosen. Did it require that he tell Abraham what he was about to do? Well, either Abraham was his man in the world, his human agent, fully trusted as the covenant bearer, even *partner* of sorts, or he wasn't. So, in or out? Which would it be?

Making his choice, he turned to Abraham and said, "The outrage of Sodom and Gomorrah is so great . . . ," then went on to say that he, meaning through the agency of the two who'd accompanied him, would go into the city and see for himself whether the "outcry" he has heard was true. Just then, as if on cue, the other two began making their way toward Sodom. Perhaps Abraham sensed the deepening of Yahweh's resolve and was himself emboldened by it, because he now stepped up and took him on, asking, "Will You sweep away the innocent along with the guilty?" The question begins a dialogue, the subject of which is nothing less than justice: What sort of justice is it when the means of punishment destroys the innocent along with the guilty? Abraham pushed (though not too hard). *Will you spare the town if fifty innocent people can be found? Yes? How about if forty can be found? Yes? Thirty? Twenty? Ten?* Abraham, "like one of the prophets of Israel, eloquently demands justice from God, and pleads for mercy [arguing] . . . not that the guilty be punished and the innocent spared, but rather that the lord *forgive* [the entire city] *for the sake of the innocent . . . who are in it.*"⁵⁵

Justice? From Abraham? This is the same man who, rather than face his wife's wrath, allowed his pregnant consort-wife to be driven into the desert. Is he a brave man who has days when he is a coward, or a coward who has days when he steps up? Is he a scoundrel with a decent streak, or a decent man who keeps the trickster in the closet until it's time to bring it out? Yes (to all the above), meaning that this old man may have greater depths than we imagined. What I love most about this sort of discovery in a literary character, a historical figure, a friend, or just someone on the news, is how it goes against the arrogance in my near certainty that we humans are doomed to die of our own shallowness. When I don't like this sort of revelation, it's because I've made up my mind that someone is a lightweight. I like being right; it's my only godlike attribute.

57

EDDIE, MY FATHER, A POOL GAME, AND ABRAHAM.
I DISCOVER THERE IS YET MORE TO KNOW

Though I'd known my father and lived in his house since birth, I met him again one day when I was sixteen, in the basement of a friend's house, around a pool table. His children—there are four of us, three sons and a daughter—

remember him as the odd combination of honest man whose word and hand-shake was gold, and a born hustler who early in his life had mastered the art of helping any opponent, business and otherwise, into the trap of underestimating him. When it came to anything requiring dexterity and hand-to-eye coordination, he was a natural: he could throw a ball equally well with either arm, was Dallas All-City first baseman in high school, went to college on a football scholarship, and served as a master welder—a ranking earned in record time—during World War II in the shipyards at Orange, Texas. With either hand he could deal cards with such dexterity and speed that you couldn't tell which side of the deck they came from and was a dead-on shot with a rifle or shotgun. More than any of that was his ability at the game of pool. When he was a young man, he made his living in part by hustling pool. Part of the family lore is that he was one of the best pool players of his generation, and that he once played Minnesota Fats. Part of the reality was that he refused to teach any of his sons what he knew about pool or the art of the hustle. In fact, before the day in question, I had him pegged as a hopeless square who drove the minimum legal speed on freeways, who thought no music worth listening to had been written since swing, and who refused either to tell or allow to be told even the mildest off-color joke if a woman was within earshot.

My friends and I were fifteen when we'd begun hanging around the pool halls in South Houston, drinking beer, acting bad-ass, playing eight ball, nine ball, rotation, and pocket billiards. Eddie was the best of us, and in 1962, the year we were sixteen, he got a pool table for Christmas. One Saturday afternoon in January, he, Greg, and Paul were already playing when I arrived.

"Thought you weren't coming."

"Dad brought me."

Eddie's eyes brightened. "Your dad's here?" None of us had seen him play, but through stories told by men and women who'd seen him play in earlier days, Dad's skill was legend.

"Yeah. I think he's gonna stay and have a drink with your dad."

"Think he'll come down and play a game?"

"Not a chance." We'd been over this already.

"We'll see about that," said Eddie, already moving toward the stairs, pool cue in hand. The three of us followed him to the living room, where our dads sat with their drinks.

"Hey, Uncle Dick." Since our parents had known each other before we were born, we addressed one another's parents as "Aunt" and "Uncle."

"Hello, boys. What're you fellas up to?"

"Playing pool. How 'bout coming downstairs for a game?"

"No, thanks."

"Aw, c'mon."

Dad shook his head.

Eddie paused, broadened his grin, and said, "Whatsa matter, old man? You scared?"

Both fathers looked up at Eddie, and the room, as if becoming a snapshot of itself, seemed simply to stop. It was a time and a place in which speaking like that to an elder, even playfully, was seldom tolerated. After what seemed like no more than a few years, our dads looked at each other, grinned, then looked back at us with the bemused looks of fathers who knew it was time to teach the pups another lesson.

"Okay. Let's play some pool."

Downstairs, my father chose a pool cue as Eddie racked the balls for a game of rotation, the object of which is to sink the balls in numerical order. If you miss or, except on the break, sink a ball out of order, the turn passes to your opponent. The one who sinks the most balls is the winner.

"Tell you what," said Eddie, affecting the same smart-assed tone, "you break."

"You want me to break? You sure about that?"

"Yes, sir."

Dad nodded, walked to where the chalk cone was mounted on the wall, and rubbed his hands over it so that the chalk dust was on his palms and between the index and middle fingers of each hand. Then, running his dusty palms up and down the length of his pool cue, he stepped up to the table, rubbed a small blue square of chalk around the tip of his cue stick, and said, "You might as well put your stick back in the rack, son. You won't be needing it."

Eddie snickered and leaned against the wall with that cool *I ain't worried about it* look we'd studied in pool halls. He'd not noticed that the humor had gone from my father's face, replaced now by a focus so intense it was as though he were someone else. The break was clean and violent, sinking two of the balls. Now he began moving around the table, calling every shot, chalking his cue stick between each stroke, shooting left- and right-handed, sinking straight shots, bank shots, combinations, applying "English" that seemed to incarnate each ball with a corporeal presence. His control was so exact that, before taking one shot, he'd know the precise spot where the cue ball needed to be for the next shot and would direct it there. It was as though, after the initial break, he'd taken a mental picture of the table, the position of each ball, created a strategy, and executed it in his mind. Since the house rules were that the winner breaks to start the next game, for three games Eddie never got a turn.

We were dumbstruck, my friends and I. We'd played and watched sports for years, played pool two and three nights a week for a year and a half, watching players who seemed outstanding. But we'd never witnessed anything close to what we'd just seen. Not in a pool hall, on a football field, a baseball diamond, a basketball court, or any other athletic venue had we seen anybody as good at anything as my father was at pool that day. I remember the thrill of knowing that this would be talked about at school, that my dad would, for a while, be a celebrity, and that some of his glow would shine on me. More than that, however, was the change that had come over him, that Eddie had missed, that had left me strangely unsettled and awed. It had begun with his decision to play—a shape-shift not of his physical self but revelational of a closeted self I'd never suspected, the cold, ferocious, artiste-hustler who, during the Depression, to put money in his pocket and food on the family table, had ridden boxcars from the Dallas rail yards to play pool in Oklahoma City, Kansas City, St. Louis, Omaha, and the like. Until that moment I was certain that everything there was to know about him was known to me. From that moment until his death some thirty years later, I would on occasion catch myself staring at him, wondering, *Who is this man?* Even now, my answer is only partial.

At one point during the third game that afternoon, my father made a shot by striking the cue ball in such a way that it leapfrogged another ball in its path. It was wondrous. Later, when I asked him about it, he said only that it was a trick shot and wouldn't have been necessary if he hadn't hit the previous shot a little too hard, leaving the cue ball out of place.

It is now more than forty years since my first serious reading of Abraham's dialogue with Yahweh, and it can *still* leave me breathless. Abraham "comes forward," steps up—*shape-shifts*. While it is easy to admire Abraham's cleverness, until this moment in his story there seems little, if anything, to justify Yahweh's confidence in him. Then, this! Not only does he have the moxie to bring the question about justice, but he clings to it, forcing the divine presence itself to commit to a course of action. It is wondrous. I want to cheer, to ask him, *Where did that come from? Was it hidden? Was it new to you?* I want to know if it was a youthful brashness suddenly breaking out, like Eddie's unexpected, foolhardy, gutsy "Whatsa matter, old man? You scared?" None of us had *ever* spoken like that to any of the men in our world. "Will you sweep away the innocent with the guilty?" No one had *ever* stepped up to Yahweh and, however gently and measured ("I am but dust . . ."), taken him to task, called *him* out. Jack Miles suggests that the forcefulness of the questioning is not driven by "Abraham's or the Lord's mercy [but] . . . to show the depth of Abraham's resentment of the broken promise of fertility and his contempt for what he sees as an eleventh-hour attempt on God's part to abrogate the promise."[56] Whatever J's intention here, when I imagine Abraham in that moment of confrontation, he is different—fuller somehow, textured, more interesting.

I'm not comparing my father to Abraham, but I *am* comparing human being to human being, asking the question at the heart of this book: *What good are these stories if we can't connect with them first at that primal, human level?* Nor am I working from an assumption that growing older is an automatic process of plumbing and revealing one's hidden depths. Time and experience relieved me of the naïveté that aging is idiotproof. Some decades ago, Hugh Downs, former host of the *Today* show, reporting on the results of a study on aging, said that one of the more surprising findings was that, while age *can* bring wisdom, the probability is that a young dolt will simply become an old dolt. Think of it as evidence of the power of free will, that even something as natural—*as biologically encoded*—as learning from one's experience, especially one's mistakes, can, with practice, be overridden. But it doesn't have to be overridden—so, *what do you think?* Had we been standing there, with Abraham, watching as he asked that first question, would the world have seemed to stop, as ours stopped that day at the moment of Eddie's question?

My friends and I were in that time in a boy's life when he needs to be breaking free of attachments that hold him back *not* from what he wants, but from the path to manhood. While Eddie's challenge was far more smart-alecky than a direct assault on authority, he took a step that day that none of us had yet taken, and he did it in front of his own father, a man known for his draconian approach to child rearing. Likewise, while we can hardly characterize Abraham's action as confrontational, it was far more than anyone else in Genesis had done. Eddie lost the pool game, though I wonder if, even unconsciously, he was wanting something else—self-respect, perhaps, and the respect of the men. As for Abraham, his bargaining will not save the cities—the agreement was that if he could find ten virtuous men the cities would be spared. As for his motive in stepping up, we just can't know. But if Armstrong is right about *faith* in the ancient world relying not on dogma but *faithfulness*, and assuming she means by that a *mutual* faithfulness, then I wonder if Abraham was really out to save the two cities, or if he was wanting something else—to test Yahweh's own willingness to be in a relationship that was entirely new between the humans and the gods, not equal but at least interactive, even symbiotic. Just as Eddie's stepping up was a brand-new thing in our world and hinted at the opening of a new dimension between us boys and the men in our lives, especially our fathers, Abraham's willingness to step up and Yahweh's willingness to enter into a bargain initiated by a mortal announces a new dimension in the relationship between the humans and the divine.

58

A FAILED TEST, AND TWO CITIES ARE NUKED

By the time the two men arrive at Sodom, it is evening. Lot is waiting at the city gates, greets them, and invites them to his home for the night. They tell him no, that they will stay in the square, but he insists, so they go with him to his house, where he prepares a meal for them. Then, the hospitable mood of the story gives way to a nightmarish scenario as "the townspeople, the men of Sodom, young and old—all the people to the last man," having gathered themselves into a mob, are now outside Lot's door, demanding that his guests be served up for what promises to be nothing less than a gang rape. Lot goes out and asks that they leave his guests alone, offering instead the two of his daughters still living at home, who are virgins. But Lot has lived there a relatively short time, and this uppity outsider who seems to be telling them what to do only enrages the crowd, who now promise to do worse to him if he doesn't get out of their way. Then, just as the crowd surges toward him, the two men open the door, pull him in, and slam it shut. As for the people outside, the two men "struck [them] with blinding light, so that they were helpless to find the entrance."

The men now tell Lot to gather up his family and get out of town immediately because they will soon destroy it. Lot goes to tell his sons-in-law, husbands of his two older daughters, but they assume he is kidding. When dawn finds Lot still procrastinating, the two men take him physically by the hand, along with his wife and their daughters, and drag them away. Once outside the city, one of the men says, "Flee for your life! Do not look behind you, nor stop anywhere in the Plain; flee to the hills, lest you be swept away." At this, Lot balks, saying essentially, *Don't think that I don't appreciate all you've done for me. But I don't want to live in the mountains! How about that little town over there?* (He means the town of Zoar, and we can only suppose he was pointing.) The one to whom he'd spoken agrees to spare that town, but tells them to get moving because he can't do anything until they get there. Sure enough, just as they enter Zoar, the cities of the plain are annihilated. Watching from the heights, did Abraham say to himself, *There weren't even ten virtuous men?*

Meanwhile, Lot's wife, having looked back, was transformed into a pillar of salt—a bit of local color with origins in "an old folklore motif of what happens when humans see God (or his actions), made popular by the many pillars in the region around the Dead Sea."[57] One of those pillars, in biblical times, was said to resemble a woman turning to look back.

59

A GREEK MYTH, LOT'S WIFE,
MY COMPLAINTS, AND A HAWK

In the Greek myth of Orpheus and Eurydice, Eurydice is killed on her wedding day by a viper's bite. Heavy with grief, Orpheus travels to the underworld in order to plead for her release from the dead. He succeeds, then loses her again because he fails to obey the single condition that he not look back at her before reaching the world of the living. Joseph Campbell makes the point that this myth, like hundreds of similar tales throughout the world, suggests that while the *possibility* of success is present—Orpheus and Eurydice *were* on their way out; Lot's wife was safely away, in Zoar—in each of these it is "some little fault, some slight yet critical symptom of human frailty, that makes impossible the open inter-relationship between the worlds; so that one is tempted to believe, almost, that if the small, marring accident could be avoided, all would be well."[58] *If only she hadn't looked back!*

The same theme is reflected in Kurt Vonnegut's *Slaughterhouse-Five*. The protagonist, Billy Pilgrim, like the author, had participated in the firebombing of Dresden, Germany, a city brimming with the innocent and the guilty—refugees and, no doubt, war criminals. Looking through the Bible for tales of great destruction, and coming across the annihilation of Sodom, Billy's simple commentary is "And Lot's wife, of course, was told not to look back where all their homes had been. But she *did* look back, and I love her for that, because it was so human . . . So she was turned to a pillar of salt. So it goes."[59]

Well, it *was* "so human," wasn't it? Imagine that someone in great authority comes up to you and says, *Whatever you do, don't turn around!* Your first impulse? Now, imagine that, from behind you, comes the sounds of massive explosions, as if the entire area were being carpet-bombed. Fur-thermore, back there are two of your children, their families, your home, and everything you possess. Would you turn your head? Even if *angels* had told you not to? Ellen Frankel, in her meditative commentary, imagines an answer: "I looked back to all that I had left behind—my other daughter's grave, my friends and relatives, my home with its cherished mementos, my childhood—and I wept. And so hot was the desert sun and the brimstone torching Sodom that my flowing tears dried instantly, turning me into a pillar of salt."[60] Responding to the interpreters who claimed that Lot's wife had brought this fate on herself by indiscreetly going to a neighbor to borrow salt to cook for the two visitors, thus giving away their presence, Frankel has Lot's wife answer: "No, it was because of my thoughtfulness—at the wrong time."[61] Likewise, "Jewish commentators on the tale say that her mother-love made her look behind to see whether her married daughters were following; and Christian commentators on Luke 17:32 also see the source of her move in remembrances of family and relatives, personal subjectivities of feeling."[62] Vonnegut's Billy Pilgrim might have agreed with these interpreters. Identifying with Lot's wife, he goes on to say, "People aren't supposed to look back. I'm certainly not going to do it anymore. I've finished my war book now. The next one I write is going to be fun. This one is a failure, and had to be, since it was written by a pillar of salt."[63]

But she *does* look back, and it's not just *her* looking back, but the act of looking back *itself* that is "so human," that poignant "little fault," the "slight yet critical symptom of human frailty" that we can never grow out of, not all the way, because it is too human. We just can't help but screw things up from time to time. Mulling over events long past, *returning to the scene of the crime*, reliving it, revisiting old hurts, dwelling on insults, regrets, those moments *if only I/he/she/we had*—"the small marring accidents."

Sitting atop my grandmother's old letter desk in my study is a hawk's feather mounted in a picture frame. One Saturday, about ten years ago, my wife and I were on a day trip, meandering the country roads to the west of Houston, listening to a book-on-tape. Something about one of the characters brought to mind an old resentment, one I'd been revisiting of late with some regularity, and around which I'd managed to store and keep alive an impressive reserve of hurt and anger. Stopping the tape, supposedly just to acknowledge the resemblance, I was still yammering on when a hawk went blazing past the bow of my pickup, moving port to starboard. About twenty feet away, maybe three feet above the pavement, he was a rocket moving at dive speed toward an impenetrable line of tall pines and dense undergrowth about sixty feet, or one second, away. A pilot in a comparable situation might say that it's too late even to kiss yourself good-bye, but the hawk, as if it were nothing, broke left, then up and out of sight. *Wow!* I shut up, and we drove on. Then, *Just to finish the point I was making*—as if Pam had not heard it before, *ad nauseam*—I started up again. No more than half a minute comes the hawk again, from the same direction, only slower, and closer by half. Again, up and away, and out of sight. Again, *wow!* Then, silence, drive on a bit, and *Just to finish . . .* Then, the hawk—same direction, still slower, this time so close I was sure we'd hit him. But, no. Then, making a sudden, very tight U-turn, he was back in front of the truck. Whether I hit him or he flew into me, I don't know. He was dead. We put him on the side of the road, against the tree line. I mumbled clumsily about being sorry and *You dumb bastard, you were clear! Why did you turn back like that?* Then more about being sorry. Then we drove home. *Why did he do that?* I didn't have a clue. Still don't. Before leaving, I took one of the feathers knocked loose by the impact, the one now in the frame, as a totem, a reminder of that beautiful creature, and, corny though it sounds, of the price extracted by some *goings-back.* That night I dreamed about the hawk, though it seemed more of a haunting than a dream, and several more times over the next few weeks. I can't say the incident cured me of that sort of going back, though even now I'll start up about this or that unsettled thing, and I'll see the hawk: *Turning back like that gets you killed.*

As epilogue for the story of Lot's wife, we have a lovely touch of irony that Vonnegut would've loved. Rabbi Cynthia A. Culpepper suggested that she was never told not to look back! She wrote that the command, in Hebrew, "is in second person masculine singular, addressed grammatically only to Lot and not to his wife or daughters. Only he is known to have been on the scene when the directive was given."[64]

60

MOTIVE?

"Those were vile people in both those cities, as is well known, the world was better off without them." So says Billy Pilgrim. Define *vile*, please. Were they homosexuals? Was that it? (Some of them had to be at least *bisexual*; otherwise where would all the little Sodomites have come from?) If *that* was the problem, should we assume there'd have been *no* problem had the men of the town made a habit of gang-raping their neighbors' *female* guests? To be sure, women were held in low esteem; just look at how Lot was ready to placate the mob by handing over his two virgin daughters, "to do with as you will." There's no mention of whether anyone in the house thought that to be vile—we can assume the exchange was loud enough to be heard through the door. Then again, things were moving pretty fast: The two men had pulled Lot from harm's way and blinded the mob, but for how long? The town's obliteration, that zero hour was getting close, and the business of getting out pretty much became *the* priority. *Later* would be the sensible time for talking out whatever issues might have arisen from the incident. But there would be no such talk, because the daughters had no standing. Ellen Frankel, playing devil's advocate, writes,

"If we look at the problem through the lens of the social scientist . . . when the wicked Sodomites call for Lot's guests . . . he must choose among several competing pressures: to placate his neighbors, safeguard his guests, or protect his daughters. Since daughters lack the power to either jeopardize or strengthen his position, it is no wonder that Lot chooses to sacrifice their future marriageability rather than dishonor his guests or provoke his neighbors. Such a move is certainly politically expedient . . ." Frankel then counters with "On the other hand, [he] is yielding only to wicked neighbors and social convention."[65]

Perched as we are atop human history, and from the perspectives of our own time and place, it is inconceivable to us Westerners, is it not, that a father would consider such a thing? That the mother would stand for it? That the men being protected would allow it? In response to such a mob, Great-Uncle Ralph and any of the men my brothers and I met in his home over the years would have armed themselves, barricaded the doors and windows as best they could, called the police — *maybe* — then shouted out something John Wayne heroic, such as "Come and get it!" No kidding.

Of course, to contemplate this story for long inevitably brings the question around to one's self: *What would I do? Would I give up someone in my home to a mob?* Would you?

Back to motive. Why did Sodom, and the entire valley, have to go? The standard answer, the one still being taught in Sunday schools and from pulpits, is the residents' homosexuality. Friedman, however, sees "no basis for this whatever. The text says that two *people* come to Sodom, and that *all* of the *people* of Sodom come and say, 'Let's know them.' The homosexuality interpretation apparently comes from misunderstanding the Hebrew word *'anasim* to mean 'men,' instead of people."[66] Kugel writes that the early interpreters were "perplexed about the city of Sodom. God destroyed it because of the terrible things that were being done there — but what exactly were those things? Strangely, the Genesis narrative does not say."[67] What we're told is that the people of Sodom were evil, a stigma that, when you think about it, probably would attach itself to the reputation of any town whose citizens practiced organized gang rape on out-of-town guests. "[T]here was another tradition," Kugel writes, "that held that the Sodomites' sin actually had nothing to do with homosexual acts or adultery or fornication. Instead, their fault was pride or stinginess, an unwillingness to help the unfortunate of this world."[68] Hospitality was foremost, expected both of one's own household and from others. It was a social bond and, in an environment that could be quite harsh, even a matter of survival, the lack of it, especially a systematic negation, was no small matter.

A reader hoping that Lot's already strange story will not end on some pedestrian note will not be disappointed. Afraid to live in Zoar, he and his daughters leave the town and go to the high country, where they take up residence in a cave. There, the older daugther says to the younger one, "Our father is old, and there is not a man on earth to consort with us on the way of all the world. Come, let us make our father drink wine, and let us lie with him that we may maintain life through our father." Note the verb— not *know*, but *lie with*, which is "a rather coarse (though not obscene) verb for sexual intercourse in biblical Hebrew."[69] Whether they assumed the cataclysm that took their home had been the end of the world or simply wanted to maintain their father's lineage is unclear. While the text itself does not pass judgment on them, "the fact that they are not named implies censure."[70]

A note about the origin of the story: In his book *How to Read the Bible*, Kugel writes, "For modern scholars . . . the whole tale . . . looks like an etiological narrative, that is the recounting of some incident from the distant past that serves to explain the way things are 'now,' at the time of the story's composition, when Sodom was a ghost town."[71] Because ancient cities were located where water was sufficient and the land was fertile, their sites often reveal layer upon layer of successive civilizations. Seeing all those old, ruined city sites with evidence of some ancient catastrophe suffered in common by the early biblical times, the people living in the plain had brought forward an old story to explain why the cities had never been rebuilt. As for the nature of the catastrophe, Gerhard von Rad speculated that "perhaps a tectonic earthquake released gases (hydrogen sulphide) or opened up the way for asphalt and petroleum,"[72] which, ignited, would have made it seem that the air itself was ablaze. This story, then, may have been born in the wake of some bizarre geological event. Survivors and witnesses, like all ancient people, would have assumed it had been caused by the same divine forces behind *all* the mysteries pervading their world, and that the motive would have been punishment. Over time, as the memory of the event was passed between the generations, the story as it now appears may have evolved.

61

ABRAHAM AND SARAH GRIFT ANOTHER KING

Moving on from there, Abraham and Sarah settled for a time in the northern region of the Negeb (or *Negev*). From there they made a trip to Gerar, a city-state to the north, and the stage is set for the second of the wife-sister stories. Using the identical premise—*If he thinks you're my sister, he'll take you (and pay a bride-price), but if he thinks you're my wife, he'll kill me and take you anyway*—this time the mark is Abimelech, king of Gerar, and that rarest of birds, a truly "just" ruler. That Abraham surely would have known this about Abimelech rather strips away any pretense of needing to save themselves from an evil king, does it not? So why did he do to Abimelech what he'd done to Pharaoh? Was it to show that he could? Already he had tricked the most powerful man on earth, so there was nothing to prove about his ability. Was it the money? Already he was wealthy. *Who was this man* who'd taken Yahweh to task on the issue of justice, but now puts at risk a just king, the king's entire family, court, and kingdom?

As before, the honey trap worked, and Sarah was brought to Abimelech. He discovered he'd been had when, in a dream, God said, "You are to die because of the woman you have taken, for she is a married woman." Abimelech's reaction—*Married? I didn't know! I haven't laid a hand on her!*—says a great deal about his innocence, or so the divine must have concluded, given that, with his next breath, the death sentence included that magic word, *If*. Only a moment before, he and most everyone he knew were as good as dead, but now, *If you give her back to her husband, we'll call it even*.

Abimelech might have simply sent her back to Abraham, along with the booty. Instead he had Abraham brought before him. I see him exhausted, his body still shaky from the adrenaline overload, his eyes narrowed, a quiver in his voice as he says, "You have done to me things that ought not to be done." That any unsteadiness in his voice might well reflect outrage is evidenced by the verb forms he employs, the very same used much later in the narrative by Jacob's sons on hearing of their sister Dinah's rape.

Always the careful one, Abraham must have known there was no need for him to respond to Abimelech; no need for anything but to collect Sarah, the booty, and be on his way. Instead, as if the king's words or tone had found a way through the patriarchal demeanor, Abraham seems to shrink, to lose himself in mealymouthed self-justification, saying, essentially, *Yeah, well, about that, Sarah really is my sister. I mean, we have the same father, just not the same mother.*

Was it regret shaping that response? Did he hope to gain some modicum of the king's respect? Even self-respect? Did mighty Abraham look into the face of his own hubris and feel shame at what he had done? Maybe. The moment passed. Abraham and Sarah departed, taking with them Abimelech gifts (*payoff, booty*) of sheep, oxen, slaves, silver, their very own protection detail, and royal permission to live anywhere in the kingdom.

62

SARAH GIVES BIRTH TO THE BOY NAMED LAUGHTER.
HAGAR AND ISHMAEL ARE SHOWN THE DOOR

Abraham and Sarah's son's name, *Yitshaq*. "'He laughs,' or 'He Will Laugh,' or 'He Who Laughs,'"[73] is Yahweh's idea, a reference to the moment when Abraham laughs at the notion of his ninety-year-old wife giving birth to a son. The name is to be a signifier, but we don't know of what, exactly. In *The Beginning of Wisdom: Reading Genesis*, Leon Kass writes that "it is not obvious what He wants the parents—and the son—to be reminded of by means of the name 'He Who Laughs,' partly because the (grammatically male) subject of the verb 'he laughs' is unclear."[74]

So, who's laughing?

Sarah seems tickled enough, saying, "God has brought me laughter; everyone who hears will laugh with me." However, *Tsehoq*, usually translated here as "laughter," also means "mockery," so she may have been caught by the existential absurdity of a woman giving birth at ninety. "[P]erhaps God is doing something *to* her as well as for her . . . All who hear of it may laugh, rejoice, with Sarah, but the hint that they might also laugh at her is evident in her language."[75] Abraham was so pleased with the outcome that he "held a great feast on the day that Isaac was weaned." Hagar, though, was not laughing. At some point after Isaac's birth, Sarah, having noticed Ishmael, Hagar's son, "playing," demanded that Abraham "cast out that slave-woman and her son, for the son of that slave shall not share the inheritance with my son Isaac." *Cast them out* (in other words, leave them in the desert to die) *for playing?* No. But for "Isaacing," yes. "Playing," writes Jon Levenson, "is another pun on Isaac's name. Ishmael was 'Isaacing,' or 'taking Isaac's place.'"[76] He would not be in a position to do that if he were, say, dead.

Poor Abraham. Ishmael was his son. What he felt for Hagar is not known, but they had been lovers and she was the mother of his son. What was he to do? *Just do whatever Sarah tells you to do*, he is told. *And don't worry about the boy and his mother*, because "I will make a nation of him, too, for he is your seed." The next morning, Abraham gave Hagar some bread, a skin of water, put Ishmael in her arms—even though the boy was now sixteen— and turned them out into the desert. Ibn Ezra, a twelfth-century scholar born in Moorish Spain, surmised that the miserly provisions were Sarah's idea, and that Abraham went along because "otherwise he would have violated God's command [to do what Sarah told him to do]."[77] If he is right, given Sarah's knowledge of the ways of the desert, she would've known that to leave them with so little food and water was, for each of them, a death sentence. Sure enough, when the bread and water were gone, they began to die. Hagar, not wanting to watch her son's final moments, left Ishmael under a bush, then went off a distance, sat, and wept. Then "an angel of God," on hearing her, repeated the earlier promise and showed them a well. They were saved. The boy grew up, became a bowman, lived in the wilderness, "and his mother got a wife for him from the land of Egypt."

Isaac will become more his mother's son than his father's, not an unusual arrangement in ancient and so-called primitive societies, though here it seems as much an outcome of the child migrating to the mother because the father has not offered a similar welcoming. In fact Abraham will never bless his son. Though Isaac will receive a blessing and inherit the Promise, these will come from Yahweh. His father's focus is elsewhere.

It's a reasonably consistent historical axiom that "great men" make lousy fathers. It's not that they don't love their children, though some have not; it's that whatever obsession has driven them toward greatness is a jealous, consuming mistress. Neither in secular nor holy history is it unusual to find that the firstborn son of such a man has been crushed by the father, then judged a disappointment. Even when it was not the father's intention to crush the son, the weight of his shadow may have been enough. These flattened-out sons may become rebellious, troubled, troublesome young men, or like Isaac, rather passive, even hollow, a condition usually traceable to a pattern of physical and/or mental abuse.

Isaac's experience with parent-inflicted childhood trauma is one of the best-known, and perhaps least understood, stories in the Bible.

The Test

63

ABRAHAM IS TOLD TO SACRIFICE ISAAC

One day, Elohim* put Abraham to the test. "Take your son, your favored one, Isaac, whom you love, and go to the land of Moriah, and offer him there as a burnt offering on one of the heights that I will point out to you." The next morning, Abraham split the wood for the fire, saddled his donkey, and with Isaac and two of his servants, set out. On the third day, he spotted the place they were to go, told the servants to wait, saying that he and the boy would go up the mountain, worship, then return. Loading the firewood on Isaac's back, he took the knife and the firestone, and the two of them set off up the mountain. As they were walking, Isaac recognized the implements of a burnt offering and asked his father, "Where is the sheep for the burnt offering?" Abraham told him that "God will see to the sheep for His burnt offering, my son." Reaching the spot where the offering was to take place, Abraham built an altar, laid out the wood, bound Isaac, and laid him atop the wood. Then he picked up his knife to slay his son, but an angel of the Lord called out his name, stopping him, because "I know now that you fear God, since you have not withheld your son, your favored one, from Me." Seeing a ram caught in the thicket by its horns, Abraham offered it in place of his son. Then, once again, he received the promise that his descendants would be as numerous as the stars of heaven and the sands on the seashore.

"Take your *son*, your *favored one*, Isaac, whom you *love* . . ." Why the emphasis instead of the simpler "Take Isaac and . . ."? Is Abraham being reminded, with a touch of cruelty, perhaps, how much this boy means to him? Is the divine voice saying, *I know how important the boy is to you, and how much you love him, but . . . ?* Probably not.

In fact, classical Midrash suggests that the chain of words used by Elohim seem to be the record of a one-sided dialogue; they imply the attitude of the one being addressed. Using that implied attitude, they imagine a

---

*Most of Genesis 22, which contains the story of the sacrifice of Isaac, is from the E (for "Elohist") source, whose name for the divine throughout Genesis is "Elohim."

dialogue between Elohim and Abraham. Rashi's version of that dialogue is:

> "[Take] Your son.
> "I have two sons."
> "Your only one."
> "This one is an only one to his mother and this one [read, *that* one] is an only one to his mother."
> "[The one] Whom you love."
> "I love both of them."
> "Isaac."[78]

In the end, of course, Elohim gets what he wants, but looking at this interaction through Rashi's lens, Abraham makes him work for it. While his interpretation does nothing to soften the story's outcome, it does help to make sense of its beginning, which I've always found unsettling. Abraham is told to *take Isaac, go do this thing,* so he packs his donkey, his son, himself, and walks for three days. On the third day he looks up. It's a simple enough gesture. Certainly anyone who has taken long hikes through difficult terrain will recognize it, the necessity for vigilance about the terrain immediately ahead of one's feet giving way to the need to look up for a longer view. But this lifting of Abraham's eyes is the only gesture during the entire journey, leaving "the impression that the journey took place through a vacuum . . . as if . . . Abraham had looked neither to the right nor to the left, had suppressed any sign of life in his followers and himself save only their footfalls . . . Everything remains unexpressed."[79] It is precisely this lack of expression—of *affect*—that gives the journey an air of *Twilight Zone* eeriness. Like a switched-on robot, Abraham locksteps his way from the moment of the command to the moment when, knife at the ready, the angel stops him. The text gives no indication of what he thought of the command, what he thought about during the three days, what was on his mind as he made the preparations, or what he might have been thinking as he raised the meat cleaver. E. A. Speiser notes that the noun used is "expressly for butcher knives"[80] and translates it as "cleaver," not as "knife." Alter agrees, noting that "other terms from butchering, rather than sacrifice, are used: to slaughter (verse 10) and to bind (verse 9—a verb occurring only here but used in rabbinic Hebrew for binding the legs of animals)."[81] So, Isaac, trussed like dinner, is laid atop an altar/pyre, and his father takes a meat cleaver, raises it, and . . . *what?* We know he was stopped, but before that, before he would have brought the cleaver down, did he hesitate? Did he *see* his son?

* * *

When I was a child, my Sunday school teachers and others presented the story as evidence of great faith, so I simply placed it alongside other input from the adult world that made no sense. Looking at it from my present vantage, however, it seems more the act of a madman. What!? Abraham? Imagine this: Let's say that, one evening, you are preparing dinner, half watching the news on the tube, when the anchor announces, *We have a breaking story . . .* and they cut away to a reporter in front of a house on a residential street. *Just over an hour ago, a man was arrested in the backyard of this house only moments before he plunged a knife into the chest of his young son. Apparently, he had tied the boy's hands and feet before placing him on top of a stack of firewood which he planned to set ablaze after he'd killed the boy. When asked why, the man claimed that God had told him to do it.* Would you not say to yourself, *Wow! Now there's the sort of God-fearing man we need more of! When he gets out of the loony bin, maybe he can run a summer camp for kids!*

64

STILL, SOME OF US THINK THE STORY IS TERRIFIC!

It is a bit too easy, and the story far too rich, to write it off as the biblical account of a psychopath. It is so weird, so impossibly, bloody *awful*, so indefensible, so unacceptable, that we can step away from it, see it as backdrop, a blue screen of sorts on which we might project any number of possibilities about what motivated the characters, and what they might have done. Just over 160 years ago, in his book *Fear and Trembling*, Søren Kierkegaard did just that, imagining four possibilities for how Abraham might have responded.

In the first of these, Sarah watches from a window until they are out of sight. On the third day, having reached the mountain, Abraham, by now deep in grief, decides that Isaac should be told what awaits him. As he and the boy begin making their way up the mountain, he stops, gives his son a blessing, and explains in gentle tones what is to be. Isaac doesn't get it and begs for his life, and reminds Abraham how crummy those childless years had been. Abraham tries again, but it's no good. Then he has an idea. Turning away, he walks a few steps up the mountain, puts on a crazy face, turns, grabs Isaac by the throat, throws him down, and says, "Foolish boy, do you believe I am your father? I am an idolater. Do you believe this is God's command? No, it is my own desire."[82] Isaac, shaken, cries out, "God in heaven have mercy on me, God of Abraham have mercy on me; if I have no father on earth, then be Thou my father"[83]—which is the outcome Abraham wanted.

Abraham's action, however impulsive, is not unlike the dissonance-creating methodologies employed in tribal initiation rites, the point of which, for thousands of years, has been the realization of the vast contextual shift from boyhood into manhood. Given that, this scenario does at least establish a context for Isaac's psychological/spiritual survival. Suddenly, violently, he is thrown from his father's house, as it were, thus thrown back on himself. Now, it's *his* call, *his* move: *What'll it be, boy—fold, or stand?* In this moment of high desperation, he embraces the process and so frees himself from dependence on his father. Now self-owned, as it were, he offers the new self up to another, larger ground of being.

In the second scenario, Abraham awakens that morning and hugs Sarah, who then kisses Isaac, "who had taken her disgrace from her, was her pride and hope for all generations." All the way to the mountain, Abraham is gloomy, staring at the ground. Arriving at Moriah, he prepares the altar, binds Isaac, then sees the ram, makes the sacrifice, and returns home. But "from that day on, Abraham becomes old, he could not forget that God had demanded this of him. Isaac throve as before; but Abraham's eye was darkened, he saw joy no more."[84]

For his third scenario, Kierkegaard has Abraham rising early, kissing a *young* Sarah, who kisses Isaac, "her delight, her joy forever."[85] On the way to the mountain, Abraham begins thinking about Hagar and Ishmael. Afterward, he finds himself trapped in a loop: He wants divine forgiveness for his willingness to forget a father's duty to a son, yet how could it be a sin to sacrifice the very best of what one has to God? But if what he'd done *was* a sin, how could it ever be forgiven?

In the final scenario, father and son are on the mountain, their preparations complete. Then, in a moment of insight, Isaac sees what his father intended to do. He loses his faith, and "never a word in the whole world is spoken of this, and Isaac told no one what he had seen, and Abraham never suspected that anyone has seen it."[86]

Understanding Abraham as a man caught in an existential web, Kierkegaard attempts neither to defend nor condemn Abraham's action but, rather, to *explain* it. "Abraham's relation to Isaac," he writes, "ethically speaking is quite simply this, that the father should love the son more than himself."[87] But now a divine command forces him to choose between the son and the covenant. And therein lies the rub. Abraham is not a robot but rather a man, a human, thrown back on himself by the fact of free will, which gives him complete freedom to choose. We know which option he will choose, "yet within its own compass the ethical has several rankings; let us see whether this story contains any such higher expression of the ethical which might explain his behavior ethically, justify him ethically for suspending the ethical duty to the son, yet without thereby exceeding the ethical's own teleology."[88] In other words, since there are ethics about the small stuff and ethics about the big stuff, and ethics about the stuff in the middle, might there be some way of applying these to Abraham's action on Mount Moriah that would not leave him looking like a schmuck? Not a chance, not if we bind him to the ethical standards by which we normally judge an individual's actions in society, because "Abraham's story contains a teleological suspension of the ethical. He has, as the single individual, become higher than the universal." However, "If this is not how it is with Abraham, then he is not even a tragic hero but a murderer. To want to go on calling him the father of faith, to talk of this to those who are only concerned with words, is thoughtless."[89] For Kierkegaard, Abraham's action on Mount Moriah can't be understood or redeemed within the normal channels of reason or the socially accepted morality by which we judge ourselves and one another, but only as the action of a man who has transcended the limits of what is and is not ethical.

65

ISAAC PROVES HARD TO FIND

As for Isaac, do we write him off as a victim, a late Bronze Age poster child for posttraumatic stress disorder? As a character in the larger story, he is almost a cipher, so nonpresent that the reader might wonder if Isaac noticed that he was being tied up. Imagine the scene on Mount Moriah: Abraham and Isaac have prepared the sacrificial altar. Now for the binding. Abraham would need Isaac to be supine for this, so, did he throw his son to the ground as if he were a calf in a rodeo? Or did he say, "Please lie down on the ground?" Or "Please lie down on the altar?" We read only that Isaac was bound in the same fashion used by a butcher on an animal about to be slaughtered, and we can assume that this trussing was familiar to him. When I fall into my imagination and follow the logical sequence of events from the moment when Abraham turns to Isaac to the moment when the arc of the cleaver reaches its apex, I still expect Isaac, like a character in slapstick, to snap and grok to what is happening. At first I imagine that Isaac, *not* in charge of what happens next, is not paying that much attention, and hardly notices when his father starts sliding the rope around *his* ankles instead of the usual lamb or ram. Then, suddenly, Isaac's face goes slack, his eyes bulge, he looks at the rope, then the altar, then the cleaver—then back at the rope! the altar! the cleaver! He yelps, squirms backward, pushing with his bound feet, and shouts, "Hold it!"

But in the text he's depicted as silently facing a grisly death at the hands of his father; as if he were dead already, he neither protests, resists, nor seeks an explanation. Afterward, as Elohim tells Abraham that he's passed the test, neither shows a whit of concern for this boy who, to put it as charitably as is possible, had been ill used. Karen Armstrong argues that "the primary casualty of Mount Moriah was Isaac. How do you cope with the fact that your father was prepared to kill you in cold blood? How can you relate to a deity who treats you as a mere pawn in a test of his chosen one?"[90] Isaac's near-comatose passivity as his father prepares him for slaughter signals the likelihood, indeed, the near certainty, that he was a casualty well before the events at Mount Moriah. It's a signal I learned to recognize in my work, sure, but first I had to learn to recognize it in my own life. In Isaac's deepest passivity, I recognize a closeted piece of myself.

Fall 1960, Spring 1961

My grandfather had a heart attack as he walked home from church on a Sunday in the autumn of 1960. He died the following Friday night, just after asking, "Where's Johnny? Where's my boy?"—or so my mother told me, pulling me aside, whispering it in secret. Mumbling it, really; she'd gone up the day of his heart attack and had spent the week in a barbiturate-induced haze. Actually, she'd told a few dozen people the same thing, that he'd died asking about *them*. It was one of those cultural niceties within eastern Texas Protestant society, a thing that was polite to say when somebody died, especially somebody important, like my grandfather, the former Mayor Cook. No one was supposed to *believe* it. But I'd been closer to him than to anyone else, ever, so I did believe it, convincing myself that I'd failed him just at the last and would never be able to make it right.

My mother was increasingly addicted to pills, and my father was steadily darkening from that and from the frustrations of his business. Already I'd begun to feel a creeping hopelessness and, now, with my grandfather's death and my failure, as I saw it, in my duty to him, quite suddenly it was all too much. By the time we returned home from the funeral, I was slipping into a depression. Within a week all I wanted to do was sleep, and after a few months I was barely able to function. My parents knew nothing of such things and thought I should just snap out of it. But I fell deeper. The following spring, when my report card showed a six-week average in math of thirty-nine—this was the simplest of math—*If a+2=3, what is the value of "a"?*—my mother signed it, tossed it in my direction, and, her tone dipping and lilting in all the right places, said, "I'm just so glad your grandfather didn't live to see the shame you've brought to this family." From where I lay on my bed, she appeared to be at the end of a tunnel, and I thought how curious it was that I should feel neither shame at finding yet another way to let my grandfather down, nor anger toward her for being so cold about it. I couldn't find the energy to give a damn about school, about her disappointment, or Dad's, or anyone else's. Able now to put words to the experience, it was as though I was steadily losing mass, dissolving—*not* dying, mind you, but, bit by bit, ceasing to exist. Had my father walked in that day and begun trussing me up with the intention of killing me, there may not have been enough of me left to resist him. I might even have welcomed it.

66

SARAH AND MOUNT MORIAH

As for Sarah's response to the event, the text tells us nothing. Kierkegaard imagined her in one scenario watching from a window as her husband and son departed, and in another as a young woman. The interpreters, however, found it curious that she died so soon after the events on Mount Moriah, leading to speculation that the two were connected. "According to the Midrash," writes Rona Shapiro, "Sarah dies of grief when she learns of what Abraham nearly did to Isaac, her only son, the child of her old age."[91] She goes on to quote the Midrash (*Tanhuma Vayera* twenty-three), which tells of Satan appearing to Sarah and telling her of what Abraham had intended to do, and that, had the angel not intervened, he would be dead. Before he could finish telling the story, Sarah died. Does this mean that she was not the soldier Abraham was? Perhaps she was made of less sturdy stuff? Hardly. Shapiro suggests that Sarah is made of different stuff, heart stuff, which Abraham *would* come to understand, then *become*, but only after Mount Moriah, itself an awakening experience for him, and after Sarah's death.

Ellen Frankel, in *The Five Books of Miriam*, presents the same Midrashic story, then adds, "But others teach that Satan reveals to her that Abraham has spared her son from his knife; and then her heart bursts from Joy. Such is the anatomy of a mother's heart."[92] Then, to the Rabbis, "Sarah the Ancient One retorts: What do the Rabbis know of a mother's heart?"

67

SARAH'S DEATH AND BURIAL. ABRAHAM SENDS
HIS SERVANT TO FIND A WIFE FOR ISAAC

Sarah died, at the age of 127, "in Kiriath-arba—now Hebron—in the land of Canaan." But Abraham, "a *resident alien* without hereditary land-rights or a secure place in the social and legal order,"[93] had no place to bury her. However, he is recognized as "the *elect of God* (v. 5), to whom the whole land has been promised."[94] Consulting with the local council, he gained permission to purchase a site, and he "buried his wife Sarah in the cave of the field of Machpelah, facing Mamre—now Hebron—in the land of Canaan."

That complete, Abraham now turned his attention not to Isaac, but to Isaac's future. His son needed a wife, so he sent for his servant and instructed him to "go to the land of my birth and get a wife for my son Isaac." In one of those moments when everything works out so perfectly that it's downright providential, the servant met Rebekah, Isaac's future wife. By necessity, the servant also met Rebekah's father, Bethuel, and Laban, her brother, who will prove to be one of the great sleazeballs in biblical literature.

Everyone including Rebekah agreed that she would accompany the servant to meet Isaac, who "brought her into the tent of his mother . . . took her as his wife . . . loved her and thus found comfort after his mother's death." From this verse alone, we can see that Isaac is not his father's son. In Genesis 26, when Isaac and Rebekah attempt to play *She's my sister, not my wife*, their effort is derailed when their mark, King Abimelech (yes, the same one whom Abraham and Sarah tricked), sees them making out in public. Understandably, Isaac is unable to perpetuate the same subterfuge as Abraham. Though he is one of the patriarchal trilogy that includes Abraham and Jacob, Isaac's role is less that of a leading man than a supporting character. He is a foil to his father and (as we will see) his son. Some interpreters speculate that, because he is so weakly drawn, he must have been a later invention, and that Jacob must have been Abraham's son. Others argue that he must have been part of the original story because no one would have invented so weak a character to occupy such a high place. However, I see his character as subtle, not weak, his presence in the narrative the sort of essential segue that holds together this intricate story. As you will see, there is an argument to be made that he is more complex a character than he appears.

68

THE DEATH OF ABRAHAM

Following Isaac's marriage to Rebekah, "Abraham took another wife, whose name was Keturah," about whom nothing is known, though "a midrash identifies her with Hagar."[95] With Keturah he had six more sons, about whom nothing is known beyond their names and descendants. Then, having put his affairs in order, "Abraham breathed his last . . . was gathered to his kin," and taken by his sons Isaac and Ishmael to be buried with Sarah.

Abraham is not a nice man, which can be said of many secular and religious leaders. Unlike other leaders who rise to power, however, he has no particular charisma, no warmth to draw the reader to him. To be sure, we do see one-off glimpses of a softer side—when he laughs so hard that he falls down, and again, when he presses Yahweh on the issue of Sodom and Gomorrah. In the confidence game he runs on Pharaoh, a wild, risk-taking side emerges, but in the game he runs on Abimelech, he shows an absence of concern for the consequences of his actions on the population of an entire kingdom, which is different only in scale from his lack of concern for Hagar and Ishmael when Sarah decides to leave them in the desert to die. Again, these are characteristics of many "great" men and women throughout history—the disregard for other people's money, safety, dignity, jobs, and the willingness to play risky games for uncertain gains. My own default image of Abraham is that of an old man with no affect, plodding along for three days on the way to Mount Moriah, where he will kill his son. By the normative standards of our own time, were the events on Moriah made known, Isaac would be removed from the home, while Abraham would almost certainly be judged as a danger to society and placed for an indeterminate time in a state mental health facility. Yet three of the world's religions are rooted in him, and whether one regards him as a historical figure or a literary character, he remains one of the most influential figures in human history.

PART III

THE BLESSING THIEF: A STORY IN THREE ACTS

The Grifter

Nice guys finish last.
—Leo Durocher

69

THE NAME, EARLY CHARACTER,
AND ASPIRATIONS OF SAID THIEF

Isaac's first sons are twins. The name of the second-born, Jacob (*Yaakov*), means "Heelholder," and is a triumph of irony, serving both as a lovely word-picture—an infant clinging to his twin brother's heel at the moment of birth—and a mnemonic of sorts, an unbroken reminder of his second-place finish. Jacob is obsessed with being first, however, and this seemingly sweet gesture of sibling love may well have been baby Jacob's attempt to pull his brother back in.

Jacob was the smart one, conniving, ambitious. He was the obvious and best choice to assume his father's place as patriarch of the clan, but *Tradition* had another idea. Order of birth, it said, trumped brains and competence. Their father's blessing, therefore, with all the inherited perks—supremacy in the clan, control of its property and wealth—would pass to Esau, older by seconds, a doofus that he, Jacob, would be obliged to address as Lord—unless he could outmaneuver his brother. Getting around his father could prove another matter, though not insurmountable. Tradition, after all, could be bypassed. Look at Isaac, his own father. He had not been Grandfather Abraham's firstborn son, but had nevertheless received the blessing. Moreover, the bestower of the blessing had been Yahweh, not Abraham, thus lending a certain air of divine imprimatur to the practice of *bypassing*. So, while Tradition could be a cornerstone with which to build an orderly life for all, or a rock against which an upstart could smash in his willfulness, it could also become, in the hands of one clever enough, soft as sculptor's clay. Jacob's *intention* to supplant his older brother is understandable, and it is not nearly as coldhearted or ruthless as the *means* by which he does so.

70

THE RED STEW INCIDENT, WHEN THE INCONVENIENT BROTHER, A MAN OF SIMPLER AMBITION, PROVES AN EASY MARK FOR THE BLESSING THIEF'S DARK TRICKSTER

Beyond his primacy in the order of birth, Esau ("the mantled one," so called because of the red hair encasing his body at birth) had little going for him. His culture believed hairiness to be "a sign of uncouthness"[1] and a sign of future character. Sure enough, not only would he grow to be a hairy adult, he would discover a singular passion for hunting, also considered loutish, and show a vast incuriosity toward everything else, including the wealth and responsibilities he was due to inherit.

Esau shows none of his brother's shrewdness. In one of the better-known episodes in Western literature, Esau, returning from a failed hunting trip, stumbles upon Jacob's camp. Not having eaten in days, on seeing a pot of his brother's signature reddish-brown stew, he says, "Give me some of that red stuff to gulp down, for I am famished." Jacob agrees, but on the condition that Esau sell his birthright for the stew. Esau agrees, saying that the birthright would be useless to him if he were dead. Jacob says, "Swear to me first," which Esau does.

Only seven verses in length, the episode is remarkably layered. Rabbi David Wolpe suggests that a closer look at what transpired reveals that Jacob took more from his brother than the birthright.[2] The deal they struck, he points out, was specific—the birthright for the stew. But Jacob also gave Esau bread and drink, creating for himself the superior position of having given an unreciprocated gift. In a single stroke, Jacob not only gained the status of primogeniture, but put his brother in the inferior position of debtor. *Dark* genius, but genius, still.

Whether the bargain was valid is unclear. Wolpe says the agreement was technically valid, as does Walter Zanger, who adds, "Even today in the Middle East there are places where an oath, a promise, a blessing, a curse—solemn declarations of the mouth—are not revocable. You don't swear to do something and then take it back—you don't do it!"[3] And Esau *did* swear. But Wolpe tells us, "Even the Rabbis of the Talmud say that a deal made under duress is not binding."[4] And Esau was under duress—unless he was just being dramatic.

And what about Jacob? If he believed they'd made a binding agreement, why didn't he tell his father of the new arrangement? It occurred to me that the answer lies in the character of Jacob. Throughout Jacob's story, he is shown to be a man who prefers a game in which he controls the outcome. By involving Isaac, he would be giving up control. And then what might happen? I can imagine Jacob pondering when to reveal this to his father, running risk analyses, rolling them over and over in his mind, following the possibilities, seeing various outcomes, one or more of which would end in disaster. For instance: *Jacob goes to his father with the story of how he'd scooped his brother. Isaac is impressed, but dismayed. Being old, not stupid, he sees the bargain for what it is—naked greed and ambition, a gross attempt by a son to steal his brother's rightful inheritance by subverting not only his father's will, but the divine will.* Now, add in the fact that Isaac, as patriarch, has the power to curse, to banish, or put to death, and what you've got is a sort of Russian roulette, an uncontrolled risk—not Jacob's style. (Later, however, his own *mother's* risky style will take him on just such a nerve-racking ride.)

Jacob never intended to tell his father. Still, if securing the birthright wasn't the point, what was? Given his talent for misdirection, perhaps Jacob's intention was nothing more than mental warfare, a raid of sorts, a chance to test his brother, to toy with his head. Whatever his purpose— and there are centuries of speculation—in the end Jacob would need a subtler way in, a strategy for procuring the blessing before his father and brother knew what was happening.

That's the thing about a blessing—it is *organic*; the passing of a blessing is *received*, then *held* within one's own body and spirit, then, before one's own death, *transmitted* to another. Once given, it could not be taken back, only transferred "to the one for whom it was intended."[5] Isaac, blessed by God, not Abraham, "was communicating his life essence to his son, breathing his very soul"[6] into Jacob. Clever Jacob would have been aware of that, would have known that once he'd received the blessing, he'd be safe from Isaac. As for Esau, Jacob may have assumed that even such a dimwit as his brother would be able to see and accept that it was *game over*, and that he'd lost.

I've known a few exceptionally bright but emotionally unintelligent individuals who have made this very assumption in a moment of triumph. They believed that the loser would give up after having been outsmarted. As Jacob learns, it's always best to know how someone will react *before* you act, and before the person you're intending to ruin makes it his life purpose to murder you.

Does the narrator intend this story to be a sort of subtle, ironic stew? By this time the narrator has revealed to us readers that while Rebekah, Isaac's wife, was still pregnant with the twins, Yahweh had dropped in to say that her *second*-born son was to receive the blessing. But Rebekah has not told this to her husband or sons. Along with power and wealth, the son who received the blessing would also be the sole bearer of the covenant that Yahweh had made with Abraham, *the* centerpiece of the Hebrew narrative. Yet neither son has shown even a passing interest in the covenant.

71

WITH HIS MOTHER'S AID, JACOB STEALS THE BLESSING
(UNLESS WE'VE ALL BEEN DUPED)

The central event in this first part of Jacob's story is not his manipulation of his brother, but the defrauding of his father, now quite old and nearly sightless. One day, Rebekah overhears Isaac tell Esau to go hunting for wild game, then prepare his favorite dish, "So that I may give you my innermost blessing before I die." This is it! As if spring-loaded, she goes to Jacob, tells him what she's heard, and what to do. *We'll fool your father into thinking you're Esau!* she tells him, then hurries him out the door with instructions to slaughter two lambs so that she can begin preparing the meal.

But Jacob folds, saying, essentially, that *Even a half-blind old man can tell the difference between his smooth skin and his brother's hairy skin.* Perhaps this seminal moment has been more fun to anticipate than execute. But it's now or never. Saying she'll take the blame, Rebekah takes Esau's best clothes for Jacob to wear, wraps his hands and neck with the lambskins, hands Jacob the stew, and pushes him into his father's tent. After a moment's hesitation at hearing what sounded like Jacob's voice, not Esau's, Isaac puts his hands on Jacob and says the words of the blessing. The ruse has worked—unless Jacob and Rebekah were being had. For the story to make sense *as written*, the reader must be convinced that Isaac is too blind and too senile to recognize his sons either by sight, scent, or voice, unable to discern the tactile difference between lamb's wool and a hairy arm, or to notice that the stew he's eating is prepared *not* from wild game with its telltale pungency, and with Esau's recipe, but from domesticated lamb, and by his wife's familiar hand. Then the reader must dismiss other evidence: Isaac having the presence of mind to know that the time had come to bestow his blessing; his sending Esau out to hunt wild game in order to prepare a meal that was not part of the blessing ritual. Finally, the transmission of the blessing itself called for the recitation of an extended, complicated discourse that in an orally transmitted culture was said with a certain exactitude. Was Isaac secretly playing along with his wife and second son the whole time?

According to Rabbi Wolpe, "There is a tradition claiming that a father knows his children, so Isaac knew *exactly* what he was doing."[7] The custom of the firstborn son inheriting the lion's share of the father's estate was ancient even in Isaac's time and may have emerged from the need to keep the clan together and to prevent interfamily warfare. But what if the firstborn son was incompetent to assume such responsibility? Though in a nomadic culture such as Isaac's, tradition provided meaning and structure, it is conceivable that the patriarch's duty to the future of his clan was greater than any duty to tradition. So, might Isaac have known Rebekah was listening, and what she would do? When he sent Esau out on the time-consuming and unnecessary task of hunting and preparing wild game, was it to remove him long enough to prevent his interference in what had to be done? Did he know the blessing *had* to go to Jacob?

Maybe. We just don't know.

72

I DISCOVER A HIDDEN TALENT FOR TRICKSTERISM, AND THE THRILLS OF THE DARK SIDE

I have my own history of duplicity, though one significant incident is somewhat reminiscent of Jacob, Esau, and the stew. What troubles me about my behavior is that thirty-plus years after that incident occurred, it doesn't trouble me more.

Tyler, Texas

After my graduation from seminary in 1973 and my ordination, my first position was as assistant to the rector of Christ Church, Tyler, Texas. Having spent four years in and around the progressive atmosphere of Washington, D.C. and St. Mark's, Capitol Hill, I arrived in northeast Texas something of an iconoclast, with a thirst for shaking things up. Yet rather than the high road of direct confrontation with people who opposed me (which could have ended my career), I saw that the low road of political subterfuge was sometimes a wiser path.

The first women had been ordained to the priesthood that same year, opening the gates for the ascension of women in the church to positions of power previously unavailable by custom or canon law. One of those positions at the local level was the vestry, the lay governing body elected by members of the parish. Like most Episcopal parishes, Christ Church held its annual parish meeting in January, the finale of which was the vestry election. Christ Church's tradition was that the slate of candidates would be made up of men nominated by the outgoing vestrymen. There would be a motion to elect by acclamation, it would pass, and that would be that. The men on the slate were often the same men who'd rotated out of office two years before and were now eligible to return. As a result, the same eighteen or so men, with the occasional substitution for age or infirmity, would run the business affairs of the parish for decades. Actually, a good many of these men were far more progressive than you might expect in that time and place, and their system had worked quite well.

One morning, about fifteen months after my arrival, the rector asked me to join him in his office.

"What do you think our chances are of getting a woman elected to the vestry?" he asked.

"In a show-of-hands election?"

"Yeah."

"Not a chance in hell."

"Yeah." He paused, stared at the wall, then grinned. "I'd sure like for Christ Church to be the first parish in the Diocese of Texas to elect a woman to the vestry."

"Everybody I've talked to assumes it'll happen first in Houston. Probably at Palmer."

"Yeah, I know. That's why it would be so sweet if we did it first."

I nodded.

"Why don't you see what you can do?"

"You want me to get a woman elected to the vestry this coming January?"

"Yeah."

"Okay."

"Have anybody in mind?"

"Yeah."

"Are we thinking about the same person?"

"Probably."

We agreed it was best if he simply stayed out of it from that point.

The plan was simple. Mary was the perfect candidate. When the time was right, I would approach her and ask her permission to place her name in nomination from the floor. Assuming the odds against her were too great, she would nevertheless accept the nomination as a symbolic nod toward a future when a woman truly might have a chance. In the meantime, I enlisted two male friends of mine, who were members of Christ Church but out of the mainstream of parish life. Carl, once a prominent member of the community, had managed to drink his way through two businesses and three families, but was now a recovering alcoholic and a spiritual mentor since my arrival. Jeff was the town's token radical liberal, who'd made his bones years earlier by declaring Tyler to be "a huge cesspool covered with rose petals." The allusion to rose petals came from Tyler having named itself "The Rose Capital of the World"—which, in fact, it was.

Once the election segment of the annual meeting was under way, the success of the plan would depend almost entirely on people who had no conscious part in the plan reacting in predictable ways to stimuli that Carl and Jeff would provide. The senior warden (head layman, a man I admired and was quite fond of) would present the slate, then ask if there were further nominations. Carl would raise his hand, whereupon we knew that the senior warden, on seeing it was Carl, would call on him with just a touch of condescension in his manner. Carl would stand and nominate Mary. If no one else seconded Mary's nomination, Jeff was to do it. On hearing Mary's name, the warden would give a slight roll of the eyes, for all to see, and an equally slight grin and shake of the head as he turned to write her name on the blackboard. The men at the front table would do likewise, though some more demonstrably, as would other men present at the meeting. Anyone watching for the room's reaction (and I would be) would also observe a significant number of the women's faces darken momentarily (and they did). The nominations would be closed and the vote called. Jeff would move for a secret ballot. If no one else seconded the motion, Carl would do it. The motion would pass and Mary would be elected by the women of the parish, most of whom, in a show of hands, likely would not have voted *for* her and *against* their men.

When the hour arrived, it was pitch-perfect, unfolding exactly as I'd predicted, each actor in the play turning in a flawless performance. Mary was elected, and only Carl, Jeff, and I knew how it had happened. Dick never wanted to know. The warden thought it was funny and came close to guessing, but I wouldn't confirm or deny. Nor did I tell Mary. However, that day when Jeff moved for the secret ballot, I was watching Mary, too, and she looked at me, gave a slight shake of her head as something like incredulity went across her face.

Did I rig that election? No more than Jacob rigged the outcome of his encounter with Esau, though each of us did play the manipulator, providing stimuli calculated to bring about a desired outcome. Because neither Jacob nor I could count on a particular outcome without our intervention, each of us required a plan that kept *un*certainty to a minimum. That planning, I suggest, is what we see in Jacob's encounter with Esau, not chance, though at first glance it appears to be a spontaneously sprung trap. Knowing the young Jacob's character, we can imagine that he'd foreseen the opportunity to obtain Esau's birthright, had familiarized himself with his brother's hunting grounds and his most likely return routes, and, during a period when game was scarce, had set up camp, made the stew, and waited.

I'm ravenous. Give me some stew.

Sure. Right after you give me the birthright.

Was Jacob as hungry for what only Esau could give him as Esau was for that stew? It was, in fact, all he wanted! Did Jacob know that his brother would make the bargain? Of course he did; Esau was entirely predictable.

This penchant for predicting what people will do has served me well in the past thirty-odd years as I've orchestrated other, similar sleights of hand, both in the church and in my work beyond it. I find it easy, thrilling, addictive. Watching the movie *Wag the Dog*, along with working up a bit of populist outrage, I was busy conniving, whispering suggestions to De Niro's character. Jacob would have done well in such high-level games of smoke and mirrors.

73

A FASCINATING CONUNDRUM
INVOLVING MACRO LOGIC

Yahweh, Creator of the Universe, Giver of the Law, et cetera, was something of a situational ethicist when it came to playing by his own rules. Mind you, he himself did not violate the rules, but he used proxies instead, people with flexible character whose moral fiber could be woven into whatever cloth was most appropriate to the situation. Already we know that Yahweh's intention all along had been for the blessing to go to Jacob and *not* Esau. But for the situation to be turned in Jacob's favor, it required an actor with brains *and* the sort of moral bankruptcy that allows one, by way of running a grift on his ailing father, to cheat his brother of everything, to do it for personal gain, and without a second thought. In short, young Jacob's sorry character was a divine asset.

It could be argued that this shows how close we've come to being made in God's image (or to imitating the gods), human history being one long stream of tribal chieftains, kings, queens, tyrants, and even elected heads of state using whoever might bring about a desired result. Implied in the narrative is that, had Jacob been a "better" man, the blessing might have passed to Esau, whose qualities, including the shortcoming of *not* being the skunk his brother was, made him unfit for bearing that responsibility.

In the time of the Patriarchs, monotheism was a revolutionary idea, and revolutions are brought off by rule benders and breakers. Look at Jacob's predecessors. Abraham *and* Isaac, claiming their wives to be their sisters, handed them over to other men, and Abraham came within a breath of eviscerating his own son. Yet however egregious their actions may seem to us, to *them*, all that Abraham and Isaac did was in the service of something beyond the self. Not so with Jacob. While he *was* used by Yahweh, and his grift *did* serve to effect the divine intentions, Jacob, the Blessing Thief, was acting on his own behalf. Although my own conniving may have served some larger intentionality, my cause was no larger than Jacob's.

I continue to bump up against this certainty that Yahweh should clean up his act. Perhaps this stems from some middle-American, bourgeois Protestant morality lingering from my youth. On the other hand, I find this portrait of the creator's slick side ironic, amusing, and even soothing with its implication that my own smarmier side is but the result of spiritual DNA inherited from that One in whose image I was made.

As I wrote about that election, the same inner voice, like a dithyramb from a Greek chorus of Southern Baptist ancestors, chanted *Be ashamed! Be ashamed!* Instead I was smiling, which calls to mind an old Hasidic saying, "There is no room for God in him who is full of himself." Am I being full of myself? I'm afraid so. Though I grew up in the end, being that cocky boy-man did have its days, and I've enjoyed myself immensely in this remembering.

I wonder if Jacob ever told anyone about how he'd played Esau and Isaac, and if he smiled.

The Mark

Everything I think I am attaining, is attaining me.
—ROBERT MUSIL, *The Man Without Qualities*

74

THROUGH THE BLESSING THIEF'S EYES

Quite suddenly, the prize you'd always wanted—your brother's inheritance—is right in front of you: a ripe peach just waiting to be plucked! Your mother and secret ally has come to you with a plan for making your nearly blind father think that you are your brother. The plan is clever, but *so* risky. *If I get caught*, you whine, I risk banishment, or death. *Not to worry*, she says, she'll take the heat. Okay, better her than you, only now that it's done, she tells you that your brother, who didn't much like you before all this, is "consoling himself by planning to kill you." This is bad on at least two levels. First of all, your focus had been on securing the inheritance, so you have no strategy for afterward. Second, you are what's called "a man of the tent"—think *Late Bronze Age metrosexual*—but your brother is a rougher sort, "a man of the field," meaning not just the physical, outdoor type, but a hunter, a guy used to bloodletting. Fact is, the only reason you're not dead already is that your brother can't touch you as long as your father lives. But Isaac is old—really old. It's time for you to leave.

Your mother wants you to go live with your uncle, her brother, until your brother cools off. But you can't just leave without your father's permission, and to get that, you'll need a convincing pretext. You'd think that *Because if I stay here, my brother will kill me!* would suffice, but when the moment arrives your mother does all the talking and, for her own reasons, doesn't mention the threat. Instead, proving again to be quite the player, she starts harping about how "disgusted" she is with the local women. Sure, your brother had married one of them, but they're just too low-class for her precious, refined Jacob, and if *you* were to marry one, *her* life would not be worth living (implying, perhaps, *and neither will yours!*). So your father, as if it were his idea, tells you to go to your uncle's place and choose a wife from among his daughters, your first cousins.

Now you must cross a vast landscape that's about as familiar to a guy like you as the surface of Mars.

75

A DREAM ABOUT A LADDER REVEALS ALL THE CARDS IN THE DIVINE HAND. THE BLESSING THIEF'S CHUTZPAH

At the end of Act One of his life, Jacob leaves home with whatever he can carry, and walks into wilderness that would have been a frightening place for this "man of the tent" even in the daylight. Then night falls. A man with his brother's field craft could have followed him, unnoticed, and could be out there, waiting, silent as a ghost. Finally, with a stone for his pillow, Jacob, exhausted, frightened, and a bit desperate, falls asleep and dreams.

In the dream, a ladder (or a staircase; the Hebrew term, *sullum*, is unique, its origin uncertain) reaches from ground to sky, with angels descending and ascending. Yahweh, standing next to the stairway (or next to *Jacob*, depending on how one reads the Hebrew pronoun), tells Jacob that he will make him and his descendants a great people who will cover the earth.

On waking, awed now and frightened, he is overwhelmed with a sense of *presence*. To signify the place, Jacob takes the stone he used as a pillow and sets it up as a pillar, a common practice in ancient Middle Eastern worship—and a pretty good trick for one man, since these stones were usually about seven feet high.[8] Once the stone is in place, Jacob pours oil over it and names the site *Beth-El*, literally "House of God."

Next, through the narrator's solemn, gauzy tone, we get a glimpse of Jacob-the-operator. Where others might be all atwitter from the divine attention, Jacob sees opportunity: *Look*, he seems to say between the lines, *don't think I'm not flattered. It's just that I have more immediate concerns, like food, water, protection from bad guys and things that might eat me.*

Given that Yahweh had promised already to look after him, this might have proved an affront, but Yahweh had different rules for people he liked. Besides, the hustler in Jacob would not have missed the fact that in his dream the divine cards had been revealed. He, Jacob, was the covenant-bearer. No Jacob, no covenant. So, *get me to my uncle's place and I'm your man*, he says. But what does he mean by his acceptance? Like "faith," the divine-human commitment into which Jacob now enters carried a different meaning than what is normative today. For instance, a young Christian who'd experienced what he assumed to be a divine vision might perceive it as a calling to spread the faith to nonbelievers. But beyond setting up the altar at Beth-El, Jacob will not even pray again for twenty years, and then only because he's in a jam, and he will not speak to anyone about Yahweh. In fact, neither Noah, nor Abraham, nor Isaac ever attempted to bring an outsider to their God. Their task, and Jacob's, was not like the Christian imperative to "Go forth into all the world and preach the Gospel," but the opposite—to create a new people, a new nation of believers, generation by generation.

At Beth-El, if only for a moment, this man of shallow waters had experienced awe in the presence of great mystery. Soon, and from the first glance, he will be overwhelmed by the equally unexpected, mysterious, illogical, near-to-bursting love for a woman he'd never before seen. The experience at Beth-El cracked the carapace of his ego; this transformative love will widen the breach. It will also leave him blind to the machinations of his uncle, who will use that advantage to play his nephew like a three-dollar fiddle.

76

THEN, ON SEEING THE GIRL,
HE FALLS INTO LOVE'S STUPOR

When Jacob nears Laban's farm, he encounters a group of shepherds and their flocks gathered around a well covered by a huge stone to protect it from dirt and debris. He asks if they know Laban. They reply that, yes, they know him, and, in fact, "There is his daughter Rachel, coming with the flock."

He looks, and the sight of her is a lightning strike to the heart. *But how do I get rid of these shepherds?* "It is still broad daylight," he says, "too early to round up the animals; water the flock and take them to pasture." In other words, *You're all goofing off when you should be watering the sheep and leading them back to pasture while the light's still good.* Pretty brassy for a stranger, though these men were likely used to taking orders and Jacob, the son of a patriarch, likely came across as one used to giving them. And traditionally, as the midrash *Lekach Tov* says, to "learn from this that if one visits a strange place and sees a wrong being perpetrated, it is one's duty to prevent it."[9]

The shepherds weren't being lazy. This was a community well and, to protect their water from outsiders and to prevent any single user or small group of locals from abusing the privilege, the covering stone was huge.

Before they could move it, they told him, they'd need more shepherds. Just then Rachel arrived, and the poor boy was stricken once again. He *had* to make her notice him! But how? What to do? Why, move the stone, of course—*by himself!* A hero who performs feats of inhuman strength is a recurring motif in ancient stories: Atlas and Hercules, for example; even Samson, who pushed over the Philistine Temple. But Jacob, this *mama's boy*, this *man of the tent?* How could he do that?

Certainly, in one so deeply smitten, there can be that momentary suspension of the limitations of self-imposed reality. Without a word to Rachel, or a *By your leave* to the shepherds—it was, after all, their well—he "went up and rolled the stone off the mouth of the well and watered the flock of his Uncle Laban." Then he kissed Rachel, broke into tears, and told her who he was. Rachel, not quite knowing *what* to think, ran back home and told her father.

77

HIS SLEAZY UNCLE, HER FATHER, PULLS A BAIT-
AND-SWITCH, AND THE BLESSING THIEF WAKES UP
NEXT TO THE WRONG WOMAN

Uncle Laban was the sleaze Jacob might have become had he stayed in his spoiled life in his mother's and father's home. Laban is "a masterful characterization—a selfish, greedy, exploiting, suspicious man of wealth, who never fails to observe good manners."[10] Even the sages of the Midrash didn't like him. According to Nahum Sarna, they considered Laban's hearty welcoming of Jacob as disingenuous, no more than a sign of his greed. Having made the assumption that Jacob had come looking for a wife, Laban further assumed he'd brought gifts. Sarna speculates that Laban's welcoming kiss on the mouth was an attempt to determine if Jacob had hidden jewels there, although Sarna doesn't share any thoughts on exactly *how* Laban might have detected this.

After Jacob had been at his uncle's for a month, it was time to work out an arrangement, so Laban went to him and asked, "Just because you are my kinsman, should you serve me for nothing? Tell me, what shall your wages be?" To which Jacob replied, "I will serve you for seven years for your daughter Rachel." Since a daughter was considered to be her father's property, any man coming with a marriage proposal was expected to pay a bride-price. Having arrived with nothing, Jacob was offering instead seven years of indentured servitude, the price to be paid in full *before* the marriage.

To Jacob's offer, Laban replied, "Better I give her to you than to an outsider. Stay with me." This apparent yes may have been no more than Laban's clever dissembling. But swooning in love's first blush, Jacob took Laban's answer as a yes and the seven years "seemed to him but a few days because of his love for her." Then, when it was time, Jacob went to Laban and said, "Give me my wife." So Laban threw a huge wedding celebration, and the next morning Jacob found himself in bed with the wrong woman.

Yikes!

As though evening the score, *Tradition*, Jacob's old nemesis, said that older sisters were to marry first, and Rachel's sister, Leah, was now Jacob's wife. He'd been played, and in a near carbon copy of the manner in which he'd played his father.

78

SPECULATION ABOUT HOW IT HAPPENED. AN APOLOGIA FOR THE BLESSING THIEF. THE BOY GETS THE GIRL HE'D WANTED

How could a fellow as cagey as Jacob have been so completely duped? It may not have been that difficult. The bride after all had been heavily veiled throughout the wedding and the day's celebration, so he'd not seen her face. With no reason to suspect the veiled woman was not Rachel, any discrepancies in behavior, voice, or body language might easily have been subsumed beneath the myriad distractions of ritual, ceremony, and wine-soaked celebration.

But what about the moment of consummation? How could he not know who was in the wedding bed? Again, in Jacob's defense, the room was dark, the bride still veiled, and he had been partying. And he had been mooning over Rachel, the woman he'd expected to find there, for seven years — seven celibate years. In the bridal bedchamber, he is folded into the warm, welcoming, perfumed, naked embrace of the woman he assumes to be his beloved. Yet even in that heightened moment, might there have been at least the whispery wondering of an inner voice, asking, *This . . . is Rachel?*

Given my former propensity for waking up next to the wrong woman (decades ago, another marriage), *and* remembering how the frenzied, needy hunger of such moments could heighten the temptation to override cautions of less subtlety, I understand how this could happen. Also, given what we know of Jacob, it's not impossible to imagine his doppelganger, that shifty, *pre*-Beth-El, *pre*-Rachel Jacob, murmuring *Maybe she is, maybe she isn't.* Still, the narrator tells us that the next morning Jacob awakened next to Leah.

Outraged at the betrayal (and, surely, at himself), he confronted Laban, whose reply essentially was *It's not you, m'boy, it's tradition for the oldest daughter to marry first. And unlike you, we keep tradition. But, tell you what: agree to give me another seven years, and you can marry Rachel right away. Next week work for you?*

Since betrothal was a legal status, a betrothed couple was considered to be already married. So when Jacob had said to Laban, "Give me my wife," his meaning had been *Give me what is already mine.* Except that Rachel, arguably, was *not* his, because Laban arguably had not agreed to the betrothal. Giving one's word was, in that time and place, a serious matter, but what Laban had said those seven years before, remember, was "Better I give her to you than to an outsider," which seems less a language of commitment than of musing. Jacob may have heard what he wanted to hear and what his uncle hoped he'd hear.

Rachel must have had some part in the subterfuge. A midrash in the Babylonian Talmud tells of Jacob and Rachel having devised a signal just in case Laban tried to substitute Leah for Rachel. "But on the wedding night, Rachel, feeling compassion for Leah and not wanting her to be shamed, shares the code with her sister. As a result, Jacob is deceived in the darkness, even as his father Isaac had been fooled in his blindness."[11] Perhaps, on reconsideration, Rachel thought Jacob needed his own come-uppance after what he'd done to his father and brother, a humbling shock to the system that said *You're not always the cleverest one in the room.* But he *was* the cleverest. In time, Uncle Laban will learn just how far out of his own league he'd strayed.

It's rather satisfying to know that *the* Jacob—of *Abraham, Isaac, and Jacob*—could be duped. Still, both from literary and psychological points of view, a few things don't add up. For instance, it seems out of charac-ter that Jacob, even lovestruck, would have missed Laban's equivocating answer to his marriage proposal. Likewise, seven years of observing his uncle's sleazy character surely would have given him *some* pause about the bargain they'd struck. Also, this business of the oldest daughter marrying first was ancient tradition, so Laban's seemingly ready agreement to violate it should have been a heads-up itself. Then again, perhaps his love for Rachel was the perfect somnambulant, making of Jacob the perfect mark for Laban's long con.

In the end, this part of Jacob's story is made plausible for me by memories of my own spells of love-blindness. His being played for a sucker is a refreshing, balancing layer of naïveté to a character who otherwise might have become predictable and tiresome in his self-important schemes and attempts at one-upmanship. Given the parallels with Jacob's behavior toward his own blind, trusting father, his frustration has an element of sweet, karmic justice—perhaps Yahweh's little joke.

79

JACOB'S WIVES, THEIR PROXIES. THE NAMING OF THE FIRST TEN CHILDREN BECOMES AN ALMOST POIGNANT STRUGGLE FOR DOMESTIC TURF

In time, it would become illegal for sisters to marry the same man. The atmosphere in a household with multiple wives could be turbulent enough without the emotional baggage that sisters might bring. In fact, Jacob's wives make the naming of their children into a years-long, raging conversation, all of which makes for one of the more deliciously outrageous and affecting dramas in the Bible.

It starts with Leah, the big sister, whom Jacob had been tricked into marrying. She knows that Rachel, her younger, prettier sister, is the one Jacob really loves, so when Leah gives birth to a son, she names him Reuben, meaning, "The Lord has seen my affliction . . . Now my husband will love me." She then bears three more sons, Simeon, Levi, and Judah, each name conveying a similar hope—and, perhaps, a raspberry to her childless sister—that yet another son will bring her closer to Jacob. By now Rachel is pretty jealous, so she goes to Jacob and says, "Give me children or I'll die!" To which he responds, more or less, *Look, I'm doing my part! What more do you want from me?* Then Rachel has an idea: *I know, I'll send my handmaiden to Jacob's bed!* Soon, the handmaiden, Bilhah, has a son, and Rachel names him Dan, meaning "Vindication"—or, in the modern argot, *"Ha!"* Bilhah has yet another son, and Rachel names him Naphtali, which roughly translates as "I won the contest." Not to be outdone, Leah sends *her* handmaiden to Jacob, and Zilpah bears a son whom Leah names Gad— "What luck!" Then another, this time a boy, Asher, meaning "Women will deem me fortunate."

Next, Rachel's anxiety at her own childlessness will seed a rather remarkable episode within this larger, multiyear drama. During the wheat harvest one year, Reuben found mandrakes, flowering plants that are "supposed to look like a small human being, with exaggerated sexual features, and to serve as an aphrodisiac with magical powers to produce conception."[12] By now Jacob is living full-time with Rachel, who, still desperate to conceive, goes to her sister and asks for some of the mandrakes. But Leah, who considers it Rachel's fault that Jacob never visits her bed anymore, lashes out with "Was it not enough that you take away my husband, that you would also take my son's mandrakes?" A bit of overkill, to be sure, though it may have been inspired by her reading an unspoken meaning into her sister's request, such as *It's obvious that* you *don't need 'em!* Then, in Rachel's desperation, Leah sees opportunity! Using the mandrakes as currency, Leah offers to buy Jacob's sexual services for the night. Done! And that evening, as he comes in from the field, Leah tells Jacob, "You are to sleep with me tonight, for I have hired you [from Rachel] with my son's mandrakes."

Who said the Bible's not colorful? Cut this episode to its essentials, and what we have left is Rachel selling Jacob's sexual services for the night to Leah. Or *Rachel-as-pimp*, a lesson never mentioned once in fifteen years of Southern Baptist Sunday school or three years of seminary. Cut a bit more away and we see two women trying to survive the relentlessness of a life that seems determined to break them—Leah, rejected and lonely despite the sons she has borne, and Rachel, forced to share her husband and childless in a culture that valued women by their ability to produce children, especially sons.

Jacob seems helpless, caught in the middle. I picture a Gahan Wilson–like cartoon in which the wife-sisters, their handmaidens alongside them, Jacob between them, lob baby names like hand grenades at one another. Jacob holds a placard on which a hand-drawn map displays a bold X, to which he is pointing. Above the map reads a message: *Dear Esau: You're still dumber than dirt, you stink, and Mom always liked me best! Your brother, Jacob. PS: If you still want to kill me, I am right here. Please, hurry!*

Poor Jacob. At every turn, he'd known what he wanted, set goals, and gotten what he'd asked for. Yet contentment eludes him. Always he'd gotten the *unwanted* with the thing he'd wanted, including exile from his home, a brother who wanted to kill him, not one but *two* wives, who hated each other, two proxy wives, a zillion children, and a four-flushing father-in-law.

This was how Yahweh treated his *chosen* one?

Yes, when it suited. Like the rest of us, even Jacob had to learn St. Mick's (Jagger) credo, borrowed from the mystics, "You can't always get what you want." But where Mick say "sometimes," the mystics say that "You *always* get what you need"—even when you don't want it or think you need it. Once Jacob's greed and ambition had served to secure the blessing, those boy-man traits no longer suited Yahweh's purpose. So, in what one might think of as his initiation into manhood, Jacob's overstated ego was being hammered, winnowed, and refined—a process that is, as so many of us have learned, far more amusing when happening to someone else.

80

WHEN THE BLESSING THIEF DECIDES TO RETURN HOME,
UNCLE LABAN AGREES TO THE SEVERANCE TERMS,
THEN TRIES TO CHEAT HIM—*AGAIN*

Following the birth of Joseph, Rachel's first child, Jacob is ready to return to the home he'd left twenty years before. He goes to Laban and says, "Give me my wives and my children, for whom I have served you, that I may go." The implication here is that Jacob's place in Laban's household had been that of an indentured servant. As such, until he was released, he was not free to leave without permission, and his wives and children belonged to Laban, his master.[13]

Acknowledging that Jacob had fulfilled his obligation, Laban agrees to let him go. But, first, there is the matter of the severance (*manumission*) that by custom is paid to a freed servant.

"What shall I pay you?" Laban asks, likely bracing himself against Jacob's answer, as the custom called for a liberal severance.

"Pay me nothing."

Well, almost nothing. Jacob agrees to go on managing Laban's flocks for a time, provided Laban allows him to start his own flock by culling out the sheep and goats discolored by spots or stripes in their coats. Given that discolorations lowered the value of livestock, and that Jacob's management of Laban's flocks had increased their value, this was quite an attractive offer. Besides, Laban sees an opportunity to leave Jacob so impoverished that he will have little choice but to remain in Laban's service.

Having once cheated a man with such proven talents, Laban, a man suspicious by nature, might have paid extra-close attention to any deal he proposed, especially one that so clearly was not in Jacob's best interest. But Laban is blind to the situation as it evolves. Starry-eyed with love and trust before, Jacob is now clear-minded and wary. Deceit, he knows, is in his uncle's nature, as it is in his own. This begs the question of whether Jacob's weak-sided offer was, in fact, a trap. The superior strategist, since the wedding fiasco Jacob surely kept a watchful eye on Laban, studying him, and now is ready to predict what he would do in response to the offer—that he would steal his own sheep, assume victory, and fail to keep a watchful eye on his son-in-law.

Straightaway, Laban had the discolored animals removed and hidden, to be watched over by his sons. Then he put three days between himself and Jacob. (*Three*, like *seven*, was symbolic of a considerable passage of time.) Can't you just see him atop his camel, swaying left, then right, a self-satisfied grin spread across his face, bursting into occasional laughter at the brilliance of the single stroke with which he'd secured his property *and* Jacob's continued servitude? He may have expected that Jacob would be outraged, which he, Laban, would answer with outrage of his own: *I did not renege on our agreement! There was no provision preventing me from culling the discolored animals! You had not yet claimed them, so were they not my property to do with as I chose?* Besides, Jacob was still welcome to all the discolored animals he could find among the flocks. That none was left was his misfortune.

But that nasty business was for another day. For now, far away from Jacob, Laban could drift into sleep each night, dreaming of the future, counting all those sheep and all that money. Meanwhile, with Laban gone, and his sons off watching over the contraband flock, sure enough there was no one left at home to watch Jacob.

Oops.

81

THE BLESSING THIEF LETS THE TRICKSTER OUT
OF THE CLOSET. UNCLE LABAN IS NO MATCH

The coloring of a cow's offspring, ancient breeders thought, was influenced by whatever the mother was looking at when she conceived.[14] If you wanted striped offspring, you'd see to it that the female, when mating, was looking at stripes; for dark or spotted offspring, you'd point them toward animals whose coats were spotted or dark in color. This is what Jacob did with his uncle's sheep, but only with the sturdiest animals, leaving the weaker animals to breed among themselves. For Laban, the end result was much the same as it had been for Esau: Jacob had the marbles that were supposed to have been his.

For Jacob, however, this time was different. Before, when he'd loosed the Trickster on his brother and father, his motives had centered in his greed. Now, however motivated by the long-term need to provide for his family, the greater, more immediate need, this one energized by years of resentment, is to leave Laban *and* his extended family in a state of near ruin. It seems excessive but it is a sentiment with which I have been intimately familiar.

82

AFTER ONE OF MY OWN DANCES INTO
THE DARK SIDE, I CONCLUDE THAT THE TRICKSTER
IS A BETTER FRIEND WHEN HE WEARS A LEASH

Loosing the Trickster is tantamount to inviting the devil to dance, to consciously summoning one's own dark side, the shadowy self, the seat of our deepest passions, our creativity, even our humor. But it can get pretty ugly, too, and the denser one's self-righteousness, the greater the danger of dancing into darker places where *any* fool, you'd think, would know better than to go, since that sort of entertainment comes with a soul price.

Fremont, California

Earlier, I told the story of discovering my own aptitude and appetite for tricksterism. Years after that political maneuvering of my flock, I was no longer an assistant but had become priest in charge of a small parish. There I was immediately embroiled in a protracted power struggle with a group of laymen who, having formed in the vacuum of my predecessor's weedy leadership, had no real intention of stepping back now that I had come to town.

It was January 1981, less than a year before I would resign and move on to another career. Once again, I'd planned a surprise for the annual meeting, but the issue this time was whom I would appoint to the powerful lay position of senior warden. By tradition, the appointment had always gone to a man or woman member of the vestry currently serving, which lent the practice an aura of canon law. Because my strongest supporters were rotating off the board, however, the scuttlebutt around the parish was that I'd be forced to make the appointment from among the board members who were part of the opposition. I had said nothing to suggest otherwise.

A week or so before the annual meeting, I phoned a young couple and asked if we could meet. Since joining the previous year, they'd become quite popular, and the husband, Mike, had already demonstrated that rare leadership brew of brains, generosity, purpose, and strength. I asked that he run for election to the board, and, if elected, which was a near certainty, that he accept the appointment of senior warden. We talked, I left, and a few days later, Mike said yes.

Though my earlier manipulations to elect a woman to the governing board had served what I considered a noble purpose, I confess that my larger

inspirations lay in showing my boss what a clever fellow I was and in the
fun of pulling it off. Now, seven years later, as with Jacob, those years of
service had pounded me until, finally, I cared about accomplishing something beyond my own gain. But like Jacob's motives, mine were layered
and conflicting. I'd convinced myself that I was in a struggle for the soul
of my parish, yet, time and again, in my imagination, I would make my
announcement, see the shock ripple across their faces, and watch their
spokesman take the bait and then soar to his feet to declare that I could *not*
do that. I would stand mute, having primed the outgoing senior warden
to read from the appropriate section of canon law. There would follow a
moment of silence, heavy as lead. Then, just as Peter O'Toole's Henry II
in *The Lion in Winter,* having again outmaneuvered his wife and sons,
shouted, "Oh God, but I love being king!" I would shout, "When will you
understand that you'll never defeat me!"

As before, minus my Henry II, it happened just as I'd predicted. In Tyler,
there'd been an element of fun, even mischief, and antic. Now in its place
was exhaustion, dark exhilaration. I smirked. Jacob had, too, I suspect.
Behind our smirks, the hurt and anger that motivated us to do what we
did, each of us was skirting the edges of that moral abyss that pulls in the
self-righteous with the gravity of a black hole.

83

HIS KIN READY TO KILL HIM, THE BLESSING THIEF MAKES
A RUN FOR IT. LABAN CATCHES UP, BUT LOSES FACE. MAKING
A PACT, EACH TURNS FOR HOME. THEN, ONCE AGAIN, ANGELS

Uncle Laban and his sons did not see the humor in their herd being
reduced to a bunch of white, scrawny animals, so it was necessary for Jacob
to make plans to go—again. The first time he had had to run, he was alone
and slipping away had not been that difficult. But now he would have to
travel with the families and belongings of two households, plus the servants
and their households, plus provisions for what would be a long trek across
a dangerous wilderness, plus all that livestock. Someone in Laban's camp
was bound to notice them packing, which would have been a source of
worry had Laban and his people not already proved themselves to be rather
dim candles. Jacob waited for the right moment, which he knew would
present itself.

The next spring, when Laban and his sons were days away, seeing to the
annual shearing of their sheep, Jacob and his family packed up and moved
out. It would take three days for word to reach Laban that most of what had

been the family's fortune was now hoofing it to the south, but after seven days, they caught up. Now, with Jacob's party in sight, they made camp and watched, waiting for morning. Whatever dark plans Laban may have had for Jacob and his family were met that night by a dream in which Yahweh told him to lay off. It was not a threat, at least not in so many words, but even Laban could read between those lines.

Still, whatever unnatural circumspection Laban had felt at waking soon dissipated, because he'd no sooner arrived at Jacob's camp than the situation was teetering on the edge of violence: "What did you mean by keeping me in the dark and carrying off my daughters like captives of the sword? Why did you flee in secrecy and mislead me and not tell me? Why did you steal my gods?"

Gods? Yes. Called *terafim*, these were hominiform figurines of gods. Of more significance than the sort of tchotchkes on display in modern households, they were believed to ensure the welfare of one's family.

Rachel had taken the gods; it was her little secret. Knowing nothing about it, Jacob responded to the first two questions by admitting his concern that Laban would never have allowed his daughters to leave. As for the stolen gods, he invited Laban to search anywhere he liked, and "anyone with whom you find your gods shall not remain alive." So Laban went through every tent. When he came into Rachel's tent, she apologized for not standing, claiming that she was menstruating, knowing that he wouldn't touch her if she was on fire, *or* the cushion she was sitting on, which, of course, is where she'd hidden the figurines.

Pretty clever, but why did she steal them in the first place? Once again, opinions vary: revenge for having had to share Jacob; wanting to save her father from idolatry; not wanting him to use them to divine where they were headed. Whatever her motive, Rachel's actions may have invited disaster. Already pregnant that day (so, not menstruating), she would die giving birth to another son, Benjamin, a result, claims a midrash, of the death curse that Jacob placed on the unknown thief.

When Laban finds nothing, Jacob, not a man given to confrontation, loses his temper for the first time: "What is my crime . . . my guilt that you should pursue me? You rummage through all my things; what have you found of all your household objects? Set it here, before my kinsmen and yours, and let them decide between us two." He went on a bit more, emphasizing how diligently he had worked for Laban through the years in spite of Laban's unfair treatment. Though it may have been satisfying for Jacob to vent, it was unnecessary in any larger sense. He has won. Outwitted by Jacob, Laban had run him down, threatened him, accused him of theft, searched his tents, and found nothing. This public double humiliation has shown Laban to be a fool. His authority over Jacob is at an end.

Laban and Jacob then make a covenant that amounts to an agreement about territorial boundaries. The next morning, Laban says good-bye to his daughters and grandchildren and turns for home.

When Jacob first set out from his father's house after taking the blessing, possibly the greatest risk to the covenant with Yahweh was his immaturity: he had the *body* of a man, but not the mature *mind* of a man. In any society, but especially in a tribal society like Jacob's, how and when a boy makes the transition to manhood is a serious matter. From prehistory up to today, tribal rituals of male initiation have served to identify young men as full members of their community and reflect the larger reality that the tribe's security is now or will one day be in their hands. The tribe has no place for a self-absorbed boy housed in a man's body. Nor did Yahweh, not in the long term.

While Jacob had not undergone a formal ritual of coming of age or assuming his tribal responsibilities, the years since leaving home have offered him the chance to grow up. Now, following the divine command to "return to the land of your fathers where you were born," we see what the years have made of him. Jacob, who'd avoided direct confrontation, has been forced to confront his enraged father-in-law. With this encounter, Jacob has faced an old fear, has confronted the possibility of violent death. The cagey Jacob remains, but the boy-man has passed on.

As he turns from Laban, once again "angels of God encountered him [Jacob]." His earlier *dream* of angels had marked the beginning of Act Two of Jacob's life, and this *encounter* with angels would mark its end. Beth-El (House of God) and Mahanaim (the name he gave this spot) become bookends, "a literary framework for the Jacob and Laban cycle."[15] Act Three begins as he turns toward the home he'd fled and the brother he'd betrayed.

The Seed

And when, I wondered, would I rise at last above all this stuff, the accidental, the merely phenomenal, the wastefully and randomly human, and be fit to enter higher worlds?

— SAUL BELLOW, *Humboldt's Gift*

84

NOW THERE'S NO AVOIDING A FACE-TO-FACE WITH THE INCONVENIENT BROTHER. BUT WOULD HE *STILL* BE ANGRY? MUSINGS ON RESENTMENT

The text doesn't mention whether Jacob thought of Esau over the years, though it's only reasonable to assume it. During those days in the wilderness, running from his brother's rage, surely he'd kept a close watch over his shoulder, and as the years passed, had known anxious moments from wondering who that figure shimmering against the horizon might be. His wits had been his strength and protection, along with a certain knack for just-in-time escapes. But with Laban behind him and Esau ahead, he had no escape. Besides, going back, facing his brother, was the right thing to do: he'd sensed it, and Yahweh had said it. Still, as the moment drew near, and with him not knowing what to expect from his brother and fearing the worst, he must have been frightened at the thought of Esau resolute on revenge.

After twenty years, would Esau *still* be angry? In the last mention of Esau in the text, he was "consoling himself" by planning to kill Jacob. In other words, the idea of murdering his brother made him feel better. That's a lot of rage that might not go away after a few days, months, or even years. Perhaps the initial heat had dissipated, and then Esau had faced the realities of things as they were—a life far less abundant than the one he'd imagined. Perhaps the resentment, cooler now but no less potent, had simply planted itself beneath the surface, sinking roots, dormant but ready to grow again.

It's axiomatic that, given time and nurture—even *unconscious* nurture—a resentment can gain such momentum, claim so much psychological and spiritual ground that it takes over a life, acquiring such a bright halo of normality that it becomes virtually inseparable from one's identity. I've watched people transform their lives by letting go of powerful, decades-old resentments — it was not easy for them, but worth it to finally put down the burden. And I've watched resentment junkies recommit their lives to the bottomlessness of resentment as a wellspring of blame for their failures in love, in work, as excuses for their most unconscionable behavior.

I need only look in the mirror. My own resentment against my mother for her addiction to alcohol and pills was *the* organizing principle in my life. Prolonged immaturity, extramarital affairs, failure in my first marriage, my core belief that women were fundamentally untrustworthy — through the illogic of resentment, I believed *all* of it was my mother's fault, none of it mine. It was foolish, yes, and unreasonable, but the resentment gave me leave to behave as I please. More than that, it fed my need for things to make sense by providing a sensible answer for how it was possible to be successful and unhappy.

Imagine, as Jacob might have imagined, that each of the more than seven thousand days since the day he had stolen the blessing had brought Esau some reminder of that other life that should have been his. Now, see yourself in Jacob's present circumstance. There is no 911. You and your extended family are in the open, vulnerable, at the mercy of this man of the field, this hunter accustomed to killing and blood and who may have spent years nurturing his hatred.

To deal with his fears and protect his family, Jacob needed on-the-ground intelligence, so he sent messengers ahead to tell Esau that he was coming, where he'd been, and what he was bringing with him, along with the toadying salutation, "I send this message to my lord in the hope of gaining your favor." The messengers returned with nothing more to say than that Esau was coming to greet him — Esau and *four hundred armed men*.

85

THE BLESSING THIEF REVERTS TO WHAT HE KNOWS BEST.
BUT THIS TIME HE IS DIFFERENT

Now what? For the first time in twenty years, Jacob, who had depended on little other than his brains, prayed. And a lovely prayer it was, though it comes as no surprise that he began and ended it with a reminder to Yahweh that he had been promised a big future. Jacob finished. Waited. No answer. So, with *that* behind him, he went into high gear, doing what he did best — managing the outcome, playing with the other guy's head, giving him, or seeming to give him, what he wanted. The Trickster was *back*!

Jacob began his play with a gift, a mixed herd made up of male and female goats, ewes and rams, camels with their colts, cows and bulls, and male and female donkeys—some six hundred animals. But this sort of gift giving in that culture was a tricky affair, and it had to begin with the right word. Jacob told his servants to use the word *minhah*, which could be interpreted by the receiver as an "expression of friendship and respect . . . [or] a tribute in recognition of the donor's subordinate status. The ambiguity . . . is intentional. Esau is free to interpret it as he wishes."[16] In other words, between the lines, Jacob is telling Esau, *Look, if you want to think of me as your friend, that's okay by me! If you want to think of me as a sycophantic, simpering loser, that's okay, too!*

When Jacob had called on the Trickster to steal the blessing, he had been greedy and ambitious. With Laban he'd used his wiles to gain property and revenge. Now, however, what he most cares about extends beyond his own well-being, to the well-being of all those who depend on him. Now, with Esau approaching, his intentions unknown, Jacob's motive is life, *more life*—for himself and his family, and his servants and their families. He is *not* out to cheat Esau, but to cheat death. The Trickster he now discovers could be used for purposes other than self-service.

86

LIKE THE BLESSING THIEF, I DISCOVER THAT THE TRICKSTER CAN SUPPORT A GOAL NOT *TOO* ETHICALLY CHALLENGED, OR, "HOW TO LOSE A BIG CLIENT IN THREE DAYS AND BE (ALMOST) HAPPY ABOUT IT"

Houston, Texas

Several years ago, my second-biggest client asked that I conduct a team-building workshop for a group of blue-collar men who'd been chosen for an experimental project. Like any program designed to bring about change, the workshops that my colleagues and I conducted regularly delivered the sort of shock to the system almost certain to bring out the surliness in any group. These guys, however, *arrived* surly and I'd soon had enough. With another group I might have tempered my tendency to be blunt, but these were rough, worldly men, like my father, my uncles, and most of the men I'd known in my youth. So, deciding to throw propriety to the wind, I said, "Look, we've got two days together, and I've already had enough of your shit. You all can either come clean about the bug you've got up your collective asses, or I'll end this thing right now, and you can explain it to your superiors." Sullen expressions gave way to angry glares, which either meant they'd start talking, or they'd cross their arms and legs and stonewall, or they'd simply get up and walk out.

Their anger was short-lived. A few, the team leader among them, now appeared to be studying me, as if deciding whether I might be trusted. Then he began talking. They were a handpicked team, brought together for this particular project. Right away, they'd discovered a flaw in the plan—namely, that without additional team members, the project would fail. When they had reported this up-line, however, they had been told that if they were as competent as management assumed them to be, their numbers would be sufficient. *But we are that competent,* they'd replied, *which is why we can see problems you can't see!* Management responded with a veiled threat of termination if they didn't get on with it.

It was all so unreasonable that they had begun digging around, asking questions, finally finding their own Deep Throat, who'd told them that the upper management who'd designed the project weren't about to be told by anyone at their level that they'd made a mistake. When the project failed, however, the blue-collar men would be blamed, perhaps even terminated for incompetence. Since I'd been hired by corporate, they'd assumed I was part of it. I told them I was not part of it, that I too was outraged, and that my past experience made it easy to assume some of the company brass were capable of such a thing.

What to do? Given the situation, it would serve no purpose to go forward with the team-building workshop I'd planned. When one of the group mentioned that the executive committee would be meeting on Friday of that week, I had an idea. I asked if any of the committee members were good guys who might listen. They said yes. Then I asked if they were absolutely certain of their need for more people. Yes. How many? Three. Could they prove it? Yes. Well, since we had three days on our hands—the workshop was a Tuesday and a Thursday, with Wednesday off—why not build team cohesion by drawing up a plan for turning the game back on the bad guys? They *liked* that—but how? You step out of your world and into theirs, I told them. You create a presentation, using facts and reason *only*—no emotion, no recriminations—in which you make an airtight case for why you must have these additional team members. Then, on Friday morning, you show up in suits, ties, and polished shoes, and ask, *politely,* for time on the executive committee's agenda. Once inside, unless one of the bad guys asks a question, ignore them and focus your attention on the good guys, as if making your presentation to them. Then again, the committee might refuse to see you, so you'll need to decide before you arrive if it's worth it to crash the party.

Let's do it, they said. So we began laying the groundwork.

That was Tuesday. On Wednesday, while one group spent the day in research, another went shopping for clothes, and another for various supplies. We finished our preparations on Thursday. On Friday, four of the team members, dressed to the nines, made their presentation. Since their proof was undeniable, their case was made, and they got the additional people they needed. They were thrilled. They phoned me with the news and I was thrilled. Several in upper management were not thrilled. On Monday I was told I would not be invited back.

Idiotic? Quixotic? My options had seldom seemed so clearly defined. Option one was to follow the original plan, get through the two days, then go home and try to convince myself that I'd not *really* played a role in the possible ruin of their careers. Option two was to propose a plan that might have shown them how to save their project, maybe even their jobs, spend the two days working with them, then go home, wait for corporate to call, and try to convince myself I was not a moron.

Did I care that I lost the account? Yes. It was a dependable income stream that might well have increased. And there was a time when I would have gone through the motions just to keep that account, but just as Jacob was no longer the man he'd been, neither was I. To borrow a lovely biblical image, the years had given each of us a new heart. I knew that walking away from those men would've haunted me to distraction for years to come. So, less money, fewer ghosts. I got more than I lost. It was worth it.

To dispel any lingering miasma of sanctimony, however, let me say that my so-called new heart was doing battle with a dark impulse, that same "crouching beast" about which Yahweh had warned Cain. Along with helping out those men, I also wanted—*needed*—to defeat those other men, the ones who'd assumed they could do with us, with *me*, as they pleased. Just as Jacob had left Laban nearly destitute, if I could've hatched a plan that would've left *them* without jobs, I'd have done it. Even now, on reflection, I'm aware of a residue of that resentment and find myself wondering just how many I've left in my own wake, wishing the same for me.

87

A STRANGER ATTACKS FROM OUT OF THE DARK,
CHEATS A LITTLE, THEN GIVES THE BLESSING THIEF
A NEW NAME

The next day would bring the meeting with Esau. But first Jacob took some time alone, and he sent his wives, children, and servants across the river, the Jabbok. Then night fell. Suddenly, from out of the dark, a stranger attacked Jacob. They would fight all night, neither gaining the advantage until, with dawn breaking over the hills, the stranger "wrenched Jacob's hip at the socket." Still, Jacob held on. Alarmed by the approach of day, "almost as a vampire or a ghoul would,"[17] the opponent pleaded to be let go. Jacob agreed, but with the caveat that he first receive a blessing. Asking Jacob's name, he said, "Your name shall no longer be Jacob, but Israel, for you have striven with beings divine and human and have prevailed."* Then, depending on how the Hebrew verb is translated, the opponent either "leaves" Jacob or "blesses" him. Either way, it was over and, "Jacob named the place Peniel, meaning, 'I have seen a divine being face to face, yet my life has been preserved.'"

But with exactly *whom, what* had Jacob been face-to-face? Opinions vary. Since the idiom *face to face* is reserved for divine-human encounters, and since the stranger, at will, dislocated Jacob's hip, maybe it was Yahweh. Or, as one midrash suggests, this was "a wrestling match with 'the Prince of Esau, Esau's guardian angel.'"[18] Or it was Esau himself, or Sammael, the angel of death, as Harold Bloom suggests in *The Book of J*, "or if Yahweh, then from that dark side of Yahweh?"[19] Or the story may have originated in a "well-known tale of a hero fighting a river divinity."[20]

Whatever the opponent's identity, he was in equal parts life giver and life taker. Jacob's claim that his life had been preserved in the encounter is balanced by an equal motif of death—which fits the observations of mystics from every great religion that the attainment of profound insight, transformation, or spiritual depth (as opposed to religiosity) is a *means* rather than an end or purpose in itself. It is impossible to achieve without a struggle with the self, with the Other (God, Life, the Universe). *And* that struggle is a continual, evolving, and often unpleasant process of birth, death, and rebirth of consciousness, identity, and connection.

---

*That he will still be called Jacob is explained in the Babylonian Talmud (folio 13a): "This does not mean that the name Jacob shall be obliterated, but that Israel shall be the principal name and Jacob a secondary one."

88

WHICH HE'LL THINK ABOUT IF HIS PLAN
FOR SURVIVING HIS ENCOUNTER WITH THE INCONVENIENT BROTHER
AND THOSE FOUR HUNDRED MEN SUCCEEDS

Jacob now crosses the river Jabbok and rejoins his family. Despite having just brawled with *who-knows-who* in human form, on seeing Esau he becomes obsequious. Jacob goes out ahead to meet Esau, fully prostrating himself seven times as he approaches. And "Esau ran to greet him. He embraced him, and falling on his neck, kissed him, and they wept."

Next, Esau refuses Jacob's gift. This is awkward, given that Esau's acceptance of the gift would mean that everybody gets to live. But Jacob is ready with just the right word for the occasion. Having instructed his servants to use *minhah* ("gift") when presenting the herd to Esau, Jacob himself now, face-to-face with his brother and the four hundred, pleads with him to "take my present." This time he uses the word *berakhah*—literally "blessing"—which "signals to Esau that the present is in a way a reparation for the purloining of the paternal blessing twenty years earlier."[21] In other words, what Jacob had taken in the past, he now symbolically and humbly returns.

Then, surprisingly, Jacob says to Esau, "For to see your face is to see the face of God." It's a strange metaphor, this. Was he pointedly implying that *I know it was you last night*? Or did Jacob believe that he *had* seen the face of God, meaning that he could no longer be the same man who'd stolen the blessing? Esau doesn't ask. Our enigma-loving narrator won't tell. Finally, Esau accepts Jacob's gift, and does *not* offer a gift in return. Hardly an affront, this was *the* sign that, for Esau, the gift "is the settling of an old score, not a polite exchange of civilities."[22] It was over.

Or was it? Now Esau will invite Jacob and his family to accompany him to his home, some distance away. Jacob accepts but tells his brother that it will take a bit of time to get themselves together, so he and his men should go on ahead, and they'll catch up. Esau agrees, leaves, and then Jacob leads his group away from Esau and toward the home of his father and mother.

The text does not explain Esau's invitation, though it fits with the cultural demand for hospitality and with what might have been Esau's desire to extend his time with his brother. Nor does it explain Jacob's ruse, though interpreters have speculated that Esau was laying a trap and that Jacob sensed it. While Jacob's wariness is understandable—I'd likely have done the same—there is no hint of danger in the text. Besides, Esau is a man without subtlety. If he'd wanted Jacob and his family dead, he and his four hundred mercenaries could have made quick work of it on the open ground where they met.

89

THE NEED TO SPIN THE BLESSING THIEF'S BEHAVIOR NECESSITATES PAINTING THE INCONVENIENT BROTHER AS A SCOUNDREL

Rabbinic sources regard Esau as a bad guy, but we should consider the story itself. Let's go back to the moment of their reunion—for which, in my youth, my Sunday school mates and I, from boredom, created a Hollywood schmaltz version: *The brothers, smiling, weeping, arms wide open, run toward one other in slow motion, Jacob flopping facedown on the ground, getting up, flopping, getting up—seven times. Finally, they embrace, weep, and there's the kissing on necks.* Ancient interpreters took a more earnest tone. Jon Levenson points to a midrash suggesting that Esau meant to *bite* his brother. Nahum Sarna points to another midrash, this one claiming that his kiss was the *only* thing Esau ever did that was motivated by love, and not hate.

The biblical text reveals little about Esau in these later verses, just as it tells us little about him at the beginning of his and Jacob's story. He was redheaded, hairy, and a hunter, characteristics that were considered uncouth and dangerous. We know he gave up his birthright at so cheap a price that it became a metaphor for selling out, which suggests a weak character but not an evil one. We're told of his poignant grief at learning that Jacob had stolen the blessing, and how it had given way to thoughts of murder. Yet Esau has been made by interpreters to appear so loathsome that Jacob's actions, in contrast, seem to rise to the heroic—*Jacob didn't really steal the blessing, he rescued it! Indeed, he saved it!* Right. Think of this as politics—image making.

One more thing about Esau. If his forgiveness was genuine, then the man he'd forgiven was the one who'd robbed him, not the man Jacob had become. If so, it was the mature gesture of one who, like his brother, had undergone a radical change of consciousness and character.

Surely Jacob's youthful visions of life as the blessing-bearer had been grander—*easier*—than what he had actually lived through. In the years since Beth-El, he endured the machinations of Laban, the discontent of Rachel and Leah, and the burdens of a growing family, yet he always steps up and does what is required. You'd think he could catch a break.

90

DINAH

Leah's seventh child, her youngest, and the only daughter among the four women with whom Jacob had children, Dinah is a mute, diaphanous presence who becomes a pawn in an alpha struggle that plays itself out as a sort of poor man's *Iliad*. We're told that one day she left their encampment and "went out to visit [to *see*] the daughters of the land." What was she up to? Nahum Sarna writes that "the verbal stem 'to get out' . . . can connote coquettish or promiscuous conduct."[23] This venturing out by a young girl, presumably in her early teens, who was not local but rather from a nomadic family, puts her in danger of rape. Why would she take such a risk? We don't know what motivated her excursion or how she managed to slip away unnoticed, only that she was seen by Shechem, the son of Hamor, ruler of the nearby city-state *also* named Shechem, who "saw her, and took her, and lay with her by force." Or not—once again, the verb is ambiguous. Where some scholars read "force," Leon Kass suggests that the text implies that Dinah initiated the encounter, but in Richard Friedman's opinion, while the wording leaves us guessing about exactly what transpired, "Shechem's act, taking place before the request for marriage, is regarded as disgraceful by Dinah's family."[24]

Whether the sex had been forced or consensual, when it was over, Shechem the boy was in love, so he asked his father, Hamor, king of Shechem, to "Get me this girl for a wife," meaning *Please tell her father, Jacob, that, in spite of my having already violated her, I want to marry her, okay?* Hamor agreed and, along with his son and, we can presume, guards, servants, and possibly gifts, paid a call on Jacob's encampment.

Though the text doesn't reveal how he knew, not only was Jacob already aware of what had happened, he'd sent a runner to tell his sons of it, so that by the time Hamor and his party arrived, they had come in from the fields and were present at the meeting. Leaving out the part about the sexual violation, but sweetening the deal by proposing a general exchange of daughters, that is, intermarriage, between the two peoples, and the financial gains that would accrue for Jacob's family—a sort of *Why don't we turn this to our mutual advantage?*—Hamor asked that Dinah be allowed to marry Shechem. Now it was Shechem's turn to speak. As the boy who'd caused the problem and violated the honor of Jacob's family, as well as the one who was now asking for the favor of an alliance with Jacob's family, he might be expected first to apologize then plead for forgiveness. Instead, apparently hearing the muse whisper some Late Bronze Age version of

"If you want to run with the big dogs, you have to get off the porch," he jumped in and says bluntly, "Do me this favor, and I will pay whatever you tell me."

You violate my daughter and . . . ask me to do you this favor!? You're not dead! How's that for a favor? But Jacob did not speak. His sons, however, said they could go along with the marriage provided Hamor and Shechem and all the men of the city "become like us in that every man is circumcised." *Consent to that*, they said, *and we can get to trading daughters, becoming one kindred—the whole enchilada.* And were they ever *lying!* For one thing, while the request was reasonable enough, Jacob's family was still a relatively small band. Any marriage that resulted in the commingling of their cultures would have threatened their identity. Besides, at play beneath their offer was their real strategy, a plan containing an exquisite irony in that "the organ that committed the rape is the device by which Jacob's sons avenge their sister."[25] Avenge their sister, that is, *and* walk off with the wealth of the entire city in their pockets. So, deceit, revenge, plunder, and a "battle over intermarriage . . . fought by men over [Dinah's] passive body."[26] Comical, cleverly vengeful, and profitable, it seemed to be a plan worthy of the Blessing Thief.

Yet unbeknownst to Jacob, his sons had a darker motive. Believing the sons' offer to be legitimate, Hamor and Shechem agreed to circumcision, went back to the city, and started cutting. On the third day, when the newly circumcised men of the city were at their weakest, Simeon and Levi armed themselves, entered the city, and killed all the men, including Hamor and Shechem. Then the brothers seized the entire wealth of the city, plus the women and children, who would now become their property.

Jacob was not happy with this outcome. Turning Shechem into a ghost town was over the top, and his sons had acted without his permission, which could make him appear weak. When word of this massacre got around, not only might it ruin his reputation, the other city-states could decide to form a coalition and wipe them all out. To their father's objections, Simeon or Levi gave a simplistic answer: *So we should have just let our sister, your daughter, be treated like some skank?*

And there endeth the story. The text does not point out that Jacob's more subtle yet sweeping decrees had already fully avenged Dinah's and the family's honor, and that the sons themselves had violated that honor by violating Jacob's agreement and usurping his authority and judgment. Are we to believe that Jacob, *the Blessing Thief*, always the smartest guy in the room, did not suspect his sons were up to something? Even with circumcision, intermarriage would inevitably bring a melding of cultures, including religions. Was he suddenly timid and weak, giving his headstrong, violent sons room to take their own initiative, or was he "seeing here an occasion for collective action that could unify his sons in defense of their own"?[27] If Jacob had sanctioned a plan that took revenge on only the boy, Shechem, who, after all, was a prince, this action "would unquestionably have resulted in countervengeance; one could hardly expect the Shechemites to regard his killing as just."[28] In other words, to kill him and not take out the men who surely would be roused to come after them would have been foolish. It just didn't work that way, not there, not then, and not now.

Genesis's interpreters are mainly perplexed at the story's lack of both human and divine direction. There's not a single indication of the divine will, and the narrator, J, simply reports the story, telling it "with a chilly neutrality, so that even at the end there is no way to know whether the Bible is seeking to claim that the reaction of Simeon and Levi was justified or not."[29] But the interpreters needed to know, and in the phrase "such a thing ought not to be done," the very same phrase used by Abimelech when he'd protested to Abraham about the patriarch's duplicity, they found a satisfactory answer. Kugel tells us that the phrase could be ascribed to the brothers as an "implied quotation," that is, the syntax might imply that they'd said to each other *words to the effect that* Shechem had committed an outrage and that such a thing ought not to be done." But that would mean that Jacob's sons had taken it on themselves to slaughter and plunder a city. However, "read in a somewhat different way . . . these words can take on a different meaning. For if . . . one believes that the entire text of the Bible is divinely inspired or in some other way comes from God, then it might appear that 'such a thing ought not to be done actually represents God's own judgment on what happened . . . ' That is what the ancient interpreters said:

'You [God] gave a sword to take revenge on the strangers who had loosed the adornment of a virgin to defile her . . . *You* said, 'It shall not [ought not] be done thus'—yet they did so.'

—Judith 9:2"[30]

For Jacob's clan, Dinah's violation is a crisis of the first order. Their own patriarch's daughter has been dishonored, and so the tribe shared in that dishonor. Their identity as a separate people and their physical survival are at stake in the resolution of this crisis. Their options, as they perceive them, are either reconciliation through intermarriage or bloodletting. The former, however liberal the terms in their favor, means the beginning of the end of themselves as a separate, covenantal people. The latter means not a little blood, but an ocean of it.

Still, did these sons of Jacob slaughter a city and feel *nothing*? Standing next to their father, their robes drenched with blood, their reply to his concern *is* defensive, certainly, but more than that it is immediate, unreflective. There is no admission that they had acted without forethought. Despite having just hacked to death an untold number of men, having heard the pleading and wailing of wives and children, these sons of Jacob and Leah appear to be unmoved by what they've done, as if they are wholly incapable of remorse. In his monumental *Joseph and His Brothers*, Thomas Mann does not present the brothers as men seeking revenge on the one who'd raped their sister, nor as defenders of family honor, but as opportunists who saw a window through which they could sack a city for personal gain, while claiming it was a justifiable act. That the men of the city had to be slaughtered and their own sister's life destroyed was of no concern to them.

Bible scholars offer a number of reasons why we can assume that the story of Dinah and Shechem was itself to be a later insertion. For instance, in Genesis 34, Jacob has nothing to do with the raid and is furious with his sons for what they've done, then, in chapter 48, verse 22, "almost as if these two texts in Genesis . . . had never met,"[31] he takes credit for fighting the Shechemites. For another, Shechem will show up later in the Bible as a prosperous center of trade, with no hint that it had ever been a ghost town. Furthermore, without the Dinah story, when Jacob says of Simeon and Levi that "their weapons are tools of lawlessness . . . when angry they slay men" (Genesis 49:5–7), then curses their anger and their wrath, his words would make no sense.

Jacob was not a violent man, so it is impossible to imagine him having any part in the sort of violence wrought by his sons in this story. As he did with Laban, he might have relieved the king and his son of all their possessions and, while they'd have never seen him leave town—probably at a gallop—they'd certainly have been left standing. Once again it is time for Jacob and his household to pack up and go, a departure welcomed by neighboring city-states that were too terrified to pursue him as Laban and his sons had. They go back to Beth-El, where Jacob, in an insertion from P, again builds an altar and names the place, and for the second time in the narrative is given the name "Israel." After they leave Beth-El, they begin making their way toward a place called Ephrath when Rachel goes into labor and dies giving birth to Benjamin, her second son, and Jacob's twelfth. Soon after, Reuben, the firstborn son, "lay with Bilhah, his father's concubine, and Israel found out." The Talmud sees this as an attempt to "defile the slave girl of his mother's rival, Rachel, and so make her sexually taboo to Jacob,"[32] but modern commentators recognize it as "a way of making claim to his [a ruler's] authority."[33] Once again, as in the story of Dinah, the verb arguably indicates forced sex—rape—and "the same verb is used when the report of the rape of Dinah is brought to Jacob." Jacob, as before, remains silent about the matter—that is, until, on his deathbed, his sons gathered before him, he says, "Reuben, you are my first-born, my might and my vigor, exceeding in rank, and exceeding in honor . . . ," *but you climbed into my bed and brought disgrace, so you're out!* Finally, they reached Mamre, Jacob's childhood home, where after a time, his father Isaac died and was buried by Esau and Jacob.

91

THE BLESSING THIEF IS THE IRONIC
TURNING POINT IN THE LARGER STORY

In time, Jacob would become the embodiment of the people of Israel. It is in human nature to exalt our heroes, and to spin their faults into virtues. The Americans have mythologized George Washington and Abraham Lincoln, each at the center of crucial chapters of the national story, and each partly the product of spin. Even before his death, my maternal grandfather had become an icon of wisdom and warmth for me. My own father has grown in stature since his death, as have three mentors, each of whom arrived in my life at just the right moment. These men had brilliant personalities and extraordinary flaws. Each had a vital, vibrant presence, but each could be a superior ass—except for my grandfather. Yet these negative attributes do not detract a bit from what I gained from my time with them.

Whether viewed as literature or history, Jacob's life is a reason for celebration, not spin. Yes, he was a self-centered, sleazy thief, and then he changed, matured to become a useful, *balanced* adult—that is, a *semi*reformed sinner, whom I'll take every day of the week and twice on Sunday over one who's never cussed, smoked, lied, gotten drunk, been in jail (or close to it), and at least *had* adulterous yearnings. (I think of Emerson: "The louder he talked of his honor, the faster we counted our spoons.") Indeed, Jacob's strength of character, his humanness, is the product of this transformation. The narrator makes no attempt to wash away Jacob's darkness but draws a character who, with time, learns to contain it, manage it, and balance the dark with the light. Jacob evolves. We see the self-absorbed boy-man transformed by a dream, by falling in love, by cruelty and betrayal, by the vagaries and responsibilities of family, and by embracing what he most feared.

Because he evolves, Jacob is a new creature in the Genesis narrative. His predecessors are at times and of necessity a sneaky lot, but they had neither his independence of mind nor the breadth of his self-sufficiency. And they certainly lacked the sort of cheek he'd demonstrated at Beth-El, when he'd made his faithfulness a commodity deliverable on Yahweh's completion of a to-do list. Until Jacob, the characters of Genesis are far more rigidly drawn. But now we watch a spoiled, corrupted young man stirred by mystery, by love, and by the sting of a betrayal that, ironically, mirrored his own. All of it would mature him, prepare him, and, finally, deliver him to Peniel and the defining moment of hand-to-hand physical and internal struggle that would *take* his life, then give him *more* life. Before the dream at Beth-El, he was a boy in a man's body. Before the incident at Peniel, he had evolved to become Jacob, the man. Afterward, he is both Jacob *and* Israel, a man and the seed of a nation.

Jacob will now move into the background, making way for the emergence of his son, Joseph. More by default than through the ritual of formal blessing given Jacob, the responsibility for the promise will pass to Jacob's eleventh son, who, in his short life, has managed to eclipse even his father's capacity for self-absorption and the fostering of fraternal hatred.

PART IV

THE DREAM READER

He was a better man in his dreams.
—JIM CRACE, *Quarantine*

The Brat

His self-confidence . . . never needed that overhauling and lubrication that is called probing one's conscience.
— ROBERT MUSIL, *The Man Without Qualities*

92

JOSEPH PROVES HIMSELF TO BE HIS FATHER'S SON

Joseph can epitomize every self-absorbed little creep you've ever wanted to ask, *Who the hell do you think you are?* but didn't because his answer would be an impenetrable arrogance. Yet with some perspective, you may come to realize that you particularly dislike him because you're just seeing in him that part of *yourself* that you hate.

Joseph's brothers must have really hated themselves—given what they felt for him, which was off the chart of any normal sibling rivalry. They despised the ground he walked on and the air he breathed. In the crass vernacular of my own childhood, they pretty much hated his guts.

But who *was* he? And who did he *think* he was?

The narrator's idea of Joseph's place follows the solemn declaration: "These are the generations of Jacob." Where one would expect a full list of Jacob's sons, however, only Joseph is mentioned. Early interpreters took this simplification to imply "that Joseph was Jacob's son *par excellence* . . . the one who was like Jacob himself."[1] In fact, in the *Testament of Joseph*, written as though by Joseph's own hand, the author writes, "And [God] preserved me to old age in strength and in beauty, for I was like Jacob in all things."[2] Next we're told that Joseph is not only seventeen, but "youthful"—a *young* seventeen, immature for his age. A small boy when his mother died, Joseph had been pampered by his father, made a daddy's boy in the way that Rebekah had made Jacob a mama's boy, his childhood a suspension between his brothers and their father. At seventeen he was suspended between the world of children and the world of men, with little pushing him to develop the attributes of the latter. Certainly his being the first son of Jacob's beloved Rachel gave him an automatic leg up on his brothers. Within families showing a large age span between oldest and youngest siblings, it's not unusual to find that the parents are far less strict with the latter, to the dismay of the former. In my own family, my sister and I, born three years apart, caught the brunt of our parents' desire to raise properly behaved children. To our parents, the idea of an adult striking a child was barbaric, so with the exception of the time when I was three or four and my mother washed out my mouth with soap for saying "damn," we received no physical punishments, only the tedium of long hours in my room in order to *think about it*, and days with no dessert, and sometimes writing "I won't (fill in the blank)" a hundred times or more. (Our mother taught second grade for twenty-five years.) Eight years after I was born came a second son, but it was the third one, three years later, for whom a trend toward relaxed parenting became what I took to be a license for getting away with murder. "You'd have killed me for that" became a mantra, my protest at the injustice of letting my baby brother get away with things for which I'd have incurred at least a lecture from my mother, one of those looks from my father—followed by exile to my room. Just out of their line of sight, my brother would be making faces, trying to get me to blow my stack and chase him, which would draw a lecture from Mom, the look from Dad, and more of the same from little brother. At the same time he *was* a cute little boy—freckled, happy, big-eared, smart—and my parents were seasoned now, less obsessed about the small things, and *tired*. Maybe Jacob too was tired, and maybe Joseph was the cute, bright kid onto whom he could transfer his affection—a light in the ocean of grief following the death of Rachel who, but for his mother, had been the only person to whom he'd ever been close.

93

JOSEPH TATTLES ON HIS BROTHERS, GETS A TECHNICOLORED COAT. HIS RELATIONSHIP WITH HIS BROTHERS APPROACHES THE TIPPING POINT

My neighborhood gang of five was so tight that we didn't worry about one of us ratting out the others. Cub Scouts, school, and Sunday school were different, as if the larger, more structured social systems required the added dynamic of a tattletale—not an integrity watchdog, but one willing to barter information for favors and power. In Jacob's huge family, that tattletale was Joseph.

Right away the author tells us that, when Joseph was seventeen, he "tended the flocks with his brothers, as a helper to the sons of his father's concubines, Bilhah and Zilpah. And Joseph brought bad reports of them to their father." Exactly what they'd done we're not told, though interpreters speculated that "Joseph must have reported something concerning their conduct as shepherds."[3] One thought they might have slaughtered one of the better animals for their own use while another wrote that, yes, they had slaughtered a sheep, but one that, already mauled by a bear, was beyond saving. Whatever they'd done, Joseph's "report" has the earmarks of a boy telling on his big brothers in order to incur his father's favor. Imagine the brothers in question standing before their father, his face wearing *his* particular mix of disappointment, anger, and disapproval: "So, I understand that you boys . . ." Whether Jacob mentioned Joseph as their accuser, they'd have known it was him: *So, he's watching everything we do? Reporting every little infraction to our father?* Now they hated him more. Next Jacob made for Joseph an "ornamented tunic," or "coat of many colors," and "they hated him so that they could not speak a friendly word to him."

When most everyone in a social system as enclosed as a family of desert nomads so despises one of its members, you'd think that that member, for reasons of companionship or personal safety, would adjust his behavior within the group, but Joseph did not. Isolated from all but his father, he changes nothing, but goes forward, as if he were living in a sort of dream state, aware of what he was doing, even of its effect, yet driven to continue, to force his brothers' hand so they would do what had to be done.

94

JOSEPH DREAMS

Jacob's dream at Beth-El was a prophetic vision given during a divinely induced coma. Next to it, Joseph's dreams, made up of symbols, are downright pedestrian. That the symbols in these dreams are as much emblematic of the lad's inflated self-image as they are prophetic seems self-evident; as he describes them to his brothers, he is "self-absorbed, blithely assuming everyone will be fascinated by the details of his dreams."[4] To his brothers, who already see him as an overconfident, self-important weasel, he says: "There we were, binding sheaves in the field, when suddenly my sheaf stood up and remained upright; then your sheaves gathered around and bowed low to my sheaf." The brothers take this to mean that he intends to reign over them and rule them, and they hate him even more. Oblivious, he tells them of yet another dream: "And this time, the sun, the moon, and eleven stars were bowing down to me." Even his father doesn't like that one, saying, "Are we to come . . . and bow low to you to the ground?" And, yes, his brothers, the very same fellows who'd had no problem slaughtering a city, hate him still *more*.

*   *   *

Joseph may indeed have been no more than an egomaniacal boy-man impervious to signs that he was pushing his brothers too far. In *Joseph and His Brothers*, Thomas Mann writes that Joseph's "blissful self-confidence was, despite all unambiguous signs to the contrary, a kind of self pampering that told him that everyone loved him more truly than they loved themselves."[5] Thomas Harris, in his bestselling *I'm OK, You're OK*, identified the ego position, "I'm OK, You're *Not* OK" as potentially dangerous, a pathology that requires no empathetic consideration of others, no meaningful examination of self or motives, and from which, having no equals, one cannot be meaningfully criticized. Was this Joseph? Probably, but only for part of his life. Think of it as the young Joseph's temporary interpretation of reality, which, as it does for most of us when we're young, cocky, and stupid, will bring reality down on him like an anvil.

Not long ago, my wife and I went to see a movie about a dog that, as the story begins, doesn't realize that he is a character in a television series about a dog with superpowers. His belief that his powers are real makes it impossible for him to be in a realistic relationship with things as they are. For him to be effective in the real, that is, *nontelevision* world—in this case, to rescue his friend from the fiendish bad guys—he is required to see himself as he is. Not less than he is, just not bulletproof. Mann's Joseph is in roughly the same fix. Created in the belief that others love him more than they love themselves—which would, indeed, qualify as a superpower— Joseph's world does not contain rancorous brothers who truly hate him, whose hatred automatically predetermines how they interpret his dreams and react to the coat. In Mann's novel, Jacob shows the robe to Joseph but, concerned about how his other sons might react, decides that he should not wear it for now. But sent on an errand to see his brothers, Joseph, as deaf to voices wiser than his own as he is blind to the rage all around him, takes out the coat, puts it on, and heads out.

95

AS A SIDE NOTE, DID YOU KNOW THAT KING DAVID— *THE* DAVID—WAS ANOTHER BIBLICAL BRAT?

Joseph and David were cut from similar bolts of cloth, David's being a rougher weave. Also in his teens, he enters the biblical narrative in 1st Samuel, when the eponymous Samuel is told, "Fill your horn with oil and set out; I am sending you to Jesse the Bethlehemite, for I have decided on one of his sons to be king." Jesse had eight sons, and when Samuel arrived in Bethlehem, Jesse presented the seven oldest sons, but when David, the youngest, "ruddy-cheeked, bright-eyed, and handsome," arrived from the fields where he'd been tending the family sheep, "the Lord said, "Rise up and anoint him, for this is the one" (I Samuel 16:12).

A cursory reading of the story might tempt the reader to assume that David's conceit began in that moment, though the boy in the story does not appear to understand what has just happened. A closer reading produces some hard evidence that the lad's high opinion of himself went to the bone already and was every bit as rapturous as Joseph's. In the moments before his fight with Goliath, we get a full view of this arrogance. Sent by his father with provisions for his brothers and a gift for their commander, David arrived in the Israelite army encampment just in time to hear Goliath's challenge and witness the ensuing panic among the Israelites. Goliath's threats and boasts were a daily occurrence now, and it was a source of shame for the Israelite army that the Philistine giant, encased in a hundred pounds or so of battle armor, and sporting his oversized weaponry—javelin, spear, and sword—would step unhindered onto the field between the two armies. "Choose one of your men," he'd shout across the distance, "and let him come down against me. If he bests me in combat and kills me, we will become your slaves; but if I best him and kill him, you shall be our slaves and serve us." The guy was nine feet tall *before* he put on the armor, and he'd probably been a soldier since he was a boy. The Israelites themselves were good soldiers, but they were citizen soldiers, not professionals, and we can assume they were men of average size.

To David's mind, however, only a prize chump would fight Goliath on *his* terms. Forget the armor and the big pointy things, and forget the difference in strength and experience in battle. None of that mattered when a sling in the right hands—*his* hands—could hurl a projectile of the proper size, shape, and weight with uncanny accuracy, and at a velocity (about thirty-two meters per second) sufficient to cause extensive brain trauma, killing even a giant. Therefore, if David chose to accept the challenge, Goliath, the invincible, the mighty warrior, the pride of the fearsome Philistine army, would be bringing a sword to a gunfight. Who's the chump?

As the frightened soldiers pass him in retreat, David overhears a few of them mumbling about the reward promised to whoever killed the giant. It was huge, but was it real? He asks another group of soldiers, "What will be done for the man who kills that Philistine and removes the disgrace from Israel? Who is that uncircumcised Philistine that he dares to defy the ranks of the living God?" Or, without the religious, patriotic sentiment, *What's in it for me if I put this guy down?* Wealth, they told him, *and* the king's daughter in marriage, *and* no more taxes for anyone in his father's family. David was inspired.

But his brother, Eliab, overhears David speaking with the soldiers. Until then he had not known that his little brother was in the camp. His response, immediate and bitter, contained the history of a relationship beyond redeeming. The oldest of Jesse's sons, Eliab has no brotherly affection for or trust in his youngest brother. Working from the assumption that David was incapable of motives that are not entirely self-serving, he concluded that his brother's presence could mean only that, having decided he'd rather be here in camp, watching the battle, than back there, tending the family sheep, he'd simply walked away, leaving the flock to fend for itself. Eliab had no need to verify any of this because "I know your impudence and impertinence [literally, *badness of heart*]."

Unless we assume an imbalance in Eliab's mind or character, we're left with the fact that this man who'd known David since birth had come not merely to dislike his baby brother, but to consider him to be of such low character that, on an impulse, and without a pang of conscience, he would abandon the sheep left in his charge to the whims of weather and predators. As an older brother, my own feeling toward a much younger brother tended, in large part, to be paternal, protective — for David to have earned that depth of contempt from Eliab would have taken some doing. But just as Joseph was guilty of nothing more than egotism and naïveté, David was guilty neither of abandoning the sheep nor of leaving them unattended. About his conversation with the soldiers, David might have said to Eliab, *Look, it's just business, an opportunity worth exploring — certainly not worth getting yourself worked up about.* Instead he replied with a curt "What have I done now? I was only asking." Then, without waiting for an answer, turned his back to Eliab, and continued his conversation with the soldiers. It was a brush-off, a classic dismissal.

Having been the recipient of similar dismissals from people who are masters of the technique, and with whom I've had a "history," I can imagine Eliab's state of mind as David turned his back to him — the instant, near-to-violent rage that Esau felt at Jacob's betrayal, the same outrage that occupied Joseph's brothers time and again. Eliab did not act, of course, and Esau cooled with time, but Joseph's brothers' anger soon will pass the point of no return, when *Who do you think you are?* will explode into a murderous fury.

96

I SPECULATE ABOUT OTHER,
MAYBE DEEPER REASONS FOR HATING JOSEPH

Whether from nature or nurture, Joseph appears to be the brightest and most gifted of all Jacob's sons, who otherwise seem crude and rather oafish. None is shown to have Joseph's brains or his sense of self. They may have hated him, in part, for being Rachel's son, as six of the twelve brothers are Leah's sons (two of these by Zilpah, her slave girl). Surely Leah's bitterness toward her sister, her certainty that Rachel was the reason that she and her offspring were not as loved by Jacob, would not have gone unnoticed or unabsorbed.

Worry about their inheritance could also have influenced them. Did the brothers perceive Joseph as a usurper? Being Rachel's firstborn son, might he take what, by tradition, belonged to Reuben, Leah's firstborn son? Already we, and probably they, know of their father's proven willingness to go around *that* tradition. Also, we, and probably they, know of Reuben's violation of Bilhah, though Jacob's silence on the matter has left it unsettled, and left the brothers and us readers to wonder what their father was *not* saying.

Jacob's family was simmering with resentment and fear: Rachel was dead, but hardly gone, kept alive by Jacob's love, Joseph's presence, and Leah's hatred; Leah no doubt resented Joseph for the favor showed him by Jacob; she and her sons surely resented Jacob for what he would not give them—the affection she craved as his wife, the attention they craved as his sons. All that had gone to Rachel was now poured onto Joseph, who bore it all with a maddening air of entitlement. By the time Joseph strides into the narrative, he has already come to represent something bad to his brothers and, perhaps, someone who is just a bit evil. If only they could rid themselves of him, wouldn't their lives become sweet as new wine and honey?

97

AT TWENTY-ONE, I LEARN WHAT IT IS TO BE HATED

I've been disliked here and there in my life for various reasons, but only once have I known it to rise up to that level of virtuous contempt that can make group violence so cathartic an option. Not unlike Joseph, my part was a mix of naïveté, youthful insensitivity, arrogance, and stupidity. My antagonists saw me as a scapegoat for frustrations that, like that of Joseph's brothers, had been building for most of their lives.

Houston, Summer of '67

By mid-June, needing to make money for college, I'd found a job with a company that made asphalt-based roofing shingles, whose general manager was a friend of my father's. Entry-level hiring for the factory being way below his pay grade, by the time I started word was out on the factory floor that for the next few months they'd have to make room for some college boy whose daddy was a friend of the big boss—which, in fact, was true.

I was to be the stacker, the guy at the end of the manufacturing line. On the line, raw materials for making the shingles were transformed into their final form and wrapped. The packages passed by the man responsible for gluing the proper label and placing it just so on each package as it passed his station at the rate of about fifteen to twenty per minute—a far more difficult task than it appeared to be. Next, the stacker properly arranged the packages on wooden pallets. No big deal, I told the fellow who was showing me how to properly arrange the packages on the pallet. I'd done the same job at my father's dry-mix concrete plant for years, and with ninety-pound bags.

Most of the men I worked with that summer were pleasant enough, but a significant core of the younger men saw me as the incarnation of what they feared and despised and blamed for the disappointments of their lives. I would not be allowed to escape without a reckoning. At first, the hostility manifested itself in the jibes like "Must be nice having a daddy who can get you a job by picking up the phone," in the stares, and in the way "College Boy" became not so much a nickname as an epithet, and a gauntlet thrown at my feet. I wonder now if, floating inside all the enmity, waiting not to be asked but unleashed like some primal scream, was *Who do you think you are?* just before pounding me into the dirt.

I assumed it would pass, that once I proved my willingness to work as hard as any of them, they'd accept me. Instead they began running the line faster than I could take the packages off and properly stack them. Production slowed as packages rolled off the belt and broke open. After a few choruses of "If you can't do the job, College Boy, go back to your daddy," they'd run the line even faster. More broken product, more lost production, until "You break another package, College Boy, and your ass is mine."

Finally, the plant manager saw what they were up to and its effect on production and put a stop to it. The trouble might well have ended there, but my father, who was not the rich man they seemed to think he was, and who, while generous, had never been one to give the "big gift," astounded me with a 1965 Mustang convertible for my twenty-first birthday. The smart thing would've been to ride an old bike to work, but, like Joseph, I was naïve and showed up in that gleaming car. When asked about it, I said, "Yeah, my dad gave it to me for my birthday." I may as well have said, *Yeah, my dad gave it to me for the day when I say "Ciao" and go back to college and all those gorgeous girls with the long, long legs that rich guys like me get to play with as we ready ourselves for the goooood life. Bet you wish you had one.*

Compared to them, I did live a life of privilege. Unlike Joseph, I worked as hard as any of them while I was there, but it was only through my father's influence that I was there at all. My parents valued education, so I would leave that place and return to school for my senior year. My future seemed wide open, but without a university degree, theirs appeared limited to a job in that shingle factory, or another factory, or a refinery. I was already a symbol of both real and perceived injustices that left them feeling helpless, but with the arrival of the Mustang, I became a means for expressing their outrage at this inequality. Like Joseph's coat, my car served as the tipping point for their anger. And where Joseph's life was saved by his brother Reuben, I would be saved from a beating by an unlikely friend.

Part of the shingle-making process is the application of a layer of colored grit, which, at least in 1967, came in bags, and which the company bought by the boxcar load. Since unloading the boxcars required the use of forklifts, which were needed during the weekdays' production operations, the unloading was always carried out on a weekend, when the plant was otherwise closed. Given its unpopularity with the regular crew, the task of unloading the latest shipment fell to me and another new guy. About twenty-five, a Vietnam veteran known for keeping to himself, he had a nasty scar he wouldn't talk about and already had earned a reputation for being a little spooky. Right away, I liked him. Both of us were quiet sorts, so, once we'd agreed on the details of how we'd approach the task, we worked more or less in silence for half a day, making the occasional joke about this or that.

When we broke for lunch that first Saturday, he began to talk. He'd served in the crew of a brown-water boat, the small, well-armed, but vulnerable craft that patrolled the rivers of the Mekong Delta. His service had begun in the days when the standing orders were, if fired upon, you were not to return fire unless given permission by the commander in chief, Pacific. Off and on, for the rest of the day, I listened to his stories. One stands out. As he and his mates were taking their boat through a shallow river narrows, they were ambushed and taking fire from each bank. Though I don't remember why—perhaps their engine had been damaged—they were unable to make speed. Now Viet Cong swimmers began making their way toward the boat, carrying what looked like American hand grenades. Manning a .50 caliber Browning machine gun, and already returning fire, he let loose on the swimmers, shooting at their heads, some of them at little more than point-blank range. It's not that he thought about it much as it was happening, he said, but the memories of what the .50-caliber bullets had done to their faces wouldn't go away. Still, if you wanted to live, he said, it's what you did. You sure as hell didn't wait for permission to shoot back, so he'd lose his stripes, win them back, and lose them again. Trying to rebuild his life after all that had been hard.

During the following week, in a tone he might have used to talk about the weather, he told me of having overheard five of his co-workers discussing their plan to be waiting by my car after work that afternoon, where they'd pick a fight and "put you in the hospital." I didn't feel frightened so much as resigned. I had no doubt they'd do it, nor any illusions I could do anything to stop it—that is, short of running to my car and leaving, or phoning my father, or going to the general manager who'd hired me. I was too proud for any of that. Not knowing what else to say, I asked him what I should do.

"About what?" he asked, shaking a cigarette from its pack, his manner so nonchalant it was as if he'd already put the incident far behind him.

"About those guys you just told me about."

"Oh, yeah." He flipped open his lighter, lit the cigarette, took a deep drag, held it for a moment, and on the exhale, said, "You ain't got to worry about them."

"What do you mean?"

"I told 'em you were my friend, and if they laid a hand on you, I'd kill 'em all."

And that was that. Over the six remaining weeks, there would be no beating, no being tossed into a pit or carried off as a slave—not even another discouraging word.

With the aid of his own champions—Reuben, who will save his life; and a man from Pharaoh's court he'll meet in prison; and then Pharaoh himself—Joseph in time will land on his feet, and at the top of the world. But to get there he will have to travel *and* go through some experiences that, however difficult, will allow the gifted, self-absorbed boy to morph into the gifted, consciously aware grown-up.

98

JOSEPH IS DRY-GULCHED BY HIS BROTHERS,
FINDS EMPLOYMENT IN EGYPT

Hearing about the second dream proved to be too much for the brothers, though it also might have been seeing the robe that last time, when their blood was already up. Sent out by his father to find his brothers, Joseph, wearing the robe, was still some distance away when they spotted him, "that dreamer," as they called him. They began laying plans to murder him, throw his body into a pit, and blame his death on wild animals. Reuben, the oldest of the brothers, who had planned to rescue Joseph later, argued that it would be better to leave him in the pit, but alive. So they waited, then jumped him, stripped him, tossed him into a pit—and broke for lunch. As they were eating, they spotted a caravan and, deciding that, Joseph being their own blood, it would be less traumatic for them to sell him into slavery than kill him, they made a deal for twenty pieces of silver.

Reuben was not around for lunch or the sale, and on seeing that Joseph was not in the pit, he "rent his clothes," and said, "The boy is gone! Now what am I to do?" Good question. What *was* Reuben, as the eldest son, to do? One option was to get Joseph back, but his brothers might kill him first and there was the risk that Joseph would blab to their father. Another option was to tell Jacob the truth about what had happened, with the downside that he might have them all killed. Or they could go with the original idea, revised—just slit a goat's throat, soak some of its blood into Joseph's coat, take it to the old man, and, pretending to be really broken up about it, claim that some wild animal ate him. Yes, that could work. Sure enough, Jacob bought their story, then "rent his clothes, put sackcloth on his loins . . . and refused to be comforted."

More irony: just as Jacob had fooled his own father by using his brother's clothing and lambskins, Joseph's brothers, in "one of a series of paybacks for deception that form a chain in the J narrative,"[6] now use their brother's coat and the blood of a slaughtered goat in order to fool Jacob. Meanwhile, the people who'd bought Joseph (in E it's the Midianites; in J the Ishmaelites) finally reach Egypt, where they sell him to an important member of Pharaoh's court, whose randy wife sees their handsome new slave boy as a tasty addition to their household.

Try this: Take the story of Joseph up to this point, place it in a contemporary setting, give the characters contemporary names, and change the family business from sheepherding to, say, automobile repair. Now put yourself in the shoes of a family friend who, for years, has observed how the older brothers are required to work long hours every day, without so much as a nod of approval from their father. The second from last son, however, by comparison gets a free ride, reports any indiscretion he sees to their father, and gets the fatherly attention and affection denied his brothers. Whether it's because some piece is missing or underdeveloped, leaving him unable to understand how his brothers have come to despise him, or because he doesn't care, the younger son seems unaffected by the ill will swirling all about him. Put that way, except for the part about selling the little brother, the family in question could be the neighbors down the street when I was a boy.

99

JUDAH AND TAMAR

Some modern scholars regard the story of Judah and Tamar in Genesis 38 to be an interruption in the Joseph narrative. Others say it is a sort of parallel story taking place within the same time frame in which Joseph is making his life in Egypt. Either way, it reveals the place of women in that culture as reflected in the tradition of "levirate" marriage, and tells the story of a woman who, caught in an impossible situation, gets out of it by pulling a fast one on the men.

Judah, "the only one of Jacob's sons besides Joseph to have a separate story about him,"[7] left his father and brothers and married a Canaanite woman. They had three sons, Er, Onan, and Shelah. Er grew up and married a woman named Tamar, but before they had children—*sons*—he did something "bad," for which Yahweh killed him. Now, given the law of levirate marriage, it fell to Onan, Tamar's brother-in-law (Latin, *levir*) and the next oldest brother, to sleep with Tamar, with the understanding that any children born from their coupling would count as Er's children, though he, Onan, would be responsible for the child's welfare. Not wanting that responsibility, though hardly in a position to say no, when he slept with Tamar, just as he was about to ejaculate, he would pull out, letting it "go to waste." Bad idea. Yahweh killed him as well.

To Judah, all this death was Tamar's fault, of course, her being the woman. With two sons down and only one to go, he sent Tamar back to her father's house, telling her to remain a widow until Shelah was old enough to marry her. Given that a woman's worth was measured by her ability to bear children, especially sons, for her to return childless to her father's home would have been seen as a disgrace.

In time, Judah's wife died and, after a period of mourning, he went with a friend to a place called Timnah in order to participate in the sheep shearing. Meanwhile, Tamar, still waiting for Shelah to show up, heard about Judah's plans and came up with a plan of her own. Guessing what might have been on the old man's mind, his wife having been dead now for some time, she dropped the widow's garb and, covering her face with a veil and wrapping herself up—taking on the look of a cult prostitute—she set herself at a place she knew he would be passing. It worked. Seeing her, Judah wanted her, offering to have a young goat sent from his flock as payment. Tamar agreed, but only if he would leave, as pledge, his seal and cord, and his staff, which would be returned on delivery of the goat. Done. They slept together, he left, and she put her widow's garb back on. Now Tamar was pregnant with Judah's child.

Judah sent the goat by way of his friend, but she was nowhere to be found. In fact, nobody remembered having seen such a woman. When the friend reported this, Judah, having acted in good faith, and not wanting to look foolish, decided to let the matter drop. She could keep the seal and cord, and the staff. Then, three months later, Judah was told that Tamar had become pregnant by playing the harlot. Because she was "still in a state akin to betrothal to Judah's family,"[8] the charge was not harlotry, but adultery, a capital offense. With "precipitous speed . . . and . . . without the slightest reflection or call for evidence"[9]—almost as if *he* were guilty of something!—Judah condemned her to death, the sentence to be carried out immediately. Just as they were about to take her away, Tamar produced the things that Judah had left with her and, using the very same language Joseph's brothers had used when presenting Joseph's bloodied coat, told Judah that the father of the child was the owner of these things. For Judah, it was a transformative moment. What appears to be a Perry Mason–like save would have amounted to nothing had Judah, the final arbiter in the matter, not admitted the truth. But he did, *and* he acknowledged the injustice perpetrated through his failure to send Shelah to Tamar as promised. The matter was closed. Tamar would give birth to twin sons, who helped to fill the void in the family left by the deaths of Er and Onan and Tamar. If Karen Armstrong is right in observing that Judah "had begun the painful journey from selfishness and ignorance to self-knowledge,"[10] then this is as much his story as Tamar's. Certainly, the metaphor of his embarking on a "journey" fits the biblical theme of exodus from bondage to freedom—the liberation of spirit, of soul, as well as body. Likewise, the new man that emerged from Judah's willingness to see the truth about the man he'd become since the death of his sons fits with the argument made by Socrates at his trial, some five hundred years later (about the time the first of the postexilic interpreters began their work), that "the unexamined life is not worth living."

The Slave-Inmate

100

JOSEPH IS SOLD, RISES TO A HIGH PLACE,
THEN FALLS—AGAIN

In Egypt, Joseph was purchased by a man named Potiphar, Pharaoh's chief steward, who was so impressed with Joseph that "he made him his personal attendant and put him in charge of his household, placing in his hands all that he owned." Potiphar's household prospered under Joseph's management. In fact, everything was going along swimmingly until Potiphar's wife came up with yet another idea for what Joseph could do with his time. "Lie with me," she said one day. He refused, saying that his master trusted him, had been good to him, so "how then could I do this most wicked thing, and sin before God?" So she let him get away—that time. It is the first time in Joseph's story that he, or anyone else, had invoked the divine name.

"Good looks," writes Levenson, "are often a sign of divine favor in the Tanakh, but here they set the one who bears them up for a potentially catastrophic temptation."[11] He goes on to cite a midrash that doubts Joseph's innocence, likening him to one "who would stand in the market place, put make-up around his eyes, straighten up his hair, and swing on his heels."[12] Joseph wore eye makeup? (What a showstopper of a topic that would have made in my southeast Texas Baptist church!) The fact is that Egyptian men of the period dolled up with heavy eyeliner—even the macho, *macho* men. If the midrash is correct about Joseph's behavior, then not only would he have used it, but "Mrs. Potiphar's proposition was thus a punishment for his narcissism and machismo."[13]

Poor Joseph. As my paternal grandmother might have said, *That boy was just too good-looking for his own good.* And poor, randy Mrs. Potiphar. Hearing no from a slave might have been a turn-on, especially from this hottie. She simply had to have him, so day after day she kept after him, pleading with him, "Lie with me." Day after day he would refuse, and she would relent—until the next day. Even Joseph, who'd spent his life in the shallow end of the pool, must have sensed that this could not end well, and it didn't. One day, with Potiphar at work and the other household servants outside, he entered the house. "Lie with me," she said, but this time, the two of them alone in the house, she grabbed a handful of his garment.

Startled, no doubt, and frightened, Joseph made for the door, leaving her holding the garment. Outside, the other servants, who could hardly have missed her daily attempts to bed the lad, likewise would not have missed it that he'd gone into the house fully clothed and come out half naked. Oops.

But *that* sort of trouble could swing both ways, so, thinking fast, Mrs. Potiphar called out to her servants, and said, "Look, he had to bring us a Hebrew to dally with [or *fool with* (Friedman), *play with* (Alter)] us!" In one short sentence, she managed to divert guilt away from herself and onto the *Hebrew*, who would not even have been around to mess with *us* [you servants and me] if *he*, Potiphar, hadn't brought him. When her husband arrived home, she met him with "The Hebrew slave whom you brought into our house . . ." Still holding the garment as evidence, and as Friedman points out, using "the same device that Adam had used when trying to exonerate himself in Eden when he said, 'The woman whom *you* placed with me . . . '"[14] she again deflected all blame and responsibility from herself and onto the *Hebrew* that *you* [Potiphar] brought here! It was a brilliant display of obfuscation—so brilliant that one might suspect that she'd done this before. Surely the servants rolled their eyes at one another. As many times as I've read this passage, I still half expect Potiphar to pause, sigh, shake his head, and say, *Will you give me a break?* But, no. We're told he was furious with Joseph and sent him to prison.

Like his father Jacob before him, Joseph seems to make his way through life by attracting one disaster after another. And, as with his father, I see in Joseph enough of my own youthful folly to leave me a little nervous. Perhaps you, as well? Have you ever been accused of something quite serious that you did *not* do, the ramifications of which could, and likely would, change the course of your life? While I could say that such times in a life are moments for growth—and they can be, I suppose—I will say that if such an opportunity for deepening has not come your way, you really haven't missed a thing.

101

I MANAGE TO ATTRACT YET *ANOTHER* NEAR DISASTER

Tyler, Texas: Winter 1973–Spring 1974

As would prove to be true in each parish I served, most of the members of Christ Church, Tyler, proved lovely and welcoming; some, not so much. From the former group would come several good friends and mentors;

from the latter would emerge the few ready to do whatever was necessary to move their agenda forward. In other words, power politics, church-style.

I arrived in Tyler just after my bishop had placed his hands on my head, making me part of the Apostolic Succession, that unbroken chain of one generation laying hands on the next, going back to the beginning. As the assistant to the rector, I was in charge of the Sunday school and the high school youth group, and tasked with designing a series of adult education classes to be offered on weeknights. I was fired up! Insensitive! In a *hurry*! And I was certain I could win everybody over to my point of view, even the few in that latter category. In other words, politically I was a moron.

During the first week of Advent, I was invited to attend a weekly prayer and Bible study group. Being a savvy politician, and a teacher willing to let me make my own mistakes, Dick, the rector, my boss, asked if I was serious about going.

"Sure," I said. "Why not?"

"I just wouldn't advise it."

"But, why?"

"Let's just say you won't enjoy it the way you think you will."

The meeting was informal, in a cozy setting with couches and easy chairs that could be arranged to form a circle. The group's usual agenda was to open with a prayer, then read and discuss the Bible passages set aside in the Episcopal lectionary for the following Sunday. After the prayer, and a few welcoming words for me, the moderator proceeded to read the Annunciation–Virgin Birth passage from St. Luke's gospel. Following the reading, beginning with the reader, then moving around the circle, each member shared his or her impression of the reading. Their common ground being a literal interpretation of the Bible, each spoke of his or her belief that the events had happened exactly as written. Then it was my turn. I wanted to impress them with what I knew about the subject, wanted to give them historical-critical facts I assumed they didn't know, wanted them to say, or think, *Wow, you're really smart! We're so glad you came tonight!* I began by saying that Luke's gospel had a strong classical Greek influence, that the image of the Virgin Birth was archetypal, so it could be found in the myths of many ancient cultures, including the Greeks, and that Luke had used it here because his audience would see it as allegory, a conduit into the rest of the story. Besides that, the only other *direct* reference to the Virgin Birth, Matthew's, is based on Isaiah 7:14, which does not say "virgin" but "young woman." I simply *couldn't* have been more pleased with myself!

Silence. Then, "Yes, but . . . do you believe it to be *true*?"

Ready for that one, I said, "I believe it doesn't matter whether it's true or not true," and went on about how arguing about the story's literal truth was to miss the point that something brand-new and transformative was entering human history.

Silence. "So . . . you . . . *don't* . . . believe . . . it's true."

"You want to know if I think the Virgin Birth happened, in history? An actual event that could have been filmed or tape-recorded?"

"Yes."

"Then, no, I don't."

More silence. Finally, the person to my right began speaking, saying essentially what the others had said. The moderator offered a prayer. I was thanked for attending, and the meeting was adjourned. As I was making my good-byes, one of the members pulled me aside and said, "Someone like you has no business in the ministry. We intend to see to it that you are *gone* in six months!"

It was so odd. I'd experienced the usual threats from schoolyard bullies, threatened with expulsion from my seminary, with bodily harm by coworkers. But I'd never been threatened for *not* believing what other people believed. I couldn't get my head around the sheer unreasonableness of it, the injustice, the un-Americanness at the heart of it. Then there was the attack on my character encoded in *Someone like you*. I wanted to ask, to shout, *Someone like me? Like what? Like WHAT? Who the hell do you think you are?* But I kept my mouth shut. Besides, the dissonance between what I'd assumed these people to be and *this* was dizzying, giving the encounter a sense of unreality, as if I'd gone to sleep for a moment, and dreamed. But it was real, and the *we*, as I would learn, was a small, determined group within the group. I told my wife about what had happened, as well as my boss, who, grinning, said, "Told you so." Life went on.

It was about five months later that a friend with his ear to the parish gossip mill dropped by my office to tell me about the sordid affair I was having with a parishioner's wife.

"Where am I having all this fun?

"Your place."

"My house?"

"Yeah, while your wife's in the other room. That's at night. During the day, you're doing it right here in your office, on the floor. Sometimes you don't even bother closing your door all the way."

That spring, I'd begun a counseling relationship with a young woman from the parish who was in a deeply troubled marriage. We'd met once or twice a week, always in my office, and always during the day when there were plenty of people around. That she was an attractive woman provided the rumor with a bit of spice.

It was about six weeks after the counseling began that she and her two children showed up at our front door in the middle of the night, still wearing their nightclothes, robes, and slippers. When her husband, an alcoholic, had come home drunk and violent, then threatened her with a pistol, she'd grabbed the kids and made a run for it. We talked for a while, then, as my wife was getting them settled in the guest room, I called my boss and informed him of the situation. We agreed that, beyond letting the senior warden and his wife know what was happening, it was best to keep her location a secret for the present. They would stay with us for about a week. When the crisis had passed, and word had got around about where she'd been, it became a near-perfect medium in which to grow a rumor.

I was professionally vulnerable. I'd been told by several colleagues that our bishop was a man who neither forgot nor forgave, and the falling-out three years before over the issue of where and how I would spend my intern year had never healed. As with any human organization, advancement in the church depends a great deal on being noticed, which itself depends on being in a position to be noticed. If he got wind of the rumor, there was a chance he would pull me out of Tyler, place me in some backwater, and forget that I existed.

Rumors behave like viruses. Gaining access to a host, they live in it, feed on it, duplicate, and morph. Some rumors leave the host largely unaffected while others incapacitate for a short time, a long time, or permanently. Some leave scars. A rumor introduced into one's place of work, place of worship, or neighborhood might hurt the intended target, but collateral damage to a host has been known to produce a surprisingly intense blowback from the host and onto the rumor starters. Especially when the target, with little to lose, is willing to play *really* dirty.

For reasons I've yet to discern, I'd gained a reputation for being a loose cannon. I was not that, but perception being the creator of its own reality, it did provide a powerful image. Also coming to my aid, pushing up, as it were, through the persona of the sophisticated Episcopal clergyman, ready to augment that image, was the junkyard dog from blue-collar roots, my father's son, who was not about to go quietly. Threatening to wreck the joint seemed entirely appropriate. I took a few minutes to gather my thoughts, then went to tell Dick, the rector, the news.

"Yeah, I heard about that. You know how these things go. I figure it'll just blow over."

"You know damn well it won't! You know where it's coming from, and what'll happen if the bishop hears about it."

"Nah. You're making too much of it."

"Hell, I am."

"What can you do about it?"

"They wanna get literal, okay by me." I went on about how, in Matthew 18, Jesus says that if your brother sins and won't stop, then take it before the congregation. "So, here's the plan: Today is Tuesday. If I haven't heard from you by Saturday that the rumor has not only been stopped, but reversed, I'll stand up Sunday morning, call 'em by name, and tell the whole congregation just what the bastards have been up to. It'll be the biggest stink this town has seen in decades. You know I'll do it. I've got nothing to lose."

I wasn't at all sure I had the moxie to actually do it; I just wanted them to be sure. And they were, I suppose, because on Saturday morning Dick assured me that it had all been taken care of. The matter was closed. Still unanswered is the degree to which those who started the rumor considered how getting at me with such a rumor would mean slandering her.

Epilogue. Like politicians, clergy who find contentment in their profession have learned to compromise without giving away the store and, when necessary, have learned the darker art of outmaneuvering the opposition. A refinement on the latter is the art of anticipating and preempting trouble that otherwise is certain to find its way to one's door. That said, allow me to point out that Dick was grinning when he advised me not to attend the meeting, and again as I told him about the threat. Months later, as I was roiling on about the rumor, he was fighting back a grin. At twenty-seven, I was still dumb enough that, if you wanted me to run headlong into this or that wall, the simple suggestion that the task might be more than I could handle would usually do the trick. Having now revisited this incident, looking at it as best I can through eyes now more than twice as old as the boy-man I was in those years, I find myself wondering if, behind Dick's "aw-shucks" demeanor, there was a puppeteer dangling me like bait in front of trouble that might one day come looking for him. Not that he would have let me take a fatal bullet on his behalf, but if it was his plan that they would give away their position by taking a shot in my direction, then hats off.

As for Joseph, Yahweh "disposed the chief jailor favorably toward him," so, before long, as in Potiphar's house, Joseph found himself in charge of "everything that was done there." The kid had talent. All he needed was the right break, the sort that might come one's way from being in the right place at the right time with just the right skill set needed to solve the problems of important people who know more important people—like, say, Pharaoh, who just then was pretty much the most powerful person on the face of the earth.

Joseph in Egypt

102

LIKE HIS FATHER AND GREAT-GRANDFATHER BEFORE HIM,
JOSEPH RISES UP FROM THE ASHES OF HIS LATEST DISASTER

But Joseph is different from Abraham and Jacob. Where they had the itch for more, the Joseph we meet in the beginning of his story seems to have had everything he wanted. Whereas the patriarchs' troubles—Esau's and Laban's fury at Jacob; Pharaoh's and Abimelich's fury at Abraham—arose from rather bold actions that they themselves initiated, Joseph's troubles arise from his day-to-day behavior. While his forefathers' skills lay in guile, in the con, in the clever manipulation of a mark, Joseph's lay in an extraordinary ability to adapt his gifts to the difficult situations in which he finds himself. Having managed a demotion from the restricted world of a slave to that of a prison inmate, Joseph will soon discover that, curiously, *ironically*, this new situation holds one of the keys to his future.

Soon after Joseph was established as the warden's right-hand man, Pharaoh sentenced both his cupbearer and baker to prison. Since they were from the king's court and not ordinary prisoners, the warden gave them over to Joseph's personal care. One morning, a few days into their imprisonment, each man had a dream that left him unsettled, especially because, in prison, they had no one who might help them understand their dreams. Seeing their distress, Joseph volunteered to be the divine conduit by which they could learn the meaning behind their dreams. The cupbearer went first, laying out the details of his dream. Joseph said the dream was telling him that he would be released in three days and restored to his former position. Then, seizing the moment, he asked that the cupbearer not forget him. Moreover, as he'd been a victim of kidnapping, and since he'd done nothing that merited prison, perhaps the cupbearer would put in a good word with Pharaoh. Next, having heard the cupbearer's good news, the baker couldn't wait to get the meaning of his dream. Yes, he was told, his incarceration would also end in three days, though he would not be so much *restored* to his former position as, well, *decapitated*, and his body impaled on a pole and left for vultures. Joseph, it seemed, had carried over from his former life that penchant for saying the truth exactly as he saw it.

As predicted, three days later, the baker was executed, and the cup-bearer went back to Pharaoh's court, where he forgot about Joseph. Two years later, when Pharaoh had two haunting dreams that none of his advis-ers could penetrate, the cupbearer remembered his interpreter and told Pharaoh of the Hebrew youth who'd solved the puzzle of his dream. The next scene beautifully captures the irony of power, a theme that threads itself throughout the biblical narrative *and* the narrative of human history: Joseph, a nobody who'd awakened that morning a prison inmate whose best future appeared to be an uncertain term of incarceration, suddenly was "rushed from the dungeon," cleaned up, given a change of clothes, and found himself standing before this most powerful of human beings, who, having exhausted all other resources, asked for *his* help.

Pharaoh tells Joseph of his two dreams. In the first, seven plump, healthy cows were eaten by seven of the ugliest, scrawniest cows he'd ever seen, who afterward were still ugly and scrawny. In the second dream, seven healthy ears of grain were eaten by seven withered ears of grain that like-wise did not benefit from what they'd consumed. What could it all mean? He was sure the dreams were important, but not even his best magicians had been able to penetrate the meaning within the dreams.

Pharaoh falls silent. Eyes turn to Joseph. The pompous self-inflation of childhood now burned away by the ignominy of slavery and prison, the self-assured young man steps forward. Without so much as a moment's pause to consider his answer, Joseph tells Pharaoh that his dreams were a divine message about the immediate future of his kingdom, that there would be seven years of abundance followed by seven years of famine. Pretty impressive. I think of the math whiz kids who can instantly cal-culate the square root of any five-, or six-, or seven-digit number in their heads. But that sort of problem has one correct answer, while dream interpretation normally requires a bit of digging and probing—that is, unless, *unlike* Joseph's dreams, but *like* Jacob's dream at Beth-El, Pharaoh's dreams weren't dreams at all, but divine downloads, if you will, encrypted visions of the future. Given that "the Hebrew verb *patar* and its cognate noun suggest decipherment,"[15] Joseph's task was less dream *interpreter* than *code breaker*—though maybe not even that, since, clearly, by his own admission, he was merely telling Pharaoh what the divine was telling him.

A common characteristic of great leaders is their capacity for recog-nizing and utilizing talent. Joseph was an outlander, a monotheist whose god was not of Egypt, but he did appear to have answers. Not only had he identified the problem in an instant, but with the same quickness and clarity, in his next breath, and as though it were nothing, he outlined a brilliant solution: *Choose the right guy to oversee a project whereby the surplus of the next seven years is put into warehouse storage in the various cities around the country. Do this right and, when the famine comes, Egypt will survive.* Pharaoh loved the idea, said Joseph was the right man for the job, gave him the authority to make it happen, put his own signet ring on Joseph's hand, had him robed in fine linen, and gave him the chariot of Pharaoh's second-in-command to ride in. He also gave him a new name, Zaphenath-paneah, and a wife, Asenath, with whom he would have two sons, Manasseh and Ephraim.

In ancient literature, it's not unusual for the gods to move things along when it suits them. Saul's ascent from a *nobody* to a *somebody*, from *sweaty-guy-out-looking-for-lost-donkeys* to king, all in less than a day, has an air of vaudeville: *Didja hear the one about the young guy who walked up to the old guy and said, "Say, I've lost my donkeys, can you help me out?" The old guy says, "Donkeys, schmonkies! F'get the donkeys! Howdja like to be King of Israel?"* Joseph's ascent is equally theatrical. Still, however spectacular the arc of that one day—from prison inmate to the second most powerful person in the most powerful nation on earth—it was the larger arc of Joseph's life, especially the difficult years in Egypt, that prepared him for that moment. Now, with the mantle of Pharaoh's authority, Joseph will spend the seven years of abundance following the plan he'd outlined. As predicted, the eighth year brought famine so severe and of such duration— seven years—that it would have brought mass starvation and even the end of the kingdom without Joseph's plan. But the Egyptians had even more food than they needed. Good thing, too, because famine was everywhere, and their neighbors would come calling.

103

JUST AHEAD, ANOTHER EYE-POPPING
DOSE OF BIBLICAL IRONY

Most of the wealth accumulated over three generations in Jacob's family will be wiped out by the famine. Nonetheless, it turns out that the criminally naughty act of selling their little brother to that caravan headed for Egypt was the best deal the brothers ever made. Not only will Joseph save his family (along with millions) from starvation, he will bring them before Pharaoh, who will give them and their families the best land in Egypt, where they will live out their days. Along with these benefits will come another, which will rescue them from a moral death. For twenty years they will be haunted by the memory of what they'd done to their brother, creating in them an individual and collective sense of *shame*—that is, the knowledge of having done something so out of alignment with what one considers to be right action that one's own sense of *Who I am*—one's identity—is dislocated, the image of self as *one-who-would-never-do-such-a-thing* proven false and, so, irreparably broken. Think "Humpty-Dumpty," the good news being that the self *can* be put back together, though in a more truthful construct, that is, without the burden of those airy-fairy notions about how impenetrably "good" one is (the mask behind which the Inquisition and other horrors have been perpetrated). Now, armed with the awareness of one's own potential for darkness, conscious choice becomes a possibility. In other words, these men are forced into the sort of painful turning inward that is necessary to complete the process of growing up. And they are forced to do it by their own actions, initiated twenty years before, having now come full circle. *That,* and they're also rescued from of starvation and are set up for life. Who says crime doesn't pay?

104

JACOB FADES, REUBEN PROVES INEPT

Just as the brute ignorance of his sons has given way to increased self-awareness and compassion, so has the Jacob of earlier chapters changed from the brash, crafty leader he'd once been. Twenty years have passed since Joseph's disappearance, and Jacob now is a weak shadow of a man, self-pitying, old, and complaining, to paraphrase G. B. Shaw, that his world will not devote itself to making him happy. While Jacob will retain his formal authority as patriarch of the family, his deterioration will beg the question of leadership. With the famine deepening, and the family presented with the very real possibility of starvation, one of the sons had to step forward. As Jacob's firstborn son, that responsibility should have fallen to Reuben, but it didn't. You may recall the mention of Reuben's having slept with Bilhah, one of his father's concubines. About the incident, the text tells us that it happened, but not what happened, or how, or why, with everything to lose, Reuben would do such a foolish thing. Jon Levenson points to two other biblical texts (2 Samuel 16:20–22; 1 Kings 2:13–24) in which "a son's having intercourse with his father's concubine was a declaration of rebellion."[16] Though the idea that Reuben was out to take his father's place seems doubtful, it does follow that, like the man, his method would have demonstrated none of the elegance of the ways of his father and grandfather. The incident, likely a fragment of a larger story that left behind just enough of itself to tease the imagination, does not come up again until Genesis 49. There, as the dying Jacob pronounces blessings on each of his sons, we learn that the incident has not been forgotten, but it is the reason why Reuben will not be given the firstborn son's double share of the inheritance.

So, beyond the report that he did it, that Jacob found out about it (again, we're not told how), and that Reuben didn't get away with it in the end, any further investigation would seem to have nowhere to go. But the original text, remember, is in ancient Hebrew, a language rich with nuance, and those who first asked the questions of what, how, and why were not forensic investigators mining the incident in search of evidence but rather interpreters mining language in order to reveal meaning. In their wake is a series of postulations from Midrashic texts that, however inspired to get at the truth, remain as thoughtful guesswork. But it is *fascinating* guesswork in that some of these ring with such familiar tones that they could as well be examining the clues and possible motives around an event that happened yesterday.

To begin with, as Jacob speaks his blessing on Reuben, he does not point to motive as cause, but to Reuben's nature, which he describes as "unstable as water." In modern English usage, to say someone is "unstable" is the nice way of saying that he's a little crazy. This seems straightforward—after all, the guy did sleep with his father's concubine—but it doesn't tell us anything beyond the obvious; what seems simple enough on the surface isn't. For one thing, scholars are unanimous in their agreement that Genesis 49 is among the most difficult passages in the Bible to translate. "Unstable, itself," writes James Kugel, "is probably neither to the original sense of the word here nor, more importantly, to the way this word was understood by the ancient interpreters who lived toward the end of the Second Temple period."[17]* The word is uncommon, but where it is used in the Hebrew Bible, as well as in several rabbinic texts, the sense of it is "wanton" or "lewd." But *how*, asks Kugel, does something go about being "wanton as water"? And exactly what is wanton about water? He goes on to cite the *Targum Onquelos*, which likens Reuben's behavior to that of a man following his own direction, just as water goes where it will. In the *Targum Neophyti*, "Reuben is overcome by water—that is, by passion— just like a little garden flooded by rushing streams."[18]

Then again, maybe Jacob meant "wanton *in* water" or "*with* water." So, something to do with wanton *in* or *with* water? Maybe. With their perspec-

---

*The Second Temple period came after the return from exile in Babylon, when the need for interpreters became obvious.

tive on holy history, the early interpreters could point to how King David's *wanton* affair with Bathsheba issued from the moment when he saw her bathing. Water, wantonness—*is that how it started for Reuben? Had he been overcome by seeing her naked and bathing?* Perhaps Jacob had pondered just such questions. Evidence for this, the interpreters surmised, was hidden inside Jacob's reference to water. Perhaps from the wisdom of his years he surmised that, on seeing Bilhah naked and bathing herself, Reuben's overwhelming lust drove him to do what otherwise he would never have done. Not that bedding the concubine of one's father was acceptable practice but, compared to what Jacob might have done, Reuben's punishment was a show of mercy. Under the Pentateuchal Law, both Reuben and Bilhah would have been put to death.

One ancient source suggests that, indeed, there *was* immediate punishment, though not by Jacob's hand. The *Testament of Reuben*, written as though by Reuben himself, tells of a "great affliction in the loins [lasting] for seven months," a divine death sentence blunted only by Jacob's plea that his son be spared. Another possibility pondered by interpreters was that punishment was self-induced, that, having repented, Reuben underwent a period of penitential abstinence. This would account for his absence during that fateful lunch break when his brothers had sold Joseph to the slavers. He wasn't there because he was off by himself, fasting.

The intense focus on this incident tells its own story of interpreters and their persistence, fed as they were by the need to penetrate the language and meaning, all in the service of the need—theirs and the community—to know what happened, and why.

If they're in the ballpark, then Reuben, unexpectedly seeing a naked woman bathing herself, became aroused. He might have looked away, but didn't. Why? A thousand times in my life, in restaurants, in bookstores, airports, train stations, in the United States, overseas, and always unexpected, I've looked up to see a woman, say, adjusting her stockings, or bending in such a way that her breasts seem ready to tumble out of her sweater or blouse. Whether she was stunning or average-looking, slim or plump, young or old, the effect has always been the same—arousing, fascinating, mesmerizing. Far from the sort of lewd gawking that has always left me feeling empty and ashamed—not the *Shame on you, naughty boy* of childhood, but of having violated her and, oddly, me, as well—this other leaves me with a sense of having looked up as a door unexpectedly opened for only a moment, allowing a glance into the heart of a mystery. In Bilhah, we have the former handmaiden of Reuben's dead Aunt Rachel, a woman old enough to be his mother, and, as the mother of two of his half brothers, his aunt. Nevertheless, the longer he watched, the more sexually aroused he became. Whatever the motivation, in the end the act, while it would not cost him his life, did bring on the humiliation of losing his place in the family.

As for Bilhah, was she complicit? Was it her idea? Perhaps, though it would not be the first or last time in the Bible that a woman used sex to get something she wanted. More likely, however, is that she was forced. Despite being one of his father's "wives," she was also a slave, a status that, in Reuben's mind, may have given him leave to do what he wanted with her.

105

THAT WE MAY LIVE AND NOT DIE—
JOSEPH'S BROTHERS SET OUT TO BUY FOOD

As the famine deepens, Jacob sends the brothers to Egypt with money to buy grain—all but Benjamin, his and Rachel's youngest. When the brothers arrive in Egypt, they find the place teeming with groups of people from neighboring countries hoping to procure grain, yet they manage to find themselves in an audience with the vizier of Egypt himself, and, ironically, prostrate themselves before him, just as in Joseph's youthful dream. While they don't have a clue that this man who holds the power of life and death over them is the brother they'd sold all those years before, Joseph recognizes them right away, but he plays the stranger, and speaks harshly. (Lingering resentment, perhaps?) The scene strikes me as having a touch of burlesque.

So, where are you from, and what do you want?

We're from Canaan, looking to buy food.

Nah— You guys are spies! You're just here to get the lay of the land!

No way! they said, we're just here to buy food! We're brothers, see, all from the same father. There were twelve of us. Ten here, our youngest brother stayed at home, and one is gone. Really, we're honest men, not spies.

Okay. Tell you what. I'll let one of you go back to get your brother and bring him here. The rest I'll release if and when the brother shows up.

With that, he puts them in the guardhouse. After three days, he has them brought back.

Okay. Tell you what. I'm a God-fearing man. So, I'll just keep one of you. The rest can go back and feed your families. But I still want to see your youngest brother.

They agree to Joseph's terms then, right in front of him, begin grumbling among themselves about how this is payback for what they've done to their brother. Reuben reminds them that he's told them not to harm the boy. What they don't know is that Joseph, who's been speaking through an interpreter, could understand every word. Hearing them, he turns away, weeps, turns back to them, takes Simeon, has him bound as they watch, gives orders to provide them the supplies they'd come for, and sends them on their way.

106

WITH THE FAMILY IN CRISIS, JUDAH STEPS UP

Arriving home, the brothers recount for Jacob all that happened. Only later, as they unpack, do they discover among their things the very same silver they'd used as payment for grain. On seeing this, with one son in an Egyptian prison, and the demand that Benjamin be delivered to Egypt, Jacob, speaking as a "prima donna of paternal grief,"[19] says, "It is always me that you bereave: Joseph is no more and Simeon is no more, and now you would take away Benjamin. These things always happen to me." Next, in a hapless attempt to rescue the moment, Reuben says, "You may kill my two sons if I do not bring him back to you. Put him in my care, and I will return him to you."

Why, one might ask of Reuben, would Jacob, who is certain that two of his sons are already dead, find satisfaction in murdering two of his grandsons? Jacob's reply is "My son will not go down with you . . . he alone remains." Imagine their shock. "My son," he'd said. What, then, were they? "The extravagant insensitivity of [his] parental favoritism," writes Alter, "continues to be breathtaking . . ." Now, with Reuben's ineptitude and Jacob's seeming to have gone round the bend, the family finds itself with no effective leadership.

As the famine deepens and the family's food supply begins running out, Jacob tells his sons to go back to Egypt. Judah reminds him that "the man"—Joseph—had told them flatly not to come back without Benjamin, to which Jacob says, "Why do you serve me so ill as to tell the man you had another brother?" The suggestion that they had told the man about Benjamin only to hurt Jacob seems to annoy the brothers sufficiently that they come back with the rather prickly "The man kept asking about us and our family, saying, 'Is your father still living? Have you another brother?' And we answered him accordingly. How were we to know he would say, 'Bring your brother here?'" *You stupid old fool!* was not said, but it was there, in the undertones, along with something like *First Joseph, now Benjamin! Are we your sons? Are we and our wives and children to sit and watch one other die just to keep your precious Benjamin from the* possibility *of harm?* These are the energies of revolution. What might have happened had Judah not stepped up? Blunting the moment while using its energies to move the situation forward, Judah, in a masterstroke, repeats Jacob's own words, uttered just before their first journey, "So that we may live and not die," and offers *himself* as bond for Benjamin's safe return. "If I fail to bring him back to you . . . I shall stand guilty before you forever . . . but . . . we could have been there and back twice if we had not dawdled."

Already, in the story of Judah and Tamar, we've seen his strength of character, so it is not that surprising that he would put himself forward to fill the vacuum left by Jacob and Reuben, emerging in a rather natural manner as though the brothers had chosen him. Judah's is a new kind of leadership. Though it is somewhat reminiscent of Abraham's manner, both Abraham's and Jacob's *preference* for gaining power was not confrontation but rather misdirection, leaving one's opposition wondering what hit them. Jacob was never so openly bold, nor was Joseph before Pharaoh's imprimatur granted him such vast power. Of the two brothers who've shown promise, Judah's strength is in his presence, a sort of alpha-male sense of leadership, whereas Joseph's leadership is maintained by his intelligence, particularly evident in his genius for planning and organization.

Seeming to snap out of a self-induced coma, Jacob not only relents, he gives them instructions about gifts they should take along with them to present to the man. He tells them to take twice the money as before in case the silver had been returned to their packs by mistake. Finally, "Take your brother too . . . and may El Shaddai dispose the man toward you . . . As for me, if I am to be bereaved, I shall be bereaved."

107

JOSEPH SHOWS A CRUEL STREAK, QUESTIONABLE
JUDGMENT, THEN REDEEMS HIMSELF

So they go, and when Joseph sees Benjamin, he tells his steward to take them all to his house, to prepare a meal, and that he will dine with them at noon. Right away, the brothers tell the steward about the money that had mysteriously reappeared in their bags. "So we brought it back with us." The steward—I can imagine the bemused look of one who is in on the joke—tells them not to be afraid. "Your God, the God of your father, must have put the treasure in your bags for you. I got your payment." Then he provides water to bathe their feet, and feed for the animals, and the brothers lay out their gifts and wait for Joseph. Everything seems quite rosy. Joseph gets home, the brothers bow, he asks about their father, they say he is fine, thanks. Spotting Benjamin, he asks if this was the brother they'd told him about, then, not waiting for a reply, says, "May God be gracious to you, my boy," and on the verge of tears, goes to another room, where he lets go and weeps.

Washing his face, he orders that the meal be brought out and returns to his guests. When they have all been served, Benjamin's portion is several times that of his brothers. Why? Was it the ghost of Jacob's favoritism haunting an otherwise splendid moment? Was it from Joseph's affection for his little brother? Or was he trying to wind the brothers up—having himself a little spiteful fun? Whatever Joseph is up to, the sense of the text is that the brothers, astonished that they were not only alive but having lunch in the home of the second most powerful man in the known world, don't notice that Benjamin's portion is larger, or they just don't care. But what if one or more of them had taken offense and made a scene? With the exception of Judah, these hot-blooded men have an appalling record for sound judgment. Whatever the motive, it seems less the behavior of Pharaoh's vizier and more that of the clueless boy he'd once been.

At this point in his story, Joseph is at war with himself, despite his accomplishments. The hostility he showed his brothers during their first visit was a mirror of their own, earlier hostility for him. Where he had been helpless in their hands, now they are helpless in his. Anyone ever betrayed will remember the emotional cauldron of grief and rage, how time can seem, finally, to put out the fires, and how it can come back in a moment. Twice, now, Joseph has wept at the sight of his brothers. This second time, the literal meaning of the Hebrew is not what we see in translation, that he was "overwhelmed with feeling," but that "his mercy burned hot."[20] Why, then, did he not identify himself? Was he being wise, wanting them fully to understand what he had gone through as a result of their actions, or was he allowing his resentment to determine the moment? Given what comes next, the latter gets my vote.

Joseph and his brothers have a fine time, eating and drinking their fill. After the party, Joseph gives his steward instructions to give them as much food as they can carry, to put their silver back in their bags and, while he is at it, to put his (Joseph's) silver goblet in Benjamin's baggage. The next morning, at first light, they depart for home, a little hungover perhaps, but how swell life must have seemed in the face of all that had happened! Giving them time to get out of the city, Joseph tells his steward to catch up to them and accuse them of stealing the goblet. In a scene reminiscent of Laban's chasing of Jacob in search of the stolen *terafim*, the steward catches them, accuses them, tells them they've repaid good with evil, *and* that it was a wicked thing to have done—just as Joseph had instructed. The brothers remind the steward that they were the same men who'd brought back silver they assumed had been returned to them by mistake. Then, making the same grand gesture Jacob had made with Laban, they tell him that if any one of them is found with the goblet, that one will remain as a slave. The steward, having put it in Benjamin's pack, knows just where to look. They all return to the city.

Again it is Judah who speaks for the brothers. Joseph asks if they thought they'd get away with it. Between the emotional roller coaster of the previous twenty-four hours, the magically reappearing silver, the goblet, and his fear about how this day would end, Judah, like his brothers, is suddenly caught in a web of unfathomable circumstance and doesn't bother to deny the crime. The goblet had been found among Benjamin's things, so, what is there to say? Now they would all be his slaves. *Oh, no,* Joseph says to him. *Not all of you. Just the guilty one. I'll keep the kid.* Judah says that if they return without Benjamin, it would kill their father. Moreover, because he, himself, had stood as bond for Benjamin's safe return, it should be he who is kept as a slave, not the boy, who should be returned to his father.

Once again Joseph begins to lose it, so he sends everyone from the room but his brothers. After the room is cleared, saying nothing to his brothers, he begins weeping so loudly that everyone in the house hears it. Imagine the brothers in that moment. There they are, probably still in a deep bow, while this guy wails on and on. Standing up would likely have seemed like a bad idea, but do they raise their heads a little, cut their eyes at one another? Does anyone mouth, *What th'*? Are they beginning to feel a little *insane*? Do they wonder if all along their lives had been at the mercy of a lunatic? The narrator doesn't say, only that Joseph cries, though he doesn't say how long it goes on.

Then, suddenly, high drama: "I'm Joseph! Is my father still alive?" Alter calls Joseph's sudden announcement "a two-word [in Hebrew] bombshell tossed at his brothers." Just how much did he think they could take? Asking them to gather around him, he says, again, "I am your brother, Joseph," then adds, "He whom you sold to Egypt." Then he says they should not be distressed or reproach themselves for what they've done, because "it was to save life that God sent me ahead of you."

Let us pause to appreciate the human dynamics of the moment. These are the same men who'd slaughtered an entire city because their sister was raped—if, indeed, it was rape. Joseph himself, not a stranger to self-absorption, the brother they'd not seen in twenty years, whom they'd hated, has sent them on an emotional roller-coaster ride that has left them ragged, confused, and terrified, to say nothing of Simeon, the brother who'd been in jail since their first journey to Egypt. Now he says, *You shouldn't beat yourselves up over what you did to me.* So, again, I wonder . . . In that interstice between sentences, the pause for breath just before saying the part about God's motive, and after telling them not to reproach themselves for what they've done to him, did any of the brothers hear a voice rising up, saying, *What we did to you? Why, you little* . . . These were not nice men, and but for Judah, perhaps not all that intelligent. Taken with the larger portion given Benjamin at the previous day's meal, it's enough to leave one to wonder if Joseph, who'd gone from prison inmate to second in command of Egypt in a day, whose every action was backed by Pharaoh's authority, had ever escaped the self-absorption of his youth, if it even now prevented him from *seeing* the people around him, even his brothers. Any management consultant worth his or her salt already would have hit him between the eyes with something like *Keep this up, and* everybody *will hate you.*

Joseph's next words to his brothers are tender, loving. He tells them to go and gather their father and their families and bring them to Egypt, to Goshen, where "I will provide for you—for there are yet five years of famine to come—that you and your household and all that is yours may not suffer want . . . And you must tell my father about my high station in Egypt, and all you have seen." And *hurry!* With that he embraces Benjamin, kisses him, weeps, kisses each of his brothers, and weeps.

When Pharaoh hears about all this, he's pleased and tells Joseph he'll see to it that his family gets the best of everything Egypt has to offer. With that, Pharaoh orders they be given wagons and provisions enough to last until the family has relocated in Goshen. In addition, Joseph gives each brother a change of clothing—all but Benjamin, of course, who gets several changes of clothing and three hundred pieces of silver. Nobody complains. Then he sends them on their way with orders not to be quarrelsome—a bit schoolmarmish, though not surprising. Rashi suggested that at the heart of Joseph's admonition was his concern that they would start blaming one another for having sold him into slavery all those years back, which might well make their hate for him return.

108

OFF TO EGYPT, A VISION, A PROMISE,
A MOMENT WITH PHARAOH. THEN JOSEPH
BECOMES DICTATOR OF EGYPT—OR NOT

When the brothers first told Jacob about Joseph, "His heart [goes] numb." He doesn't believe them, so they kept at him until "the spirit of their father revived," and he said, "Enough, my son Joseph is still alive! I must go see him before I die." With that, they pack up and set out. Once again, at Beer-sheba, Jacob offers a sacrifice, and in a night vision is assured that the move to Egypt is part of the plan, is promised that he, Israel, will be a great nation, will be returned to Canaan and, finally, that "Joseph's hand shall close your eyes."

On seeing one another, Jacob and Joseph embrace and weep, and Jacob declares, "Now I can die, having seen for myself that you are still alive." Then Joseph tells his brothers about the upcoming audience with Pharaoh. Since they are shepherds, and the Egyptians don't care for shepherds, it is important they be prepared when Pharaoh asks them about their occupation. Knowing Pharaoh as he does, and being Joseph, he tells them exactly what to say. Then he goes to tell Pharaoh of his family's arrival.

When the time comes for the audience, selecting just a few of his brothers, he presents them and his father to Pharaoh. What happens next is predictably awkward and comically human. Once again, imagine the scene: In one corner, as it were, genteel, urbane, wearing makeup, and dressed to the nines, is the king of Egypt (and who may have been harboring illusions that the family would be like his golden boy, Joseph). In the other corner, sun-baked, rather rough-looking, and dressed well—Joseph would have seen to that—we have an old desert nomad and a few of his sons suddenly in the same room with the guy who was pretty much the center of wealth and power on the known earth, who, sure enough, asks, *What's your occupation?*

Shepherds. Family's been shepherds for generations.

I imagine a nervous, cotton-mouthed pause here, then, *Since the famine has wiped out the pastures, we were hoping we could stay in Goshen.*

Pharaoh turns to Joseph and says his family is welcome to settle in Goshen. *And*, if any of them has the competence for it, he'll put them in charge of his own flocks.

Joseph now presents his father, who in the world at large is but "a mere Semitic herdsman chief."[21] You might think he'd be intimidated. Jacob, maybe, the tiresome, whiny old man of recent years but, standing face-to-face with Pharaoh is *Israel*, son of Isaac, grandson of Abraham, wrestler of angels, bearer of the divine covenant, from whose seed a nation is to rise, and who now pronounces a blessing on Pharaoh.

How old are you?

One hundred and thirty hard years, not yet as many as my fathers.

With that, Jacob says good-bye and leaves Pharaoh's presence. Once cared for by his father, Joseph will now see to his father's needs and those of his extensive family, provide them with food, and settle them on the land Pharaoh had set aside.

The famine will deepen until nothing grows anywhere. With the exception of what has been stored in the warehouses, "there was no bread in all the world." All the grain in the warehouses belonged to Pharaoh, not the Egyptian people. Growing desperate, the people came to Joseph with the offer of trading both their land and *themselves* for food. Now, with Pharaoh's proxy, Joseph will take control of Egypt, nationalizing all the land holdings except those held by the priests, and essentially enslaving the people. Quite a dramatic development, but the lack of any historical record of such nationalization in Egypt leads some scholars and interpreters to suggest E, its author, made it up. Why? In order to give his present-day audiences, who would have regarded the enslavement of the Israelites in Egypt as history, a sort of vengeance fantasy—*Whaddaya think of that? You were our slaves first! Ha!*

109

LAST THINGS

After seventeen years in Egypt, "the time approached for Israel to die." Sending for Joseph, Jacob exacts a promise that he would not be buried in Egypt, but in the promised land, the burial place of Abraham and Isaac. The text jumps forward to Jacob on his deathbed, from where he will give each of his sons a blessing. Having been told his father is dying, Joseph, with his sons, Manasseh and Ephraim, go to him. In what appears to be a separate audience, Jacob blesses Joseph, placing him over his brothers. He also adopts Joseph's sons as his own, blessing Ephraim first, placing him above his older brother. Next, with all his sons gathered around him, he will give each a blessing, beginning with Reuben (who is about to discover that his bedding of Bilhah had not been forgotten, but had cost him his place as first son, and half of what would otherwise have been his inheritance). Then having given them instructions about his burial, "he drew his feet into the bed and, breathing his last, he was gathered to his people." On Joseph's orders, Jacob is embalmed. After the period of mourning, which lasts for seventy days, Joseph asks and is granted Pharaoh's permission to go bury his father. The combined households of Jacob's sons, all but the small children, along with an escort of chariots and horsemen, begin the trek. Following the burial, they return to Egypt.

Joseph's brothers have never entirely trusted him. What might he do to them, now that Jacob was gone? Perhaps because it is what any one of them might have done, they worry that Joseph might come after them. So they send a message, telling Joseph that "your father" had instructed them to ask their brother's forgiveness. Moved to tears, and "speaking kindly to them," Joseph assures them that he will continue to look after them and their families.

As his own death approaches, and having assured his brothers that "God will surely take notice of you [meaning, "your descendants"] and bring you up from this land to the land that He promised," Joseph asks that his body be taken with them. Then, with no more fanfare than to say that Joseph was 110 when he died, and that his body "was embalmed and placed in a coffin in Egypt"—an ending more like a comma than a period—the book of Genesis draws to a close.

But life rolls on.

Throughout Genesis, both human *and* divine plans are thwarted by forces outside their control. Neither can *make* the other do his bidding. The human players manipulate and scheme; they plan for every contingency *except* the unexpected. The divine, by giving humans free will, limits his own control. He can create the heavens and the earth but he can't stop Adam and Eve from eating the fruit. He can command, rant, rave, threaten, yet the humans are free to do what they want. While each can empower the other—and here is the often unnoticed factor in the divine-human relationship as expressed in Genesis—each has the power to *limit* the other.

With Exodus, a shift in focus enters the narrative. Having set the stage on which a far larger drama will now play, Genesis becomes the prelude for what Everett Fox calls "Israel's second book of origins." He goes on to write that "Genesis had concerned itself with the beginnings of the world, of human beings and their institutions, and of the people of Israel as a tribal family. Exodus continues this thrust as it recounts the origin of the people on a religious and political level (here inseparable as concepts)."[22] Right away, in chapter one of Exodus, we're told that "the total number of persons that were of Jacob's issue came to seventy," that "Joseph died, and all his brothers, and all that generation," but that "the Israelites were fertile and prolific; they multiplied and increased very greatly, so that the land was filled with them." The new Pharaoh, who had not known Joseph, now becomes so frightened at the strength of their numbers that he sets in motion a series of events that in time gives rise to Moses, the escape from Egypt, and the years of wandering in the desert.

This is *Holy History*, the story of Israel's beginnings in the shared experience of persecution, slavery, escape, and two generations in the wasteland. Taken as metaphor, this cycle into which the narrative has already entered, of life giving way to death, giving way to new life, becomes the path taken by any human being who has tried to find a way through the world, and a place in it. It is our story.

EPILOGUE

About the author Jorge Luis Borges, translator Andrew Hurley writes, "Borges makes it unmistakably clear that every translation is a 'version,' not *the* translation . . . but *a* translation, one in a never-ending series, at least an infinite *possible* series."[1] The same must be said of this or any interpretation of Genesis or any other part of the Bible. There are thousands of interpretations—and no wonder, since, as James Kugel puts it, "The Bible says little openly."[2] This is not to say that Genesis is unwelcoming—on the contrary. But it does require seriousness of intent. I once heard a young man tell of his experience with a tai chi master in Beijing, how it had taken three years of showing up most every morning, whatever the weather, before the master would regard him as a serious student. The Torah has been spoken of in the same light—prove yourself willing to return and, in time, it will begin to reveal its secrets. That may sound strange, as if the "it" I'm referring to is a living thing, yet my experience of the last three years with Genesis has been that Genesis is alive with subtle meanings. As a theology student, I spent considerable time building a relationship with Genesis, but handicapped by the arrogance and inexperience of youth, I did most of the talking and little listening. Forty years later, I've learned the truth of Camus's declaration, "There are places where the mind dies so that a truth which is its very denial may be born,"[3] and finally know Genesis to be one of those places. I've attempted to change my relationship with Genesis, to be quiet and let it, the text, speak as I listen. I've come to trust it, to have "faith" in it, the same sort of reliance I'll have on a friend who over time has proved his faithfulness—which, you'll remember, is the ancient meaning of the word, and defined the relationship between Abraham and Yahweh.

Some of Genesis's speaking has come through the work of modern biblical scholars, men and women who have spent their lifetimes in study, though I've kept in mind Harold Bloom's caution, here worth repeating, that "perspective governs our response to everything we read, but most crucially with the Bible. Learning from scholars, whether Christian or Jewish, one still questions their conditioning, which too frequently overdetermines their presentation."[4] While I've used sources with a clear religious agenda, those in whom I've put most of my faith are those without an agenda beyond the integrity of their work. They don't ask me to believe this or that and in fact don't seem to care if I believe *them* or not.

*　　*　　*

In the introduction, I stated that the ethical and spiritual DNA of Genesis is embedded in the foundations of Western civilization, shaping our awareness of who we are as a people and as individuals, the religious and nonreligious alike, and invited you to consider whether its ancient stories resonated with your own. In considering my approach, I was particularly interested in readers who find themselves in the middle of the modern debate between religious fundamentalists and the new atheists, the marginally religious to the nonreligious who may *sense* those genetic markers, who are *curious* about those stories and characters, but want neither to be saved *by* religion nor saved *from* it. How does one provide a way into these stories that neither discourages nor requires a religious point of view—that in fact does not require the reader to believe in anything beyond his or her own experience of being human? The answer was to take it entirely as story and metaphor, the characters as ancient reflections of ourselves, their stories, our stories, mirrors in which to see our best and worst selves—different clothing, certainly, and language, and customs, yet at the level of the *human*, just as greedy and generous as we are, as gullible and crafty, as moronic and brilliant, as cowardly and brave.

Certainly the four generations of Abraham, Isaac, Jacob, and Joseph represent a generational variance that we'd recognize as entirely modern. Abraham, the patriarch's patriarch, is the terrifying, distant father who sees only the vision and proves himself willing to do whatever the vision requires. Beyond his role as "Son of the Great Man," the enigmatic Isaac seems to act in ways that always end in a question mark: Was he Abraham's and Yahweh's victim? Was he the clever manipulator masking himself as a doddering old fool? Ultimately, he strikes me as a quiet man carrying at least the scar of a traumatic event, if not the open, unhealed, Arthurian wound. Young Jacob is made of pure mercenary ambition, the sort of amphibian soul at the center of every modern political financial scandal. The older Jacob does grow into the role of patriarch, though like his father and grandfather he is a lousy father, ignoring his older sons, slathering affection and indulgences on the two youngest. Joseph is different from them all, and especially from Abraham and Jacob. Where they had the itch for more, the Joseph we meet in the beginning of his story seems to have everything he wants. His forebears' troubles—Pharaoh's and Abimelech's fury at Abraham; Esau's and Laban's fury at Jacob—arose from well-laid plans that they themselves had initiated. But Joseph's troubles begin with Joseph being Joseph. While his forebears' skills lie in guile, in the con, in the clever manipulation of others, Joseph's lie in an extraordinary ability to adapt his gifts to the difficult situations in which he finds himself.

*   *   *

The women of the Bible are smart, at times diabolically clever, and through their own machinations provide the means by which the narrative moves forward. Without them the narrative would simply stop—even though, in that culture, they were "only" women, considered property, not even second-class citizens. It's as if J and P were playing the same sort of joke on their own patriarchal culture that Beaumarchais played on the French aristocracy in *The Marriage of Figaro*, especially in the way the men go about in their assumed self-importance while the women, especially Sarah and Rebekah, manipulate events.

Even in its full depiction of a vanished world and its fully rendered human characters, Genesis does not portray every possible human challenge and metamorphosis. But it has more than I, and perhaps you, might have imagined.

NOTES

INTRODUCTION

1. Bruce Feiler, *Abraham* (New York: HarperCollins, 2002), p. 18.

PART I: THE BEGINNING

1. Tamara Cohn Eskenazi, in *The Torah: A Women's Commentary*, ed. Tamara Cohn Eskenazi and Rabbi Andrea L. Weiss (New York: URJ Press, 2008), p. 8.
2. Robert Alter, *Genesis: Translation and Commentary* (New York: Norton, 1996), p. 9.
3. Ibid.
4. Richard Elliott Friedman, *The Bible with Sources Revealed* (New York: HarperCollins, 2003), p. 36.
5. James Kugel, *Traditions of the Bible: A Guide to the Bible as It Was at the Start of the Common Era* (Cambridge, Mass.: Harvard University Press, 1998), p. 94.
6. Richard Elliott Friedman, *Commentary on the Torah* (San Francisco: HarperSanFrancisco, 2001), pp. 17–18.
7. Kugel, *Traditions of the Bible*, pp. 97, 98
8. Henry Chadwick, *The Early Church*, vol. 1 of *The Pelican History of the Church*, ed. Owen Chadwick (Baltimore: Penguin, 1969), p. 228.
9. Alter, *Genesis*, p. 16.
10. Kugel, *Traditions of the Bible*, p. 146.
11. Ibid., p. 147.
12. Ibid.
13. Ibid.
14. Ibid., p. 149.
15. Found in ibid.
16. Ibid.
17. Levenson, *The Jewish Study Bible* (New York: Oxford University Press, 2004), pp. 18–19.
18. Kugel, *Traditions of the Bible*, p. 150.
19. Ibid.
20. Ibid.
21. Ibid.
22. Ibid., p. 151.
23. Ibid.
24. Gerhard von Rad, *Genesis: A Commentary* (Philadelphia: Westminster, 1972), p. 107.
25. Ibid., p. 155.
26. Ibid., p. 107.
27. Nahum Sarna, *Etz Hayim: Torah and Commentary*, ed. David L. Lieber (Philadelphia: Jewish Publication Society, 2004), p. 27.
28. Alter, *Genesis*, p. 19.
29. Levenson, *The Jewish Study Bible*, p. 19.
30. Alter, *Genesis*, p. 22.

31. Philip Zimbardo, "How Ordinary People Become Monsters . . . or Heroes," Technology, Entertainment, and Design Conference, February 2008.
32. Levenson, *The Jewish Study Bible*, p. 21.
33. Sarna, *Etz Hayim*, p. 34.
34. *The Chumash*, the Stone Edition, Artscroll Series, ed. Rabbi Nosson Scherman and Rabbi Meir Zlotowitz (Brooklyn, N.Y.: Mesorah, 2005), p. 27.
35. Friedman, *Commentary on the Torah*, p. 34.
36. Carl G. Jung, "Answer to Job," *The Portable Jung* (New York: Viking, 1971), p. 535.
37. Thomas Moore, ed., *A Blue Fire: Selected Writings by James Hillman*, (New York: HarperCollins, 1989), p. 6.
38. James R. Hillman, "The Myth of Normalcy," in ibid., p. 149.
39. Levenson, *The Jewish Study Bible*, p. 21.
40. Ibid., p. 79.
41. Cited by Kugel in *Traditions of the Bible*, p. 185.
42. Ibid., p. 185.
43. Friedman, *Commentary on the Torah*, p. 8
44. Ibid., p. 38.
45. Ibid., p. 39.
46. William Butler Yeats, "The Second Coming," in *The Collected Poems of W.B. Yeats*, ed. Richard J. Finneran, 2nd ed. (New York: Simon & Schuster, 1996), p. 187.
47. Alter, *Genesis*, p. 40.
48. Kugel, *Traditions of the Bible*, p. 222. Emphasis in original.
49. "Zeus . . . bound his father because he unjustly swallowed his sons, and . . . castrated his father for similar reasons." "Euthyphro," in *Plato: Complete Works*, John M. Cooper, ed., G. M. A. Grube, trans. (Indianapolis: Hackett, 1997), p. 5.
50. Alter, *Genesis*, p. 40.
51. Karen Armstrong, *In the Beginning: A New Interpretation of Genesis* (New York: Random House, 1997), p. 49.
52. Ibid., p. 49.
53. Dante Alighieri, *Inferno*, Allen Mandelbaum, trans. (New York: Bantam, 1988), p. 3.
54. Friedman, *Commentary on the* Torah, p. 46.

PART II: THE WANDERERS

1. Oded Borowski, *Daily Life in Biblical Times* (Atlanta: Society of Biblical Literature, 2003), p. 65.
2. Sarna, *Etz Hayim*, p. 69.
3. James R. Hillman, *The Soul's Code: In Search of Character and Calling* (New York: Random House, 1996), pp. 3–4, 7.
4. Ibid., pp. 7–8.
5. Ibid., p. 46.
6. George Orwell, "Why I Write," *Essays* (New York: Knopf, 2002), p. 1080.
7. Joseph Chilton Pearce, *Evolution's End: Claiming the Potential of Our Intelligence* (San Francisco: HarperCollins, 1992), p. 189.
8. Ibid., p. 190.
9. Hillman, *The Soul's Code*, p. 189.
10. Rainer Maria Rilke, *Letters to a Young Poet*, Joan M. Burnham, trans. (Novato, Calif.: New World Library, 2000), p. 11.

11. C. G. Jung, from an interview for *Good Housekeeping*, December 1961, cited in E. F. Edinger, *Ego and Archetype: Individuation and the Religious Function of the Psyche* (New York: Putman's, 1972), p. 101.

12. Reinhold Niebuhr, *Faith and History* (New York: Scribner, 1949), p. 161.

13. Harold Bloom, *Jesus and Yahweh* (New York: Riverhead, 2005), p. 173.

14. Quoted by Erich Fromm, *Psychoanalysis and Religion* (New York: Bantam, 1972), p. 112.

15. Armstrong, *In the Beginning*, p. 53.

16. Saul Bellow, *Humboldt's Gift* (New York: Penguin, 1996), p. 291.

17. Thomas Aquinas, *Summa Theologica: A Concise Translation*, Timothy McDermott, trans. (Allen, Texas: Christian Classics, 1989), p. 295.

18. T. S. Eliot, "East Coker," *Four Quartets* (New York: Harcourt Brace, 1971), p. 32.

19. Stephanie Zacharek, "More than just a beautiful face," Salon.com, September 29, 2008.

20. Alter, *Genesis*, p. 51.

21. *Chumash*, p. 57.

22. Ibid., p. 57.

23. Louis Ginzberg, *Legends of the Bible* (Old Saybrook, Conn.: Konecky & Konecky, n.d.), pp. 99–100.

24. Kugel, *Traditions of the Bible*, p. 31.

25. Ibid., p. 254.

26. Ibid., p. 254n.

27. Ibid., p. 255.

28. *Chumash*, p. 57.

29. Levenson, *The Jewish Study Bible*, p. 31.

30. Jack Miles, *God: A Biography* (New York: Vintage, 1996), p. 47.

31. Ibid., p. 49.

32. Ibid.

33. Friedman, *Commentary on the Torah*, p. 52.

34. Levenson, *The Jewish Study Bible*, p. 33.

35. Alter, *Genesis*, p. 62.

36. Miles, *God*, p. 50. Translation is by Miles.

37. Ibid.

38. Armstrong, *In the Beginning*, p. 57.

39. Erich Neumann, *The Origins and History of Consciousness* (Princeton, N.J.: Princeton University Press, 1973), p. 174.

40. Armstrong, *In the Beginning*, p. 58.

41. Ibid., p. 56.

42. Ibid., pp. 56–57.

43. Alter, *Genesis*, p. 68.

44. Levenson, *The Jewish Study Bible*, p. 36.

45. Nahum Sarna, *The JPS Torah Commentary* (Philadelphia: Jewish Publication Society, 1989), p. 120.

46. Ibid.

47. Ibid.

48. Alter, *Genesis*, p. 69.

49. Friedman, *The Bible with Sources Revealed*, p. 56.

50. Levenson, *The Jewish Study Bible*, pp. 37–38.

51. Alter, *Genesis*, p. 75.
52. Ibid.
53. E. A. Speiser, *Genesis, The Anchor Bible*, vol. 1 (Garden City, N.Y.: Doubleday, 1982), pp. 126–27.
54. Alter, *Genesis*, p. 73.
55. Ibid., p. 81.
56. Miles, *God: A Biography*, p. 56.
57. Everett Fox, *The Five Books of Moses: The Schocken Bible*, vol. 1 (New York: Random House, 1997), p. 83n.
58. Joseph Campbell, *The Hero with a Thousand Faces* (Princeton, N.J.: Princeton University Press, 1973), p. 206.
59. Kurt Vonnegut, *Slaughterhouse-Five or The Children's Crusade, A Duty-Dance with Death* (New York: Dell 1991), p. 22.
60. Ellen Frankel, *The Five Books of Miriam: A Woman's Commentary on the Torah* (San Francisco: HarperSanFrancisco, 1996), p. 26.
61. Ibid.
62. James Hillman, "The Salt of Soul, the Sulfur of Spirit," in *A Blue Fire*, pp. 126–27.
63. Vonnegut, *Slaughterhouse-Five*, p. 22.
64. Cynthia A. Culpepper, "Vayera: Positive Pillars," in *The Women's Torah Commentary*, Rabbi Elyse Goldstein, ed. (Woodstock, Vt.: Jewish Lights, 2000), p. 64.
65. Frankel, *The Five Books of Miriam*, p. 25.
66. Friedman, *Commentary on the Torah*, p. 66.
67. Kugel, *Traditions of the Bible*, p. 331.
68. Ibid., p. 333.
69. Alter, *Genesis*, p. 90.
70. Sarna, *Etz Hayim*, p. 109.
71. James L. Kugel, *How to Read the Bible: A Guide to Scripture, Then and Now* (New York: Free Press, 2007), p. 129.
72. von Rad, *Genesis*, p. 220.
73. Leon Kass, *The Beginning of Wisdom: Reading Genesis* (Chicago: University of Chicago Press, 2003), p. 355.
74. Ibid.
75. Alter, *Genesis*, p. 97.
76. Levenson, *The Jewish Study Bible*, p. 44.
77. Ibid.
78. Alter, *Genesis*, p.103.
79. Erich Auerbach, *Mimesis: The Representation of Reality in Western Literature*, Willard R. Trask, trans. (Princeton, N.J.: Princeton University Press, 2003), pp. 9–10, 11.
80. Speiser, *Genesis*, p. 163.
81. Alter, *Genesis*, p. 105.
82. Søren Kierkegaard, *Fear and Trembling*, Alastair Hannay, trans. (New York: Penguin, 2005), p. 10.
83. Ibid.
84. Ibid., p. 11.
85. Ibid., p. 12.
86. Ibid., p. 13.
87. Ibid., p. 66.
88. Ibid.

89. Ibid., p. 78.
90. Armstrong, *In the Beginning*, p. 70.
91. Rona Shapiro, "Chaye Sarah, Woman's Life, Woman's Truth," in *The Women's Torah Commentary*, p. 71.
92. Frankel, *The Five Books of Miriam*, p. 30.
93. Levenson, *The Jewish Study Bible*, p. 47.
94. Ibid.
95. Ibid., p. 52.

PART III: THE BLESSING THIEF

1. Sarna, *Etz Hayim*, p. 147.
2. David Wolpe, In "Jacob's Ladder," *Mysteries of the Bible*, A&E Home Video, 1996.
3. Walter Zanger, in ibid.
4. Ibid
5. Armstrong, *In the Beginning*, p. 78.
6. Ibid.
7. Wolpe, "Jacob's Ladder."
8. von Rad, *Genesis*, p. 285.
9. *The Torah: A Modern Commentary*, rev. ed., W. Gunther Plaut and David E. S. Stein, eds. (New York: Union for Reform Judaism, 2005), p. 212.
10. Benno Jacobs as quoted in ibid., p. 213.
11. Sarna, *Etz Hayim*, p. 172.
12. Friedman, *Commentary on the Torah*, p. 103.
13. Levenson, *The Jewish Study Bible*, p. 62.
14. Berhard W. Anderson, *The Oxford Annotated Bible* (New York: Oxford University Press, 1965), p. 38.
15. Nahum Sarna, *The JPS Torah Commentary, Genesis*, p. 223.
16. Ibid., p. 225.
17. David Rosenberg and Harold Bloom, *The Book of J* (New York: Vintage, 1991), p. 217.
18. Daniel C. Matt, *The Zohar, Pritzker Edition*, vol. 1 (Stanford, Calif.: Stanford University Press, 2004), p. 162.
19. Rosenberg and Bloom, *The Book of J*, p. 217.
20. Fox, *The Five Books of Moses*, p. 154.
21. Sarna, *The JPS Torah Commentary*, p. 230.
22. Sarna, *Etz Hayim*, p. 205.
23. Sarna, *The JPS Torah Commentary*, p. 233.
24. Friedman, *Commentary on the Torah*, p. 116.
25. David Biale, *Eros and the Jews: From Biblical Israel to Contemporary America* (New York: Basic Books, 1992), p. 23.
26. Ibid.
27. Kass, *The Beginning of Wisdom*, p. 480.
28. Ibid., p. 493.
29. Kugel, *How to Read the Bible*, p. 165.
30. Ibid., pp. 165–166.
31. Ibid., p. 170.
32. Alter, *Genesis*, p. 200.
33. Ibid.

PART IV: THE DREAM READER

1. Kugel, *Traditions of the Bible*, p. 440.
2. As quoted in ibid.
3. Ibid.
4. Alter, *Genesis*, p. 209.
5. Thomas Mann, *Joseph and His Brothers* (New York: Knopf, 2005), p. 393.
6. Friedman, *The Bible with Sources Revealed*, p. 94.
7. Friedman, *Commentary on the Torah*, p. 127.
8. Levenson, *The Jewish Study Bible*, p. 78.
9. Alter, *Genesis*, p. 223.
10. Armstrong, *In the Beginning*, p. 105.
11. Levenson, *The Jewish Study Bible*, p. 78.
12. *Genesis Rabbah* 87:3, as quoted in ibid., p. 79.
13. Ibid.
14. Friedman, *The Bible with Sources Revealed*, p. 131.
15. Alter, *Genesis*, p. 230.
16. Levenson, *The Jewish Study Bible*, p. 72.
17. James L. Kugel, *The Ladder of Jacob: Ancient Interpretations of the Biblical Story of Jacob and His Children* (Princeton, N.J.: Princeton University Press, 2006), p. 85.
18. Ibid.
19. Alter, *Genesis*, p. 250.
20. Ibid., p. 257.
21. Ibid., p. 280.
22. Fox, *The Five Books of Moses*, p. 241.

EPILOGUE

1. Andrew Hurley, "A Note on the Translation," in Jorge Luis Borges, *Collected Fictions*, Andrew Hurley, trans. (New York: Penguin, 1998), p. 519.
2. Kugel, *Traditions of the Bible*, p. 179.
3. Albert Camus, "The Wind at Djimila," in *Lyrical and Critical Essays*, Philip Thody, ed., Ellen Conroy Kennedy, trans. (New York: Vintage, 1968), p. 73.
4. Bloom, *Jesus and Yahweh*, p. 173.

ACKNOWLEDGMENTS

I wish to thank my agent, Eileen Cope, for her enthusiastic support, and my editor, Leslie Meredith, for her steady hand and insightful questions, and of course her assistant, Donna Loffredo, who seemed able to keep forty balls in the air at any one time.

Deepest gratitude to my sister, Caroline, for a lifetime of cheerleading her younger brothers; to my brothers, Frank and Ralph, for their comradeship and love; to our parents, for their belief in their children; and to Michael Goins and Sarah Cortez, who first pushed me to write. Finally, to my teachers at The Bennington Writing Seminars—Sven Birkerts, whose gentle insights gave my work a stronger focus; Susan Cheever, whose patient coaching helped me through a difficult time; Bob Shacochis, whose not so gentle style blasted me out of a rut so that I could find my own voice; and Phillip Lopate, who reminded me of what I knew and encouraged me to begin this book.

INDEX

ABOUT THE AUTHOR

John R. Coats holds master's degrees from Virginia Theological Seminary (Episcopal) and Bennington College Writing Seminars. A former parish priest, he was a principal speaker and seminar leader for the More To Life training program in the United States, Great Britain, and South Africa, and an independent management consultant. He lives with his wife, Pamela, in Houston, Texas.